Voices from the
Heartland

Voices from the
Heartland
Volume II

Edited by
Sara N. Beam
Emily Dial-Driver
Rilla Askew
Juliet Evusa

UNIVERSITY OF OKLAHOMA PRESS : NORMAN

This book is published with the generous assistance of the Wallace C. Thompson Endowment Fund, University of Oklahoma Foundation.

"Snake Season," by Rilla Askew, was orginally published in *Flock* 18 (April 2017).

Library of Congress Cataloging-in-Publication Data
Names: Beam, Sara N., 1980– editor. | Dial-Driver, Emily, editor. | Askew, Rilla, editor.
Title: Voices from the heartland : Volume II / edited by Sara N. Beam, Emily Dial-Driver, Rilla Askew, Juliet Evusa.
Description: First Edition. | Norman, OK : University of Oklahoma Press, [2019] | Includes bibliographical references.
Identifiers: LCCN 2018052464 | ISBN 978-0-8061-6322-2 (pbk. : alk. paper)
Subjects: LCSH: Women—Oklahoma—Social conditions. | Women—Oklahoma—Biography.
Classification: LCC HQ1438.O5 V65 2019 | DDC 305.409766—dc23
LC record available at https://lccn.loc.gov/2018052464

The paper in this book meets the guidelines for permanence and durability of the Committee on Production Guidelines for Book Longevity of the Council on Library Resources, Inc. ∞

Copyright © 2019 by Sara N. Beam, Emily Dial-Driver, Rilla Askew, and Juliet Evusa. Published by the University of Oklahoma Press, Norman, Publishing Division of the University. Manufactured in the U.S.A.

All rights reserved. No part of this publication may be reproduced, stored in a retrieval system, or transmitted, in any form or by any means, electronic, mechanical, photocopying, recording, or otherwise—except as permitted under Section 107 or 108 of the United States Copyright Act—without the prior written permission of the University of Oklahoma Press. To request permission to reproduce selections from this book, write to Permissions, University of Oklahoma Press, 2800 Venture Drive, Norman, OK 73069, or email rights.oupress@ou.edu.

To Ofelia Chavoya

Contents

Preface, *by Sara N. Beam* | ix

Calibration

Oklahoma Canon, *by Merleyn Ruth Bell* | 3
Snake Season, *by Rilla Askew* | 8
Novice at Belle Point, *by Sara N. Beam* | 17
Finding a Way to Thrive, *by Jeanetta Calhoun Mish* | 22
Fidelity, *by Tamya Cox-Touré* | 27
An Outsider Within: A Culmination of a
 Multifaceted Journey, *by Juliet Evusa* | 30
I've Never Been to Heaven . . . , *by Mary Mackie* | 42
Uncertain Ground, *by Janice Willson* | 48

Advocating

Speaking Truth to Power, *by Pam Kingfisher* | 59
Marriage Equality and the Courage of
 Our Convictions, *by Sharon Bishop-Baldwin* | 65
What Is a Girl Like You Doing in a Place
 Like This? *by Kalyn Free* | 69
Roots or Wings, *by Priya Desai* | 76
Action Potential, *by Apollonia Piña* | 81

Forging Paths

Do I Belong? *by Arielle Davis* | 89
Impossible, *by Jenny Yang Cropp* | 93
Time, *by Ureka Williams* | 99
Letter to My Grandkids, *by Spring Houghton* | 102
Notes on Humiliation, Compassion,
    and Oklahoma, My Home, *by LeAnne Howe* | 107

Incarceration and Liberation

Poetic Justice, *by Ellen Stackable* | 119
Driven, *by Rhonda Bear* | 123
Walk a Mile in My Heart, *by Ruth Askew Brelsford* | 128
Pilgrim, *by Shaunte Gordon* | 135

Weathering Trauma

One Lightning Second, *by Eden Hemming* | 145
Call to Compassion, *by Katie Rain Hill* | 150
Salvation, *by Deborah J. Hunter* | 155
From This Side, *by Nancy Michno* | 162
The Struggle, *by Veronica Wolf* | 167
Diagnosis: Major Depressive Disorder,
    by Jenna Buschmann | 172

Cultivation

Silt, *by Yasminda Choate* | 179
Strong Roots: A Reflection, *by Grace E. Franklin* | 184
Teaching Topsoil at Risk of Blowing Away,
    by Lenzy Krehbiel-Burton | 188
Period, Exclamation Point, *by Amanda Ruyle* | 190

Navigation

Going Home, *by Jari Askins* | 199
Just Be Nice, *by Emily Dial-Driver* | 203
The Button, *by Aura Thomas* | 207
Don't Tempt Me! *by Sherry Morgan* | 210
Agak-agak, *by Cordelia Santa Maria* | 212
Adjusting the Bible Belt, *by Vicki May Thorne* | 216

List of Contributors | 225

Preface

SARA N. BEAM

But I will not stand by silently and allow him, in his anger, to reinvent me.
—Anita Hill, "The Smear This Time," *New York Times*, 2007

I start with these words from Anita Hill, with her voice, because she is Oklahoma-born and raised, and because she was courageous in testifying in 1991 about the sexual harassment she alleges that she endured. Refusing to be silenced, she told her story in a very public way, knowing that an unrelenting backlash from Clarence Thomas and his supporters would follow. But she did it.

And then she spoke up again in 2007, publicly, when Justice Thomas's memoir was released and included an unfavorable portrayal of her. Some—many—people said that Hill just wanted attention, that she was just causing trouble, that she should get out of the way. And then those same people criticize women for not speaking up for fear of social reprisal. It's a catch-22 for women, especially women from minority populations.

I begin also by mentioning Tarana Burke's #MeToo movement, relevant particularly to "young women of color from low wealth communities." #MeToo rightfully tells hurt, harassed, and violated women to speak their truth and stand in their power, binding them together on social media so that they can speak and claim their pain, draw attention to an epidemic of sexual violence against women, and perhaps feel support in solidarity. Like Hill's response, #MeToo is rooted in coming forward and in resisting reinvention, resisting an unfounded revisionist history.

Anita Hill's 2007 article and the inception of #MeToo both coincided with the publication of the original *Voices from the Heartland* anthology. Although the book does not mention either of these, it provides a platform for several Oklahoma survivors of sexual violence to tell their stories. What you will find in this new collection are more stories by Oklahoma women from an even broader and intersecting range of identities: identities of race, nationality, sexual orientation, gender expression, religion, neurodiversity, class, and economic status. I know this book will raise the spirits of women who recognize themselves in these narratives. Beyond that, I hope this book legitimizes these stories and narratives for people who would read them skeptically; I hope this book legitimizes *women's voices* for people who would only hear them skeptically. Or for those who would not listen at all. Although their tones and words may sound different from some readers' singular perspectives, these minor yet key voices reflect the human condition. The collection is organized by themes that play with notions of identity and direction: calibration, advocating, forging paths, incarceration and liberation, weathering trauma, cultivation, and navigation.

Before we can navigate home like writer Jari Askins or cook with the deft touch of Cordelia Santa Maria, we must calibrate, or recalculate our place in an unstable territory and atmosphere. Merleyn Bell's and Rilla Askew's stories capture the feeling of recognizing and coming to terms with the tectonic shifts that happen and reverberate after older generations die. In between their bookending thematic sections are stories of advocating causes and ways of life, forging a way where none exists yet, weathering the tests of life, and carefully cultivating the future for new generations to come. In the very center of the text's labyrinth are voices speaking on the experience of the imprisoned women of Oklahoma—here, two formerly incarcerated women, Rhonda Bear and Shaunte Gordon, discuss their time on the inside.

The collected essays all vary in content, organization, and style because each was composed by the contributor herself; the same goes for the contributors' biographical statements at the end of the text. We wanted the writers' descriptions of themselves to be individual and to reflect what *they* would want others to know about them, not what *we* would want. Our goal for ourselves as co-editors is to amplify voices without overproducing the result.

I hope the stories in this book give you pause, give you cause, give you life, like the first volume gave me. I first read the 2007 *Voices from the Heartland* anthology when I was teaching at Rogers State University in Claremore, Oklahoma, in 2014. *Voices* was edited by Carolyn Taylor, Emily Dial-Driver, Carol Burrage, and Sally Emmons, each of whom contributed pieces to the collection of fifty works. Other contributors included Wilma Mankiller, OU women's basketball coach Sherri Coale, and First Lady Kim Henry. In the book's preface, Taylor writes, "We believe we are not alone. Women everywhere are hungry for a substantive discussion of the dilemmas that confront us all." And the first *Voices from the Heartland* provides just that, covering topics such as girlhood, personal trauma, women at work, parenting, politics, and religious beliefs.

During that time in 2014, I was laboring hard to balance a forty-hour work week, a three-year-old daughter, a work commute, and a relationship with my loving and supportive partner, Brian. A typical day would begin at 6:15 A.M., when I'd rise, make coffee, help convince a three-year-old to get dressed and eat food, throw on clothes, feed the cats, and then, at 7 A.M., drive forty minutes toward the rising sun to work. I was lucky to have a reliable car, a job I enjoyed, a partner who cared for our child and kept house, a family who supported my pursuit of my dreams, and friends who took care of me (and helped me care for myself).

Voices spoke to me in a way that no other book had. In it were familiar words and landscapes. Some of the stories in the book were raw and vulnerable; others were polished and firm like packed clay. I shared the book with students at Rogers State University, and their written responses were of a quality that I hadn't seen before. This was real for them. They heard their sisters, mothers, grandmothers, aunts, and themselves speaking. When they created multimedia representations of the stories, they took big risks, drawing, creating websites, recording audio, and composing video collages.

In spring 2016, I told Emily that I wished there could be another volume of stories, perhaps a ten-year follow up. Oklahoma *still* incarcerates more women per capita than any other state. "Prisoners in 2015," published by the U.S. Department of Justice, informs readers that the incarceration rate for Oklahoma was 151 per 100,000 members of the female population, the highest in the United States. In 2015, nearly 112,000 Oklahoma women were incarcerated. People still need to know this, and they need to hear it straight from those who are in or have been in the system. Sunlight is the best disinfectant.

Furthermore, Oklahoma is still governed largely by men, leaving women without equitable and fair representation, despite the facade of female-friendliness that having a woman, Mary Fallin, as governor creates. The Oklahoma State Legislature "Senate Members" directory shows that, as of October 2018, only 6 of the 48 Oklahoma Senate offices are held by women. Only 13 of the

101 districts of Oklahoma are represented by women in the Oklahoma House, according to the State Legislature "House Members" webpage. Women are underrepresented in the State Legislature. Why is this? The patriarchy appears to be alive and well in Oklahoma.

Immigrant, indigenous, African American, Latinx, Asian American women; trans women; femme-presenting genderfluid or non-binary folks; lesbian, bisexual, and pan women; women who are not Christians; women with disabilities and differences, neurodiverse women; and women who identify as working class or poor all deserve life, liberty, and the pursuit of happiness, just as women in privileged populations (white, able-bodied, middle-class or wealthy, Christian, and so forth) do. Where are their voices today? How can we give them a platform? Our liberation is bound up in theirs, so we must act in concert. Whiteness and middle-class economic stature have afforded some of us privilege, a leg up to access higher education. Familial wealth, unextravagant as it may be, can provide access to a working vehicle, assistance in applying to college and acquiring student loan money, and a helping hand paying medical bills. These things are privileges that not every woman has. Thus, as with the original text, we plan to donate the proceeds from sales of the book. Proceeds from this volume will benefit a scholarship fund at Rogers State University in memory of former student Ofelia Chavoya.

When I suggested the idea of a follow-up volume of *Voices* to Emily Dial-Driver, her eyes lit up and she told me to go for it—she was in, but she suggested I be lead editor. Fair enough, I thought; I told her I'd do it, but she had to support me. She immediately agreed. We began brainstorming, creating a list of potential writers. We met with Carolyn Taylor at a local restaurant for lunch, and she gave her blessing. I asked her to act as editor emeritus, since the original anthology really was her baby. Though Carolyn has stayed removed from the writing and editing process, she is involved in this project as a guide and a network hub.

This book would not exist without Carolyn, Emily, Carol Burrage, and Sally Emmons. Their voices may not all be here, but they created the foundation that Emily, Juliet Evusa, Rilla Askew, and I build on. The original coeditors, and the original contributors, have my utmost respect and admiration. I thank them for modeling collaboration, for inventing a way to collect and share a multitude of women's voices, and for sharing that method freely and openly with those of us who would honor the project and carry it forward.

This book would also not exist if it weren't for the current contributors, these steel-hearted Oklahoma women who told me their stories despite the risks some took for speaking. This collection provides a platform for all, including underrepresented voices who do not fit the stereotype of what women from Oklahoma are like (that is, all or mostly white, Christian, heterosexual, cisgender, middle class, and English-speaking). The liberal/conservative binary is too simplistic for genuine understanding of what it is to be a woman in Oklahoma—or a woman in the United States for that matter. Intersectional feminism compels us to do work that highlights less-heard or unheard perspectives in the name of restorative justice, and to query binaries rather than serve them. The only writing prompt we gave these writers was to tell a story that mattered to them, something worth sharing, in a way that seemed natural and organic to them. Thus, you'll read their stories here as they want them told: in a mix of poetry and prose, in the voice of a relative, in the voice of a tired person across the breakroom table, in a secret hush, or in a voice not unlike that of your best friend or mother. They could only hang a lantern on one moment in their lives, and this is what they chose.

Remember this: the only person allowed to write you or revise you *is* you. You are the best person to tell your story, and we are listening.

Calibration

Oklahoma Canon

MERLEYN RUTH BELL

"Where are you from?"

If only I had a nickel for every time I've been asked that question. It's innocent enough, though when people ask, they're often trying to get at *what* I am more than *where* I'm from. Of course asking "What are you?" would be impolite (though it has happened). So folks say "Where are you from?" or "Where are your people from?" Either way, the answer is Oklahoma.

Picture an olive-skinned woman with hair as thick and dark as molasses, dark eyes and brows, and a broad nose above thin lips. These features get me mistaken for Italian, Indian, Mexican, and Maori (to name a few). Rarely has anyone ever guessed correctly that I have a black father and a white mother. When I reveal my biracial identity, they almost always say "Oh, I thought you were [insert race or ethnicity here]." It's curious how people insist on pointing out just how wrong they were. I recently attended a wedding reception down in Texas where a fellow guest said, "Now Merleyn, I know you're from Oklahoma, but *where* are you from? We've been talking about it at our table and I said India, but someone else guessed you might be Persian."

Uh, no and no.

Look, I get it. A thirty-something biracial woman is not what most people envision when they think of Oklahoma. More likely it's the quintessential cowboy or pioneer woman. For the longest time, even I swooned thinking of

Curly and Laurey in their surrey with the fringe on top. That beautiful couple with big dreams riding into an even bigger sherbet-colored Oklahoma sunset. And no wonder, considering the influence that the musical *Oklahoma!* has had on our state's image. Long before *Chicago* or *Hamilton* opened at the Richard Rodgers Theatre, Rodgers himself, along with lyricist Oscar Hammerstein, created a smash hit that changed the game. Their first collaboration was one of the first fully integrated book musicals, with a well-developed plot, two stirring romances, a fifteen-minute dream ballet (choreographed by Agnes de Mille, no less), and a show-stopping song and dance number. *Oklahoma!* opened on Broadway in 1943 to rave reviews and ran for a record-setting 2,212 performances. A decade later our state legislature passed a measure naming the musical's title song as the official song and anthem of Oklahoma. And so the die was cast.

I remember when I first heard the title song from *Oklahoma!* We put on a special concert at my elementary school to celebrate the centennial of the 1889 land run. All students were encouraged to dress the part, boys in their bandanas and cowboy hats, girls in their brightly colored dresses and matching bonnets. We sang "Oklahoma!" and a stirring rendition of "Oh, What a Beautiful Mornin'." I remember singing my heart out, bursting with Curly's can-do spirit. My mother still has the whole performance on VHS tape. And I still cringe every time she talks about how we need to get it transferred over to DVD.

Since that embarrassing performance, I've grown to understand Oklahoma's complexities. And two women taught me how my life exemplifies our great state much better than any show tune could ever do.

> *Oh Lord my God, when I in awesome wonder*
> *Consider all the worlds thy hands have made,*
> *I see the stars, I hear the rolling thunder*
> *Thy power throughout the universe displayed.*

My father's mother, Ruth, is a mystical presence in my life. She lived in the tiny town of Roland, in eastern Oklahoma, near the border of Arkansas. Since childhood, I've heard it called Shady Grove, though no one ever told me why. To get to Shady Grove you take I-40 east to exit 325, take the first right, then right again down a narrow, potholed gravel road. It's been nearly twenty years since I last made that drive, but I could still get there today from memory.

It's not just the directions that I remember so vividly. Each road trip I took with my parents to Shady Grove was a chance to create lifelong memories. I can still feel the warmth from the sun coming through the side window of our old hand-me-down sedan. I can conjure up the intoxicating smell of fried chicken and biscuits at the old rest stop in Okemah. And I'll never forget the awe I felt crossing over Lake Eufaula, which I was sure must be the biggest body of water I'd ever see. Each time we got closer to our destination, time seemed to move more and more slowly. By the time the pavement gave way to bumpy white gravel, we were moving at a snail's pace. I always wondered if that's why my dad drove so slowly down that narrow road to Granny's house. Maybe he too felt the slowing of time. Or maybe it was a hesitance about returning to a time and place he joined the army as a teenager to escape.

My granny raised thirteen children on her own at the end of that dusty path, in a small house tucked between an old cemetery and the local Baptist church she walked to every Sunday without fail. If you stayed until dinnertime on Saturday evening, you were expected to be in the pews with her the next morning. Sitting next to her as she rocked about and shouted in response to the pastor delivering the gospel was a revelation. Never before or since have I witnessed someone so authentically moved by the spirit. By the time the choir sang its final hymn, the chapel was filled with music and lyrics about God's wisdom and power and love. If only in that moment, I was a believer.

Granny was soft-spoken, unassuming even, but not to be trifled with. She had a regal air that made her akin to the Queen of England in my mind. She was named for one of the Bible's great women, you know, the great-grandmother of King David himself. It mystifies me how she reigned over her own ever-expanding kingdom with such a steady hand. I'm sure if I had the chance to ask her today, she'd credit the good Lord above. But she's gone now, and all I have are the traces of her I carry in my blood and my memory. And, of course, her name, my middle name.

I wish I had known her better, and I wish that she had lived until I was old enough to learn her secrets. Maybe then when I'm lost and without purpose or in need of courage I could ask myself "What would Ruth do?" and the answer would be less of an approximation. Still, I look to her for guidance, the same way I imagine she looked to Him, as one whose wisdom is concealed but whose love is ever apparent.

> *Lost and alone on some forgotten highway*
> *Traveled by many, remembered by few.*
> *Sweet, sweet surrender, live, live without care*
> *Like a fish in the water, like a bird in the air.*

My mother's mother, Viola Merle, was born in Shawnee, the first of five girls. In high school Merle (as she was called) started taking tickets at the local movie theater where her father worked as the projectionist. My grandfather, one of the ushers, eventually wooed Merle by offering to drive her home in his '33 Chevy Coupe. Grandma nearly always describes her childhood in idyllic terms, and as a result, her hometown remains picture-perfect in my mind, no matter how many times I visit. To me, Shawnee is Oklahoma's Stars Hollow, sleepy and unassuming with a cast of quirky characters to boot.

Grandma and I have always been close, so close in fact that when I dream of home, it's her red brick ranch-style house I see. She is a constant, steady presence and a soft place to land. In addition to sharing a name, we share a birthday. It's how I ended up with the name Merleyn; my parents changed the spelling of Marilyn to honor my grandmother and our unique connection and to confuse everyone forever (though that last part may have been unintentional). Merle and I also share a love of music. From Frank Sinatra to Elvis, John Denver to Tom Jones, she introduced me to all the great crooners. She taught me about polka by way of Lawrence Welk reruns. And I first saw *Singin' in the Rain* sitting on her comfy paisley patchwork sofa.

In addition to that elementary school production of *Oklahoma!*, countless other musical performances peppered my childhood. I don't recall Grandma missing one of them. She even sat through the piano recital where I played Pachelbel's Canon in D, which slowed down to a trickle in spots when my nerves got the best of me.

Ten years later, I studied music in college, where my knowledge and understanding of music theory expanded a great deal. Sophomore year, I excelled at creating counterpoint, like the Pachelbel I plucked out years before. The formula is simple: a melody provides the basis for the parts that come after it. These imitations begin to overlap, sometimes remaining faithful to the melody, but often expanding on it in surprising ways. All the while, the melody is still present, no matter how complex the variations become.

It took many more years, but I've learned to appreciate the unique melody my grandmothers crafted for me. Now, I'm building my own counterpoint upon a mashup of two of their favorite songs: the classic hymn "How Great Thou Art" and John Denver's "Sweet Surrender." It's a melody about living in wonder and humility. About rejecting worry and fear. I find that I am happiest when I live in close counterpoint to these tenets.

I understand now, too, that Oklahoma has its own canon, a symphony of sounds and stories about tribes and territories, turning points and tragedies. Mine is but one variation, but I hope that one day it will seem as quintessentially Oklahoman as those we choose to play on repeat now.

Snake Season

RILLA ASKEW

For those of us raised up on Revelation in this part of the country, the year 2011 seemed oddly familiar: earthquakes in diverse places, floods and fire and wind. Torturous heat. Crippling cold. Plagues of grasshoppers and serpents. Drought. By late October the lack of rain had leached all the color from the valleys of the Sans Bois, the small mountain range in southeastern Oklahoma where my family lives. The ridges were gray with naked oak trees. In the ditches, the tall grasses whispered, dry and thin as sloughed snakeskin. No hay for the cattle, no pasture. The ponds were disappearing. You could see the weedy, cracked outlines of their former selves. My dad said drought was why we were seeing so many snakes then.

One Sunday morning before church my sister Ruth went out to feed and water her chickens. She and her husband live across the pond from our parents' place on land that's been in our family for generations. Ruth knows not to stick her hands where she can't see—we all know that rule in this snake-ridden country—but what's familiar also comes, in time, to seem harmless, and that morning my sister was in a hurry. She shoved her fingers beneath the plastic trough to tip out the old water so she could hose in the fresh; the trough came up off the ground just high enough for her to see the fat, full-grown copperhead coiled underneath. *Whoomp!* Ruthie dropped the trough in an instant. Then she went in the house to call Daddy.

In those days I divided my time between Upstate New York and our second home in Oklahoma. Well, I call it a second home, but in fact those long valleys of the Sans Bois are my first home: their very harshness and beauty are etched deep inside me, though I had to leave for a lot of years to understand this. So I happened to be home visiting my parents that weekend, and I was the one who answered the phone. Before Ruth even got the words out, I knew why she was calling. Her voice had the snake-edge. I can't describe what it is about that pitch, that edge of fear and excitement, but I recognized it in my sister's voice that morning, along with a little hint of apology. She hated to be asking Daddy to come kill a snake before morning worship. But Ruthie's husband wasn't home, and the snake was in the chicken pen, and it had to be killed. I turned and yelled down the stairs, "Daddy! Ruth's got a copperhead in the yard!"

Our dad was in his mid-eighties then, and was by nature a slow, methodical man. When it came to snakes, though, our daddy moved *fast.* He had his cap on and his holstered pistol strapped over his sweatpants and his .22 rifle fetched from behind the basement door by the time I'd tugged on my boots and grabbed the truck keys.

We bumped across the pasture in his pickup, me driving, and when we pulled into Ruthie's yard we saw her standing outside the chicken pen with a flat big-snouted gun in her hand. Daddy took the gun from her, said, "You girls stay back out of the way." Ruth followed him into the pen anyway, but I wisely stayed outside the fence, positioning myself to get a good look at the snake.

Daddy tipped up the trough, held it high with one hand, snake-gun in the other. The copperhead wasn't coiled now but stretched out at the edge of the trough's shadow as if it had been trying to crawl away, though it lay perfectly still now, disguising itself against the dirt in the chicken yard. It was good-sized for a copperhead, maybe three-and-a-half feet long, thick around as four thumbs—large enough that its bite could kill a laying hen sure, or make a hefty human sick. For the brief millisecond I saw it alive, that snake was beautiful, its back mottled a lovely dusky-pink and copper, the chevron markings perfect. Then, *blam,* its head was blown off, and the body, headless, lay writhing and twisting in the dust, as snakes will do. We stood watching it a while, and then Daddy scooped it up with a shovel, tossed it out in the field behind the chicken yard for the crows to eat, and he and I drove back across the pasture to get ready for church.

On our way into town, Mama and Daddy in the back, me driving, Ruth riding shotgun, Daddy said, "I studied on that gun for two years."

"Yes," Mama said, "and then gave it away."

My sister and I laughed. He was talking about that snake-gun. It's a plain-looking derringer, hardly larger than a man's palm, and it shoots .44 caliber bullets or .410 shotgun shells—a shotgun derringer, basically, lethal at close range, but not much good for anything except shooting a close-range assailant, or killing snakes. The safety mechanism is designed to keep you from shooting your hand off, so it takes a while to reload—too long, if you've missed your first shot—which is why Daddy studied on it for two years. He'd been trying to conjure a way to make the gun reload more quickly so he could use it for hunting. He never found a way to do it safely, so he gave the gun to Ruth's husband, Les, to shoot snakes with. Most generally Les used a shovel to kill snakes, but that snake-gun was a good backup, especially for venomous snakes. He might have used it that morning if he'd been home. But he wasn't home, and so naturally Ruth called Dad.

The fact is, we'd been calling our daddy to come kill snakes all our lives—not just me and my sisters but also our mom. Mama had a way of screaming Daddy's name that made any of us within earshot turn to each other and say, "Snake." She was what our daddy called "snaky," by which he meant her fear of snakes was outsized—it went past normal fear or trepidation all the way to hysteria. But Mama's tone was humorous in the car that morning, indulgent; she meant her quip to be funny, and it *was* funny, and my sister and I laughed. The exchange was just so *them*, our parents: a man who would ponder the mechanics of one gun for two years, and a woman who would know that about him, and who would know, too, that he would, in his ultimate bafflement, give the gun away. We all laughed, driving to church on the gravel road that runs from our family's land to the highway, with great clouds of dust billowing behind us and the end of our world bearing down upon us and the bare-naked ridges in front of us gray and ugly with drought.

―――――――

That same afternoon Ruth and I were walking the gravel road, our feet kicking up dust. The air crackled with dryness. The weather was too hot and sear for October. These days, we're not surprised to see summer's heat in autumn, but back then—little more than a decade into the new century—it seemed beyond passing strange to feel such warmth in the fall. It made us uneasy. My sister saw it before I did. "There's a copperhead," she said, and I jumped. The snake was a young one, maybe ten inches long, no bigger around than a fat pencil, wriggling fast from west to east across the road. It felt our footsteps on the earth and stopped, reared back, turning to face the perceived danger, head lifted, tongue darting. Fascinated, we circled around it, our feet crunching gravel: we'd step this way, and *whiiipp*, the little snake snapped this way; then we'd step that way, and *whiiipp*, it flipped that way, head darting as if to strike. I knew if we got close enough, it *would* strike. Even a small copperhead can make you sick. I once knew a pregnant hippie lady who reached out to caress a young copperhead somebody was holding, murmuring, "Oh, isn't it beautiful?" till the snake whipped loose and bit her on both thumbs; her arms swelled to thrice their size, turned black to the elbows, she was sick for a week, although her baby, when he was born, turned out to be okay. I knew to be cautious, even with a pencil-sized copperhead.

The rule of the land in snake country is that you always kill venomous snakes when you see them, even baby ones. But Ruth's and my rule is: if it's not an immediate threat to your family or your livestock, let it go. I've never killed a snake, except a few I've run over with my car. I don't think Ruth has either. Our parents, though, would have crushed that baby copperhead in a second. That's a little known truth about our mother: she loathed and feared snakes beyond telling, but if Daddy wasn't around to do the deed, she'd take after the snake herself. I've stood in the dusky road and watched her hack a blacksnake to pieces with a hoe, chopping at it with such ferocity it would make your blood chill. She was, in fact, a bit like that young copperhead herself, fierce beyond all measure of her size and power; if she felt threatened, she wouldn't cower but would lash out, fearless, even when she was full of fear.

My sister and I watched the young thrashing snake. We were giants in the road. We could crush it with a rock, smash it with a stick. I said, "You think we ought to kill it?"

"Nah," Ruthie said. "We'll just wait till it shows up in my yard, and then I'll call Daddy." We laughed and started on to the house. After a moment I realized my sister was crying, silent tears running down her face.

"What?" I said.

"One of these days," she said, "he won't be here for us to call to come kill our snakes."

I was quiet a minute. Then I said, "I know."

And I thought I did. But I didn't. Not really. No matter how inevitably and forcefully you understand it is coming, you don't truly know grief until it is here.

The next Sunday I was back in New York, driving toward my house upstate after visiting my godchildren in Brooklyn. Headset on, I called the folks to see how they were doing. "I can't talk now, shug!" Daddy said, and there it was in his voice: the snake-edge, that telltale rip of excitement. "I got to get over to Ruth and Les's, they've got a rattlesnake under the porch!"

"Call me!" I said. "Daddy, call me as soon as it's finished! Be careful! Let me know how it goes!"

"Yes, all right."

"Be care—"

He was off the line before I could tell him another dozen times to be careful, *be careful!* It was already dark in New York, I knew it must be near dusk in Oklahoma—a bad light to be hunting rattlesnakes in. I wanted to phone Ruth to see what was happening, but I didn't want my call to be distracting, so I waited to hear, driving north over the Whitestone Bridge onto the Hutch and the Cross County to the Thruway, and north and north, until finally I could stand it no longer and called Ruthie's house. Her voice didn't have the snake-edge when she answered. I instantly relaxed. "Tell me everything," I said.

Their llama had been acting up in the carport, she said, making a weird, agitated, snuffling sound like they'd never heard before, and just the fact of the llama being in the carport was weird—ordinarily he stood sentinel in the pasture or the side yard—and then one of their little dogs inside the house started yipping, then the other dogs took up the commotion, and Les went outside to check. In two seconds he burst back into the house and headed for his .22. "Snake," he said. Ruthie rushed outside behind him; they stood on the porch. In the yard, their cross-eyed Siamese Manx sat on her haunches on a little stone rise, watching. A few feet away, a humongous rattler was coiled, tail lifted, rattling. The snake's attention was riveted on the cat. Ruthie said she knew that if the cat moved at all, even a twitched whisker, the snake would strike. But the cat sat frozen, hunkered down, watching the snake, entirely motionless, a timeless standoff, until Les raised the rifle. Well, the thing about that snake-gun Daddy gave him: to use it, you had to get in close. Les didn't favor walking up to within a few feet of that riled and rattling rattlesnake, so he'd fetched his rifle instead. He stood on the porch, aimed, fired, and missed. The cat leapt away, and the rattler uncoiled at once and started crawling—not *away* from the house but directly toward it. Within a few very long, helpless seconds, Ruthie said, that five-foot snake disappeared under the porch. So that was when Ruth went in the house to call Dad.

This time Daddy came armed with his twenty gauge. The twilight was fading, Ruth said, and they didn't know where under the house the snake was hiding. Their porch is three feet off the ground, skirted by lattice, the dark space underneath crowded with old farm tools and pieces of lumber. All along the lattice edge, the drought-choked weeds and zinnias were thick enough to provide plenty of cover for a big snake. And here was our eighty-six-year-old daddy crouched low, easing along the porch, poking in the weeds with his gun, trying to locate that rattler, his face and hands no more than a foot or two off the ground. He crept gingerly back and forth along the edge of the porch, trying to pierce with his eyes the darkness underneath. Ruth brought a flashlight. Les pointed to a large wooden pallet on the soft ground behind the lattice, not far from where the snake had crawled under, said, "I'll bet he's under there." Daddy said, "I'll just bet he is." They pried loose the lattice on one end, and Les held it back while Daddy poked his shotgun beneath the pallet. Then Daddy let loose with both barrels at once, and shot that snake all to pieces. He used the gun barrel to prod the writhing halves out into the yard. "Why, Ruth," he said, his voice edged with excitement, "that's a diamondback." My sister said, "Daddy, I know." Under ordinary circumstances a diamondback rattlesnake will not crawl down from the mountains into a domestic yard filled with dogs and humans and a llama. But these were no ordinary circumstances. This was unprecedented warmth, searing drought. This was summer in autumn. This was the seasons turned inside out, upside down.

By the end of the year, the plague of snakes was notorious in our part of the country. Stories of close encounters ran rampant—farmers and ranchers and folks who lived in the mountains all finding deadly snakes in their yards: copperheads, ground rattlers, velvet-tails. There were stories of a weird hybrid being sighted: bastardized offspring of copperheads mating with rattlesnakes—an unheard-of lethal kind of snake with the silent stealth of a copperhead and the deadly venom of a rattler. In November my husband and I returned to Oklahoma to spend the winter at our house on a ridge thirty miles from my family's land. On Thanksgiving Day, my three young nieces, out for a walk in the seventy-degree weather, crossed paths with a six-foot diamondback sunning itself in our yard. They rushed back to the house to tell us. Daddy leapt out of his chair and took out after it with a frog gig and a shovel, but the steel prongs of the gig couldn't penetrate the rattler's hide, they just bounced off, and the rattler disappeared beneath a large rock. We had to call a neighbor to come shoot it because nobody at my house had a gun. And the drought and the record warmth continued, on into the next season, and the next, and the next year after that.

"It'll rain sometime," our daddy kept saying. "It always does."

───────

And of course it did rain. Eventually. A little at first, and then torrents. But that didn't stop the heat or the drought or the seasons' inversion. The next year turned out to be the hottest on record in Oklahoma. Ninety-five percent of the state was declared to be under extreme drought. On October 8, Oklahoma City had its earliest freeze ever. The next year it snowed in Tulsa on May 2—the latest observed snowfall there since record-keeping began. That same month, tornadoes swept through Shawnee, Newcastle, Moore, Oklahoma City, in wave after deadly wave. The widest tornado ever recorded swept through El Reno on May 31, tossing semis along I-40 like toys, killing three veteran storm chasers, drowning women and children in the flash flooding that accompanied the torrential rains. In July, a derecho-like storm swept through Tulsa with wind gusts of eighty miles per hour. Widespread tree damage and downed power lines left some 100,000 residents without power. Rain, in that ordinarily dry month, caused flash flooding throughout the eastern half of the state. We're used to erratic weather in Oklahoma. We're used to torrential toad-stranglers and choking dust storms and prairie wildfires and twisters and searing summer heat. But the inversion of the seasons—the late snowfalls, early frosts, high heat in winter—that's new. Or it was new. Not anymore. It seems normal now, because it has become familiar, and what's familiar will, of course, in time, come to seem harmless.

───────

On Christmas Day 2000, the first year of the new millennium—a dozen years before this snake season I'm remembering—a slow, drizzling rain began to fall over southeastern Oklahoma. The temperature hovered right at freezing. We were all gathered at my folks' house for Christmas dinner. The forecasters were adamant: an ice storm was coming—*significant accumulation*, they said; *widespread outages*, they said; *be prepared*—but it was hard to believe them. The rain was so gentle, and the day was so warm. My husband wanted to go back to our house on the mountain, but it was Christmas, and I wanted to stay with my family. So Paul went on up to our house alone, driving slow in the cold rain in our car without four-wheel drive. By mid-afternoon the roads were becoming slick, but still the temperature hovered. I called Paul. "Don't you think you ought to come back down here? You know how we always lose power up there."

"I'll be all right," he said. By late afternoon, though, we could see what was coming. Perhaps if the forecasters had not used the word *storm*, we might have paid attention. Paul and I were used to winter storms, living in Upstate New York; we knew the sound of howling blizzards, muffled snowfall, the sense of that overwhelming power descending. Certainly, as a daughter of the southern plains, I'd been used to crashing thunderstorms, torrential downpours, the fierce, erratic destruction of tornadoes. This was not a storm. This was a slow, deceitful rain, not cold, not wind-driven, just a gentle accumulation of ice on the branches, the gravel, the eaves. Paul called. He had lost power already; there would be no water, no lights, no way to cook on our electric range. Daddy said, "C'mon, shug," and he drove me in his four-wheel-drive truck thirty miles along the steadily icing highway, and then up the mile-long drive to the top of the ridge to our house to get Paul. Daddy to the rescue, always, just like when we called him to come kill snakes. The three of us crammed in the cab of his pickup, we drove back, slow and slow on the icing roads, creeping along at ten miles an hour back to my family's land. By early evening, we'd lost power there, too.

Before it was over, ice would sheathe the better part of three states. Half a million homes would be without power. We wouldn't get ours back for seventeen days. But we were together, we were family, we cooked meals and boiled coffee in the fireplace, and Ruth and Les came over and brought food from their rapidly defrosting freezing, and we all ate together and read stories aloud by lamplight and went to bed at seven o'clock, because it had already been dark for two hours by then and there was nothing to do; it felt primitive, it felt endless, and also like an ending. It felt like something had shifted, like the world had changed forever, like it would always be this way.

In the night I'd awaken to the sound of crashing tree limbs—a sharp crack, loud as a gunshot, followed by the whooshing, thunderous fall as great branches broke under the weight and fell to the earth. Sometimes it was the sound of whole trees toppling, undermined by the slow accretion, those thin sheathes of ice built layer by layer to the breaking point, and it had all been so subtle, so quiet, no noise as the freezing rain fell, a silent, almost imperceptible beginning of the end. That's what it felt like—the end of the world as I knew it, the same as I'd been hearing about in Revelation all my life, except without violence, without Armageddon or the Four Horsemen of the Apocalypse. Just that slow, deceitful, gentle rain.

Our parents' aging was like that. A slow accretion of signs and changes, an incremental buildup, a gradual transformation. Oh, I could mark certain turning points, the accidental falls, the compression fractures, the obsessions and muddled conversations, forgotten medicines, lost billfolds and purses and keys, but most of it was both more alarming and more subtle than that. The first time Daddy stood in the living room holding his toothbrush, baffled about how to use it. The first time Mama asked me to open a can of green beans and then a few seconds later asked me again, and then, a few seconds later, asked me again. The gradual accretion, the slow build toward the point of no return, one diminishment added to another, until losses that would have disturbed or frightened us a few weeks earlier had become normal, had become the unsurprising, acceptable condition of my parents' inexorable walk toward death.

I wonder if the end of the world will be like that. Not cataclysm, not apocalyptic flood or fire or wind, but a slow accretion like a freezing rain, gentle at first, normal—nothing to fear, really, no matter how much the weather forecasters keep shouting their warnings. Just a slow incremental buildup, crystalline sheathes mounting, layer upon layer, until we lose power, until the trees and the powerlines and the towers that connect us all come crashing down.

Novice at Belle Point
SARA N. BEAM

In 2019, Oklahoma's age as a state is 112 years old. To put that into context, only 3–4 scant generations would separate a 112-year-old person from a child born today. Other U.S. states are more than twice that old. Nineteenth-century America is not that far into the past, especially here in Oklahoma.

Prior to statehood, the U.S. border arguably stood at the eastern edge of Oklahoma, at Fort Smith, Arkansas. Just across that border, on the other side of the wide, moving waters near Belle Point, the junction of the Arkansas and Poteau Rivers, was (and still is) Garrison Avenue with its single remaining brothel house, train station, and courthouse with gallows. Facing eastward, directly dead ahead was (and still is) the massive, arched and pointed, red brick Catholic Church called Immaculate Conception.

Immaculate Conception, remember, refers not to Jesus's conception, but to Mary's. What you view driving into Fort Smith from Roland, Oklahoma, is a medieval scene. Your implied choices are between virgin or whore, between morality as obedience to patriarchal law *or* immorality as river pirate, gambler, savage, john, and spectacle of punishment.

Oklahoma, as part of the U.S. imperial project, has *always* been a place of struggle. There's a sense that you must just roll with it and navigate the conditions, here in scratchy-grass Oklahoma, windy Oklahoma, muggy Oklahoma, with its ragweed pollen, dog hair, pin-oak-mite-bitten wild land. No matter how much pavement we may put over the red dirt or the river bottom earth, nature and time prevail.

This land can kill you. With tornadoes, fire, earthquakes, floods, and droughts.

Here, you live on the wind, forced to move according to aeronautical principles, to adjust the physics of your body and movement to accommodate the extra forces around you. So, in these ways, as someone who's lived in Oklahoma most of her life, I feel more than prepared to deal with cancer, childbirth, death and life, at their raw edges. Okies may *hate* each other but they will always help the shit out of people, as I saw them do during my childhood when I witnessed massive grassfires on the family land in 1980s Haskell County and again during young adulthood in the aftermath of straight-line winds and baseball-sized hail in 2005 Tulsa. Jealousy, cheating, feuds among family and friends . . . then those on-air warnings and tornado or flood sirens sound, reminding us that all is impermanent.

However, it's a lesson that borders are moveable. Borders change. They evolve, and each has its own history. Now Oklahoma is the United States, and we/they have to face our own history as the "United States of Lyncherdom" (to borrow Mark Twain's words), exposing and dismantling the old rationales for colonizing: the mythological narratives of "natives" in need of rescue, empty and underutilized land, white women under threat of sexual violence by men of color, and even the seemingly-positive myths, like those of the noble savage, the reformed woman, or the white savior, are toxic. The Land Run celebrations held by local schools are tributes to such a seemingly positive myth. Because these (hi)stories support the imperial project, they too are part of the bone-deep infection Okies must find a way to treat.

Oklahoma is still in development. It was colonized, but there were peoples, cultures, civilizations here prior to the middle of the nineteenth century. There was not *nothing* here. That is the lie of my childhood—nothing was here, nothing that mattered, nothing that was managed well or properly. A foundational fake story that existed to justify the land runs, mineral rights, and imminent domain. But I couldn't stop digging in the Haskell County ground and finding bottles, bullets, and bones.

I find similar vestiges of old laws and battles for power inside myself, in my inner terrain, and they are part of the song of myself. I'll tell you one of them—it's a story that begins in Fort Smith, the story of my first love and how, with the help of women who loved me, I turned that into loving myself. The story begins in the summer of 1999, and it's called "The Geometry of Lies." Here it is:

First, you have to remember from middle school math that the shortest distance between two points is a straight line.

Then, you have to know that I was seeing myself from the outside in, as most people do, at age nineteen. I sought to move from one feeling to another *within* a situation rather than to remove myself from the situation. Like so:

Yes, I'm fine with your friends.

Yes, I still love you.

It's my fault.

I lied a lot in my first marriage. To myself. I didn't mind that he lived with a man on crank, I told myself. It's okay that I said I didn't believe in marriage and he got me a ring. On Valentine's Day. And I said yes. Sure. This is fine, I said in my head. It's sweet, even.

But the circumference of the Walmart ring was too small for my finger. The diamond poked out and caught on the green threads of my video-store work apron.

I can make it work, I thought. This band that binds isn't too tight. And, no, no, don't worry—it's no matter you didn't find out my ring size. You're the first person who loved me back.

The shortest distance between two points is a straight line. But the shortest distance around my finger was larger than the size of the ring. Lies come easy when you internalize all your reactions and bluff. Everyone is happier when you agree, and you never have to learn how to say no.

If only that were not *so wrong*. But it is. Trying to analyze other people's feelings all the time is exhausting, and staying in your own skin, in your own present, is just as hard, but yields better results. Ultimately, it's better not to waste the time. Quick pain instead of lingering pain that sets into infection.

The truth: the shortest distance between two points is a straight line, heart to head. The shortest distance is trusting yourself.

Like so:

I don't have to explain my preferences to you.

I love myself more than I love you.

I didn't cause it. I couldn't prevent it. It's not my fault.

If I could travel with Doctor Who back in time, I'd find me and say, Young self, if your answer is not a confident yes, it's a no. It's okay to believe your gut if your gut is unsure. If something gives you pause, take that seriously. Do everything you want to do all the time. Love thyself. Trust thyself.

You can *always* change your mind.

When you've trained yourself to avoid "no," you forget how to know how you actually feel. Here are some clues. "No" feels like increased heart rate, stomach hurting, cold hands and feet. "I don't like this" feels like turning away, wanting to hide, falling asleep, going numb, faking pleasure so he'll get off and leave you alone.

I know now that if I hadn't been lying to myself, I wouldn't have lied to him.

After three years together, I'd gotten so used to self-deception that I convinced myself it was all right to pay for his rent and food even though we were separated because I had sent him away, to the Northeast, where I was planning eventually to join him. When he left, deep down I felt I didn't want to go with him, but I couldn't admit it yet. I didn't think it was real because I only *felt* it, I didn't *know* it. I wasn't sure, and I was mistaking pity for wanting to stay together. Pity said stay with him. Pity said pay his bills.

But it was worth it to be alone and safe with my true love. Me.

I was always here for me. Finally alone, I felt the most loved by myself and honest with myself in that rectangle sleeping bag on the carpeted floor of a 300-square-foot apartment with my dog, my cat, and my ring and ringer off.

They call it codependency, the way we love people with addictions, depression, borderline personality disorders. I am a textbook serial codependent. During and after that first marriage, I walked on eggshells. I lost touch with my friends. I always had an excuse for the men I was with—and there were more to follow. I lied for them. I carried loads for them. I was a compulsive rescuer.

"You're *very* important, aren't you?" a wise woman said to me slyly and gently after I told her I knew my addiction was to feel needed, to feel powerful. Feeling like a savior was just an ego stroke. She held up a mirror so I could see I was deluded, thinking I was magical in my ability to help others, thinking that if I was helping others I must myself be perfectly fine. I felt like the strongest woman in the world. But I wasn't helping, I wasn't fine, I wasn't at my strongest.

I kept myself at a distance from me because I was worried I didn't love myself—a revelation brought to me by studying the book *Alice in Wonderland*, where your dreams are populated by your own creations. Late in the story, Alice is in a courtroom subjected to the evaluations of an absurd monarch and a jury bench full of animals. She has a revelation similar to Sarah's in the film *Labyrinth*. (Remember that moment when Sara tells Jareth he holds no power over her? That.) Like Sara, Alice suddenly stands up literally and figuratively, as if to say *fuck this*. What was I missing, I thought? What had I subjected myself to because I didn't realize what was real and what wasn't? What enemies had

I imagined into being and put in control of me? These questions have led me to the truth and still set me free every day. I never get to stop asking myself, I never get to stop healing.

My first relationship is now marked by two dots on a timeline, 1999 and 2003. The further I get from them, the closer together they appear. In the museum of my mind, I look back on the events:

In 2001, when the jets hit the towers, I was twenty-one in Conway, Arkansas, and I was asleep. A year later, I was in Tulsa, Oklahoma, home of the "lost twin," the Bank of Oklahoma Tower, designed by the same architect who designed the World Trade Center.

A year after that, before my marriage had officially ended, I already was infatuated with someone else, everyone else but me.

By early 2004, I had extricated, exorcised myself from the marriage and my own lies. I braided my soon-to-be-ex-husband's wet hair into two Willie Nelson style plaits one last time and, when he asked if he could stay, I said no. There was nothing welcoming I could say that would not be a lie. He did good by me, in the end, by leaving—the apartment, the city, the marriage.

The takeaway—I'm still processing it so many years later—is that what seems to be foreign or undefinable can turn out to be a crucial part of yourself. Conversely, what seems to be part of you may be separate; I had colonized a part of someone else's needs, making them my own, securing a "resource" to feed my desire to feel needed.

Binarism, aka either-or thinking, is a logical fallacy that depends on imaginary walls. It's limiting. It reduces nuanced situations to black and white. However, there is such a thing as staying in your own skin, meaning you leave others to take responsibility for themselves. Personal integrity depends on loving yourself vulnerably, trusting your self-preserving instincts when you don't know what kinda state you're in but you know you gotta find your way home.

Every boundary has a story. Rethinking a border town at the edge of Oklahoma, I see my U.S. state in a new light. I see my place in Oklahoma history—this place that was "Indian Territory" before 1907, and so many other names before that. Though my maternal grandmother was born in Pawhuska, I am an outsider on land that was taken in unjust ways. Rethinking my first marriage and what I learned from my first romantic relationship, I see my personal state in a new light. I see my past actions, my old boundaries, as a point in my storyline and a point in the tale of my limits and inner terrain. I have always lived in this body, with this mind and heart, and I am a valid witness and judge of my state.

Finding a Way to Thrive

JEANETTA CALHOUN MISH

Clarity. I still remember what it felt like, to see myself and my life clearly. I had been awake except for rare hour-long naps for twenty-two days. Anxiety and grief and fear ruled my world. I got up from the bed where I was tossing and turning and walked a few steps to the door of my ten-year-old son's room. By the greenish glow of his Power Ranger nightlight, I saw that he was tossing and turning, too, whimpering in his sleep, frightened by a nightmare. Suddenly, I knew: I had to change my life to save his.

Despite the way I remember it, the process of changing the way I thought and lived did not occur in a singular (single?) moment. I had left my most recent abusive relationship a year before, one that broke me mentally and physically. After staying nine months with my mother and her third husband, I found a job and moved us out on our own. My son and I lived in the projects in Odessa, Texas, because that's all I could afford on my minimum-wage part-time job. The morass I was trying to crawl out of was deep.

Like many Oklahoma women, I was sexually, physically, and emotionally abused by a series of men, beginning when I was eight. By the time I was in high school, I found dangerous solace in drugs and alcohol. I found what I thought was love and acceptance in the backseats of boys' cars—a common reaction for abused girls. I got pregnant at seventeen and had an abortion. I was arrested a week before graduation for being high, but the charges were dropped. Two weeks after the arrest, I was sober for the first time in months when I gave my salutatorian's graduation speech.

Although I had a 4.0 GPA and high college entrance-exam scores, I was not a college success after high school, partly because I'd already developed a fondness for alcohol, other mind-altering substances, and partying, and partly because I did not know how to go to college. No one in my immediate family had gone to college—a family friend who had gone to college sat with my mother and me when we opened college invitation letters so he could help us figure out what they said. Neither my mother—who had not graduated from high school—nor I were stupid, but we were ignorant: we did not know the difference between tuition and fees; we did not fully understand which expenses scholarships would cover and which they would not; we did not know how to properly respond to offer letters; we simply did not know. My mother worried about how she would feed and clothe and support me if I went to a school far away. I worried about how I would fit in when my accent and lack of cultural capital would mark me, especially at the Ivy League schools that recruited me, as an outsider at the least, a cracker at the worst. I received one full scholarship offer, from the University of Oklahoma—but Norman was not far enough away from the hometown I'd come to hate. So I went off to Houston, largely because I'd found my birth father there, and wanted to get to know him.

Once I enrolled at the University of Houston, I was lost on the large campus that had many more students than my hometown had citizens. I had to work to support myself and I missed more classes than I attended. I struggled to understand enrollment forms and class schedules; I struggled to find a social group to belong to; I struggled in classes for which I was not well prepared. I lasted half a semester, went home over Thanksgiving break, and never went back. Shortly thereafter, I dove into my first abusive adult relationship.

From the day I returned to my hometown until the night I watched my son sleeping, my life ran in cycles: start a relationship, live with abuse, end a relationship. Start again—and do the same thing. It seemed I could neither recognize an abuser nor live by myself for longer than a few months. Or, to be more truthful, I was attracted to tough guys, to the bad boys that I found in the bars I frequented. There were brief periods when I understood I needed help—over the nearly twenty years between leaving my hometown and changing my life, I sought counseling three or four times, but always fell back into what I knew, to the kind of relationships my mother had chosen. But by the time I was twenty, my mother had changed her life: she lived alone, earned a certificate at the local community college that helped her get good jobs, then, eventually, chose better partners, and found happiness, security, and safety. I did not follow her model.

I have often asked myself, *How could I have been so stupid for so long?* How could I continue to leap into dangerous relationships? The only answer I have is an observation by therapists who work with adult survivors of child abuse: in 1994, Diana M. Elliott and John Briere observed that "symptoms adult survivors manifest are often 'logical extensions' of dysfunctional coping mechanisms developed during childhood" (quoted in Kathleen Kendall-Tackett's chapter, "Victimization of Female Children," in the 2001 *Sourcebook on Violence against Women*, edited by Claire M. Renzettik, Jeffery L. Edleson, and Raquel Kennedy; London: Sage Publications, p. 104). I knew abuse—it was familiar to me, and so I chose men whose personalities were familiar to me. As is often said in my part of Oklahoma, "Better the devil you know than the devil you don't."

It was the birth of my son and that one time when he was three, when his father pushed him down the stairs, which made me realize I was putting my son in the same kind of danger that I had experienced growing up. I had tried to take my son and leave before—but all I earned from the effort was a black eye and broken nose. This time, I waited until my partner was out of town, then moved out of the apartment we shared into a ramshackle, wood-stove-heated mid-1960s trailer house twenty miles away. I left no forwarding address. Wind whistled through doors and windows despite the plastic weatherproofing. The Vietnam-era aluminum-wired fuse box burst into flame. Nonetheless, it was the safest house I'd lived in since I was three years old.

Eight months after moving, I found myself so depressed and physically ill that I could barely get out of bed. So we moved to West Texas to my mother's house and then to HUD housing. The night I saw what my life—and my son's—had come to, the night I witnessed my son having nightmares, the night of clarity, I promised my sleeping child that the next morning I'd do something different, something better. Shortly after daybreak, I called a friend in the neighborhood and asked her if she'd keep my son for a couple of days until my mother and stepfather came back from a weekend trip. I asked her if she'd drive me to the mental health hospital out by the airport. Thirty days of intensive therapy. Thirty days of AA meetings. Thirty days of medications for depression and anxiety. Thirty days to change my life.

The stay at the mental health hospital was just the beginning, not the end, of my journey. Once I was stable, I enrolled in a literature course at the local community college, just to see if I could manage going back to school as a thirty-seven-year-old single mother. I passed the class, then with the help of disability funds, enrolled in a four-year college in the spring. I continued seeing a psychiatrist, I made friends—female friends—whose company I enjoyed at the movies, at the theater, at community concerts, or at home, mine or theirs, instead of going out to bars. However, I hadn't quite rid myself of old habits—I met a man at an AA meeting and we started dating. Later, my son and I moved in with him. He wasn't physically abusive—he was emotionally abusive. I told myself that it wasn't so bad, that I could expect nothing better, that I was not worthy of an abuse-free relationship. I don't think I even knew what an entirely abuse-free relationship looked like.

With the support of my family and a mentor-professor, I completed my bachelor's degree, then my master's. I applied to Ph.D. programs and was accepted to OU, the school I'd turned down so many years before. I left the man I'd been living with in Odessa and moved home to Oklahoma. The course work in graduate school was challenging, and my son had difficulties we had to deal with, problems arising from his premature birth and from keeping him in an abusive family situation for too long. We dealt with them the best we could. Mornings were busy, but they weren't terrifying anymore, and my son's nightmares slowly subsided. We both made friends. There was a short period during graduate school when I spiraled down into the darkness; I went back to therapy, took my medication faithfully, and emerged into the light a few months later. I met a man—this time a kind, smart, generous man. I had finally learned not only to recognize a good man but also to do my share to create a good relationship. We celebrated our fourteenth wedding anniversary in 2018.

Looking back, I can see that I was taking steps toward psychological health all along, but each step toward the light was followed by two steps back into the darkness. The moment of clarity I experienced watching my sleeping son was not the first such revelation, nor was it the last. Before I could have a good life, I had to learn that I was worthy of a good life, and that lesson slipped away more than once. I had to learn to forgive myself and that took a long time, a lot of therapy, and repeated, unflinching inventories of my own dysfunctions. Recovering from childhood abuse—of all kinds—is a process, not an event.

Even now, years later, disturbing dreams haunt me, occasionally dreams of actual violent events in my life, but most often nowadays, I dream I see a young woman crouched in a corner, shaking, her arms covering her head in a defensive posture. I go to her, squat down beside her, and put my arms around her shoulders. When she turns her face toward me, sometimes I see a younger version of myself. Sometimes I see a face from the day's news reports—yet another abused girl or battered woman. Sometimes I don't recognize her at all, but I understand why she's fearful. I embrace the women of my dreams. I tell them that it can get better, that it's not easy but it's possible. That, hidden inside their terror, they can find the strength and the smarts and the moments of clarity that will show them the way.

Fidelity

TAMYA COX-TOURÉ

Every guy I have ever dated has cheated on me. Every. Guy. Cheated. I have been in great relationships and not-so-great relationships, but cheating has been the common denominator. It has not changed since high school. I am an adult now, and this continues to happen. Habitual infidelity can take so much out of a person, and at times I believe it has taken absolutely everything from me—leaving me with an inability to trust, an uncompromising attitude toward men, a jaded outlook on future relationships, and consistent self-doubt.

I have been fortunate enough to see successful relationships up close among colleagues, close friends, and even my parents, so I do not have unrealistic views of what a healthy relationship can be. A successful relationship is one in which the partners honor and respect each other even when one person is almost out the door, or in which the partners recognize just how wonderful and tough being together is but still choose to stay together each and every time. A successful relationship allows partners to be honest with each other and themselves. I have seen them; I am a product of one. I just don't know if I will ever be a part of one.

I have amazing friends and a career that fulfills and challenges me. I thoroughly enjoy life. Do I have the right to complain when I am able to check off two out of the three "life is good" boxes? Maybe I do not need a perfect score to have a perfect life.

Like most people who have been cheated on, I intuitively knew the person I was dating was being unfaithful. I began secretly reading e-mails and checking social media accounts—everything I had promised myself I would never do *again*. Of course, I found the evidence I already knew existed. I was upset and mad as hell but not surprised. Why would I think it would be different? In some ways, this time was different. I found an e-mail where he had a conversation about me with her. I was actually going to get some constructive criticism about me; I was going to gain some anthropological feedback on myself. This was a gift, right? According to him, I was selfish and consistently emasculated him by challenging him in many ways. I was too this or too that. He suggested to her that I was good on paper: good job, good family upbringing, good circle of friends—just not good enough for him.

To this day I do not know if I am hurt or grateful for this insight; regardless, I was now aware of this. Even after finding the evidence of cheating, I stayed. I continued in the relationship as if I'd never read the emails, continued as if I didn't know what he was thinking, and continued as if I had not advised my friends numerous times to get out of toxic relationships. I smiled and laughed even though I knew it was all a lie. I said, "I love you" back and slept next to him every night despite dreading coming home. I realize now that I did the same things I swore I would never do after each previous breakup. Eventually, the relationship ended, probably two years later than it should have. Oddly enough, I have no ill feelings toward him. I honestly wish him every piece of happiness he deserves, even though there is zero hope of reconciliation.

I never had the *aha* moment or realized some huge epiphany during or after that breakup. Simply, a relationship that needed to end ended. I mourned the loss of our intimacy and decent friendship of course, but mostly I was relieved. I was not second guessing every move I made. I was not passively existing. I realized how tiring and overwhelming it was to pretend to be something other than me. Granted, I have never denied my numerous flaws or areas where I can make self-improvements, but it was so comforting to finally breathe freely.

If there is a come-to-Jesus moment to be had, it is the recognition that I am in my mid-thirties and may never be married or have kids. I process that regularly without ever coming to a conclusion on how that makes me feel.

I have no words of wisdom on how to continue after lost love. However, I am in a new relationship now that forces me to bare my soul to *myself*. I have had several of these soul-baring moments when I'm all alone. I suppose these intimate moments have been the most cathartic. All walls have no choice but to come down in those private minutes regardless if they are occurring during a morning drive to work, while I'm finishing the latest best-selling novels, or even on a short walk to the next room. I have no choice but to face them head on.

Before I could fully find myself in this new relationship, I had to do so much processing. I analyzed every move I made and every word I spoke. I processed every instance to make sure my feelings were genuine. I even talked through my process with my new boyfriend. I never wanted him to feel a certain way or not think I was sincere. At some point, though, I recognized I was driving myself crazy. Once again, I was overwhelming myself. Instead of making sure I had the perfect outer appearance as I did before, I was tiring myself with overanalyzing every move I made or every word he said.

I wish I could say this new relationship has removed all my self-doubt and insecurity that I specifically have about relationships. I wish I could say that my faith in relationships has been restored, but I can't. The truth is I may never be able to say those things, and that is just fine. I can't even promise that this new relationship won't end because of infidelity. I am done trying to check off all the imaginary boxes that both society and I have created to define the perfect life. I have been strong enough to live my life on my own terms in most areas, and I have to remind myself constantly that I can do that in this relationship as well. The pressure I continue to place on myself to "have it all" has led to bad decisions, and I am certain that those unhealthy relationships I was in were partly because of this pressure. But what I do know today is that I am stronger than I ever knew I was. While my faith in others may still be shaky, I know now, with unwavering faith, who I really am, the future I want, and the person I aspire to be.

An Outsider Within

A Culmination of a Multifaceted Journey

JULIET EVUSA

It was 5:30 in the morning. I could hear a myriad of birds chirping their heads off, our rooster crowing, and our cows mooing. I wished our annoying rooster would shut up. I did not feel like getting up that early. I had stayed up until midnight enjoying Jackie Collins's *Hollywood Husbands*—a novel my mother would not permit me to read, but I did anyway. "*Emali, vuka urombe ichai* [Emali, wake up and make breakfast]!" my mother yelled. As I made my way to our outdoor kitchen, I felt a cold chill rushing through my spine; I was shivering. Once I got to the kitchen, I began loading our *jiko* (a portable cooking stove) with *makaa* (wood charcoal), and then stuffed old newspapers into the stove's tiny front opening. After pouring two drops of kerosene on the newspapers, I lit them with matches. It took a few minutes for the stove to light. After brewing *chai* (tea) and warming the previous night's left overs, I headed back to the house to get my younger siblings ready for the day.

As I was serving breakfast, I wished school would open soon. Not only was August a school vacation time, it was also corn harvesting season in Western Kenya. I dreaded chores that I had to perform. Corn harvesting season is an incredibly labor-intensive time for peasant farmers in Western Kenya who can only afford to use primitive tools to farm. I hated spending my entire mornings and afternoons cooking meals for the few workers we could afford to pay. I had to cook two meals for about twelve individuals six days a week! Unlike cooking in industrialized nations, cooking in rural Kenya was an extremely tedious and time-consuming process. It involved walking a few miles to the nearest water hole to fetch water. Imagine balancing fifty pounds of water on your head in a five-gallon bucket! It also involved picking vegetables and taking our corn to the nearest corn mill to be ground. After cooking lunch, I had to move tons of harvested grains to our wooden corn storage structure. By the time the workers left, around three in the afternoon, it was time to prepare dinner for the family.

In the meantime, my older brother was only required to fulfill two roles—tending to our three cows and splitting firewood. That was it! None of us knew where he spent most of his day. He would only show up for lunch and dinner. Other minor chores were delegated to my younger sisters. I constantly questioned why our community expected girls to perform excessive domestic chores in comparison to what was required of the opposite sex.

I also wondered why we were subjected to cultural norms that did not attach value to our education. I struggled to understand why my society believed that educating me would enrich my future husband's family while educating my brother was perceived as enriching my own family. If my mother had not encouraged and also supported my efforts to overcome barriers set by my culture to pursue higher education, I would have become a statistic, another female in my community who had never seen the inside of high school, let alone university. At the time I was growing up, not only did my father perceive high school education as sufficient for girls, but he firmly believed that a college degree would deter my chances of getting married.

My journey to overcome barriers set up by my community began in 1989, when, upon completing my high school education, my mother begged my father to allow me to attend college. That year, two events led to an academic scholarship and a free one-way air ticket to India. It turned out that one of my mother's relatives knew of an academic scholarship program designed by Kenya's Department (Ministry) of Foreign Affairs for high school students with my socio-economic background. This meant that, if my application were accepted, I would have to attend college abroad. The application process was straightforward. After a few months I received a letter of acceptance from Maharaja Sayajirao University located in the Gujarat State of India. I could not believe it!

However, without the means to afford a one-way ticket to India, there was no way I would be able to travel. Once again my mother turned to her city relatives, who suggested that I approach major foreign airlines operating in Kenya and request a complimentary ticket. After talking to several airlines, I finally heard from *Gulf Air*. They were willing to fly me on "embargo" as long as there was an available seat on the date I intended to travel. When that day came, I was overcome with joy when the airline attendant announced, over the intercom, that I could finally board the plane. When my plane was about to land at Bombay (now known as Mumbai) International Airport, I recall something odd and unwelcoming about the airport's welcome sign. It simply read "This is Bombay," as opposed to "Welcome to Bombay International Airport." For a moment, I second-guessed my decision to attend college in India. I was afraid that the unwelcoming message was a sign of major hurdles to come. Like any other college student, I managed to overcome the social and economic hurdles faced by foreign students living away from home.

In 1993, I graduated from Maharaja Sayajirao University of India and became the third female in my home village, at that time, to obtain a college degree. After hunting for permanent jobs for about twelve months, I finally landed my first dream job. At only twenty-three years of age, I became one of eight graduates hired to serve the nation's Ministry (Department) of Cultural, Social, and Gender Services. My college degree finally paid off! My role as a social development officer with the Ministry also opened my eyes to some ingenious strategies undertaken by women's groups, which needed capital to start small businesses, to challenge cultural norms and practices that denied women access to property; without that access, women had no means to obtain collateral to apply for small loans. (These women discovered that they could qualify for small bank loans if they pooled their resources together to form a cooperative or self-help group.)

One appointment led to another. It was during my appointment with the Co-operative Bank of Kenya, between 1994 and 1997, when I witnessed firsthand some of the long-term consequences of harmful traditional practices that made it difficult for women to apply for small start-up loans that would help finance income-generating projects. One disturbing incident involved a male client who died of complications from AIDS. Customary laws dictated that in the event an account holder passed away, the bank must hand over the account to the deceased village chief, who would in turn consult with the deceased brothers to decide how the money would be disbursed. What is appalling is that the widow was not included in these discussions. One particular day, I happened to be working at the bank's front desk and hence was responsible for initiating the deceased client's account disbursement process. Luckily, that day the bank's manager was attending a seminar and a female supervisor was acting on his behalf. That female supervisor and I decided to carry out an unconventional transaction. Instead of following customary laws, we disbursed the deceased's savings to an account that we had opened on behalf of his widow! This made it possible for the widow to provide for her children. It dawned on me that I had just used my role as a senior clerical officer to challenge one harmful cultural norm that existed in my society.

After three years of working for corporate Kenya, I realized that I needed more than a Bachelor of Arts degree to challenge societal norms. Pursuing a master's degree from a research institution offering development programs, with direct affiliation to international organizations, would place me in a better position to apply for grants geared toward female empowerment. A higher level of academic experience would also enable me to make contributions through research that would assist in enacting policies aimed at eradicating harmful customary laws.

June 1997 was one of the happiest months of my life. After applying to a couple of research institutions, I finally received notification of an academic scholarship and stipend to one of them. Luckily this time I had saved enough money to purchase an airplane ticket on my own. Once again, I packed my bags and moved abroad—this time to Athens, Ohio. Ohio University offered one of the most prestigious master's programs in the field of International Affairs in the United States. I took courses with students from all over the globe!

My quest to highlight issues hampering the ability of girls and young women to realize their full potential had just begun. After I earned a dual master's degree in International Affairs and Communications Studies respectively, Ohio University awarded me yet another full tuition scholarship and graduate assistantship to pursue doctoral studies in its College of Telecommunications. Pursuing this route provided opportunities to publish and attend academic conferences where I could present research related to female empowerment. As if that were not enough, I applied for admission into a graduate program in the university's Department of Women Studies and was accepted! This program exposed me to various feminist theories that I would use in my research. There is no doubt in my mind that my academic opportunities justified my decision to leave my "cushy" corporate career in Kenya.

On August 7, 1998, exactly a year after I moved to the United States, the American Embassy in Kenya was attacked by Al-Qaeda operatives. I will never forget this day. My previous corporate employer's headquarters, Ufundi Cooperative House, was located in downtown Nairobi right next to the American Embassy. The attack gutted the rear half of the embassy and destroyed the entire Ufundi Cooperative House, as well as a couple of buildings within the four-block radius. By the time the operation came to an end, 213 people were dead, including 12 Americans, and an estimated 4,800 were wounded. I also learned that two of my former colleagues, including my former boss, perished in the attack. Some, who happened to be on duty when the attack occurred, sustained lifelong disabilities. It was heartbreaking. Those who survived e-mailed me photos of debris that was once my office.

This incident was yet another indication that I had made the right decision to move to the United States. The bombing would be one of the first major terrorist attacks on the Kenyan nation. The attack also introduced Osama Bin Laden and his terrorist organization, Al-Qaeda, to the American public. I finally got an opportunity to visit the U.S. Embassy memorial site in 2003. It was an emotional experience. Three years later, in 2006, I would visit the Oklahoma City bombing memorial and feel emotions similar to those I had experienced in 2003.

In July 2003, I finally got the opportunity to conduct field research in Kenya. My goal was to assess how new information communication technologies can be used to alleviate some of the daily challenges facing Kenyan women. This project, conducted as partial fulfillment of my doctoral dissertation, involved an extensive field study that drew upon multiple data sources. It employed a triangulation of methods ranging from in-depth interviewing, participant observation, and historical document analysis. A chapter of my dissertation is published in the book *Technology and Science in Africa*. This was a big deal for me!

July 2005 represented yet another milestone in my journey. After applying for faculty positions in the field of Media Studies across the United States, I finally received an offer from Rogers State University (RSU) in Claremore, Oklahoma. To be honest, as soon as I was done with the interviewing process, I was not sure about the prospect for me and my family of living in Oklahoma for more than five years. I called my mentor, Dr. Norma Pecora, to seek her advice. Her response surprised me. Based on her experience of living in the state (she received her Ph.D. from the University of Oklahoma), Dr. Pecora insisted that Oklahoma would not be a "race-friendly" state to raise my family. She was not the only individual who tried to discourage me from moving to Oklahoma.

After consulting with my husband, however, we both came to the same conclusion: we believed that Rogers State University had a lot to offer. To begin with, it turned out that one of the major attractions of the position was that I would be able to teach senior-level courses, such as Communication Research Methods, Representations of Women and Minorities in the Media, and Global Communications—key subject areas for my own research. The two other colleges that had offered me similar positions wanted me to teach Introduction to Mass Media and Public Speaking—both freshmen-level courses. Besides, unlike the RSU position, neither of these positions were tenure-track. My husband and I were also drawn to the fact that Claremore provided a safe haven to raise our family. One additional factor that sealed the deal related to my collegial colleagues. When my family and I moved to Oklahoma, my new colleagues were proactive in ensuring that all of us made a smooth transition to Oklahoma. I felt that I was part of a university "family." Together, my colleagues and I have written books, attended academic conferences, served on key university committees, and also assisted one another through tenure and promotion processes. Their supportive actions have exceeded the normal level of collegiality extended to most incoming faculty. This helped prove that I had made the right decision.

I have to admit, though, that I was taken aback by troubling statistics associated with Oklahoma in comparison to the rest of the country: third-worst public schools, third-highest rate of citizens working at or below the minimum wage, one of the highest child obesity rates, sixth-highest adult obesity rates, highest rate of female incarcerations, ninth-highest number of meth labs, sixth-highest teen birth rates, second-highest use of tobacco products, one of the worst states for mental health, in the top ten for divorce rates, highest increase in methamphetamine-related overdoes and drug use—and the list goes on. What strikes me most about these alarming statistics are two major similarities to the rural community where I grew up.

First, Vihiga County is known for its high rate of teenage pregnancy in comparison to the rest of Kenya. Not only does the county's school system fail to respond to the needs of its youth, the religious and traditional societal structure also makes it difficult to educate youth on matters of sexual and reproductive health. As a result, pregnant teenagers are forced to abandon their education early and in some cases engage in early marriages. Second, the county is facing its greatest threat from alcohol abuse. The National Authority for the Campaign against Drug Abuse (NACADA) reports that Western Kenya ranks second in the nation for consumption of *Changaa*, an illegal alcoholic beverage that literary means "kill me quickly." Locals opt for cheap illicit alcohol because they want to spend as little money as possible to get high. To make matters worse, *Changaa* is laced with lethal substances, such as methanol and formaldehyde, a lethal embalming fluid used in funeral homes.

It is not surprising that the death toll associated with the toxic alcohol brew continues to climb. During my recent visits to the Vihiga County, I saw skinny men with bloodshot eyes high on *Changaa* stumbling groggily and struggling to find their way home. It is not uncommon to see some of these men passed out in the prenoon shade. The *Changaa* epidemic is also affecting the county's youth. You see, boys who have undergone traditional male circumcision are initiated into adulthood when they are between seven to thirteen years old. Cultural traditions require that parents build temporary housing for them because initiated males are forbidden from sleeping under the same roof with their families. This gives them the freedom to indulge in "adultlike" activities including and not limited to consuming illicit traditional brews. There are no laws prohibiting businesses from serving alcoholic beverages to youth. The lack of such regulation has created a public concern, so much so that the Kenyan government has considered an amendment to the 2013 Alcoholic Drink Control Bill that would regulate the production, licensing, sales, as well as consumption of alcoholic drinks.

What I found interesting in Oklahoma is that my classroom interactions with college students and the local community in Claremore confirmed a "male hegemony" similar to the one I was accustomed to while growing up in Western Kenya. Prior to moving here, I had always envisioned the United States as a nation that embraces female empowerment. Although I had read about circumstances forcing women to take time off work to raise their children, I first met women who actually *chose* to stay at home, due to traditional reasons, in Oklahoma. The notion of a woman choosing to stay at home to raise her family would come as a shock to women in the least developed nations. For most of these women, staying at home is not an option. Given that Kenya's total unemployment rate, according to the "Gender Data Portal" posted on the 2017 World Bank website, is approximately 60 percent, and that only 19 percent of women were employed as of that year, very few women would forego the chance to work in the formal sector. Kenyan's current high unemployment rate explains why 77 percent of women in Kenya are self-employed, a statistic that also originates from the World Bank "Gender Data Portal." It is not uncommon to see women in rural areas spending their mornings laboring in farms with babies strapped on their backs. After spending their afternoons selling harvested produce in local farm markets, not only do they use their profit to purchase items like kerosene oil for their lanterns, they also purchase *makaa* (charcoal), soap, and cooking oil before heading back home to cook dinner for their families. Although this scenario might come across as depressing, these women believe that their involvement in the formal or informal sector makes them productive members of society and also gives them some form of independence. Besides, these women usually find it difficult to rely on their husbands.

One of my happiest moments in Oklahoma occurred when I finally achieved the ultimate American dream. My husband and I had saved enough to purchase a house. After living in the house for about five months, my son, who was five at that time, finally made friends with a neighbor's son his age. This was a big deal to my husband and me since our son is an extreme introvert. My son and his new best friend spent most of their time playing basketball and football and also riding their bikes and scooters. One day, I finally received a visit from his friend's mother. After she introduced herself, she proceeded to inquire about my religion. When I asked her why my religious affiliation was important to her, she indicated that she wanted to ensure that her son's friend shared her same religious beliefs. This shocked me! Growing up in Africa and India, religious affiliation was never an issue. In Kenya my mother scraped her savings together to ensure that my siblings and I attended schools known for their excellence in education, not their religious affiliation. I recall attending a Sikh primary school, a Hindu secondary school, and finally a Catholic high school. Students from various religious backgrounds attended these schools. What we had in common was our desire for quality education. The same was true when I was pursuing my baccalaureate in India. Because there were many foreign students attending Maharaja Sayajirao University, interacting with students from different religious backgrounds was the norm. I recall my roommates and me inviting our Hindu, Buddhist, and Muslim friends to partake in Christmas festivities. I also enjoyed attending their Diwali and Eid-Al-Fitr celebrations.

My exposure to individuals from different religious backgrounds explains why I was shocked at my neighbor's inquiry. The same neighbor paid me yet another visit. This time she stated, "I heard that you and your husband are college professors." She went on to ask "Does this mean that you are smart?" I was stunned! Despite her shocking concerns, our sons became very close friends.

That would not be the only time I would be asked about my religious affiliation. The fact that I identify myself as a Christian usually surprises most people here, especially my students. I always feel compelled to briefly explain the history behind British colonialism in Kenya, most importantly the role British explorations in East Africa played in paving the way for Christian missionaries. As a result, about 80 percent of Kenya's total population currently subscribes to Christianity.

The 2008 presidential election was yet another defining moment for me and my family. It turned out that the church I was attending was among dozens of Southern Baptist churches that had pledged to disavow their nonprofit status so that they could legally sway their parishioners to vote against Barack Obama, the then Democratic nominee and future president. About a month before the November election, I realized that the pastor's sermon revolved around a passage in the Bible that warns of the so-called Antichrist. Even more frightening were some of the conspiracy theories surrounding Obama to which the pastor alluded. My natural instinct led me to take notes. I recall one elderly gentleman, who thought that I was taking notes because I was enjoying the sermon, telling me, "I like this preacher because he is not afraid to speak the truth." He also added that I ought to make a point of attending church on a regular basis. Let's just say that was the last time we attended that church. As a Kenyan national whose ancestral home happens to be in close proximity to the home of Obama's father, I am fully aware of his father's family history.

A month after the Antichrist sermon, some of the church's female elders paid my family a visit. They brought with them a cute basket of delicious freshly baked cookies. My visitors then proceeded to ask me why we stopped attending church, and, boy, was I not afraid to reveal the entire truth! My husband, who was seated right next to me, had to nudge me to tone it down. I have never heard from my church visitors ever since. The point that I am trying to make is that it took me moving to Oklahoma to understand how my very own religion has been and is still been used by some of its followers to paint a negative picture of the "other" race. This was also a learning moment for me because it contrasted with the experiences that I had growing up with individuals from different religious affiliations.

In 2010 I became the first black faculty member at RSU to receive tenure at my institution. To be honest with you, I was just happy that I received tenure. Being a black female faculty member with a foreign accent in a predominantly white institution can be challenging. I vividly recall July 28, 2005, the first day

I reported to the institution. Part of the faculty orientation process entailed having your faculty ID photo taken. Once I got to the ID station, a student worker behind the desk asked me to produce my student identification number. At first I took this as a compliment. However, when I replied that I was faculty, she did not believe it. She proceeded to shout, "There is a woman here who claims that she is faculty!" The student worker did not even bother to privately approach her supervisor to explain the situation. Luckily, her boss happened to have met me when I was being interviewed. He was extremely apologetic.

I made other interesting observations during class sessions. I recall my first day of teaching Global Communications. I am 5 feet 2 inches tall and weigh about 120 pounds. When I walked into the classroom, I noticed that most of my students were nontraditional—local pastors, construction and factory workers, and even mothers returning to college. What struck me most was how some male students were sporting a mullet hairstyle, ripped checked sleeveless shirts, and multiple tattoos that glared at me. One particular student reminded me of a comedian who goes by the name "Larry the Cable Guy." I was intimidated by his appearance! I have to admit that, for a moment, I allowed a negative stereotype associated with individuals from the south to influence the first encounter I had with my students. And, boy was I wrong! As the semester commenced I learned a lot from my students. Some were not shy about indicating that I was the first black faculty member they had encountered. Here is what is interesting: they happened to be some of the most diligent students I had ever taught. I was also struck by the "southern manners" exhibited by my male students. Every time they addressed me they would call me "Ma'am." I was also able to relate to my female nontraditional students, many of them single or divorced with two to three children, enrolled in college in the hopes of securing a job that would enable them to provide for their children. This reminded me of Kenyan women to whom I relate who do whatever it takes to gain their independence.

My identity as the first black foreign faculty member also meant that students with international status were naturally drawn to me—a professor who, like them, was once an international student. Most of my foreign students tended to be athletes. What impressed me most about these students was that they often made the president's or their college dean's honors roll. I have also had the privilege of mentoring African American students who went on to pursue graduate school.

Students of color who felt that they were subjected to discrimination would frequently open up to me. I will never forget two female students who shared with me their racial profiling story. It happened that their new employer required that they dress formally for work. After clocking off work for lunch, they headed to a well-known clothing store to purchase formal wear. After paying for their purchase, they made their way out of the store. As they approached their vehicle, they noted that two police patrol vehicles had blocked it. Before they knew it, they were pinned to their vehicle and handcuffed. You can imagine how terrified they were! It turns out that the store's main branch had released a memorandum warning them of two shoplifters who happened to fit these girls' profiles. They were detained for a few hours. As soon as they were cleared, the police released them. I could go on narrating story after story of minority students who encountered racial profiling in Claremore, Oklahoma. I sometimes found it difficult to believe that this kind of profiling could happen in Claremore. In fact, my initial reaction would always be "What did you do to trigger the altercation?" However, this changed when I too was subjected to racial profiling.

One summer evening, as I was jogging in my neighborhood, I noticed two law enforcement personnel officers talking to my neighbors. After jogging for about a mile, I was stopped by those same officers. To be honest, I was not afraid. As a matter of fact, I assumed that they were seeking information. They proceeded to ask me to produce my identification. This threw me off. Who jogs with their driver's license? When I stated the obvious, they were offended. These officers were not afraid to declare that I met the profile of an individual harassing the neighborhood. I proceeded to point out that I too was part of the neighborhood. My reaction appeared to annoy them. When they finally let me go, I immediately called my husband. This was a very humbling experience. It made racial profiling a personal reality.

In 2014 my husband and I became naturalized citizens! Words cannot describe how we felt. This also meant that we would finally have the honor and privilege of participating in the world's greatest democracy! However, as a female who also happens to be black, an immigrant, and an intellectual, I felt that the 2016 presidential campaign brought to the surface some of the most uncomfortable norms in our society. Racism, xenophobia, bigotry, sexism, anti-Semitism, fat-shaming, disregard of facts and education, anti-establishment sentiment, tolerance of incivility, I could go on and on. The presidential campaign seemed an anomaly! I was surprised that a significant percentage of Americans embraced some of these prejudices.

A lot of questions ran through my mind during the 2016 campaign. What happened to the values that truly make America great? What happened to the melting pot? What happened to compassion? What happened to interpersonal connection? The lack of civility I witnessed during campaign rallies reminded me of the kind that are common in African nations, where dictatorships thrive. It is not uncommon for African leaders to use the "divide and conquer" strategy to appeal to their masses. Pitting whites against minorities appeared to have worked in America during the 2016 election. My seven-year-old son even asked me during that time whether our family would be "kicked out" of the country. To be honest, I was reluctant to ask him where he got this idea because I was afraid that his peers at school might have alluded to this and as a result hurt his feelings. However, I did my best to reassure him that this would never happen. He is an American citizen. On a more positive note, my fourteen-year-old son was obsessed with the election. He would wake up early to watch mainstream media. He even went out of his way to constantly update himself on the facts concerning this election. This was extremely impressive to my husband and me.

I have always wondered what my life would be like had I not gathered the courage to break loose from traditions that continue to undermine females. Although I do not yet feel that I have done enough to contribute to policies that would eradicate customary laws standing in the way of females who want to excel, I do not intend to give up. I am currently drawing on my Greg Kunz endowment for funding to conduct a video-ethnography in Kenya highlighting social norms that contribute to modern-day gender disparity in high school education. The story will be told through the eyes of ninth-grade students. I will continue to use video-ethnography to achieve my goal. If you were to ask me whether I have plans to relocate back to Kenya, I would not give you a firm response. Having first left when I was just about to turn eighteen, I have spent most of my adulthood away from home, so the country does not have the draw or pull that it otherwise might. I also want to remain close to my boys, who will likely stay in Oklahoma. Oklahoma will always be my home away from home.

I've Never Been to Heaven . . .

MARY MACKIE

Dreams.

It is our dreams that take us places we would not ordinarily go. If we are lucky, our dreams can be accomplished not far from home, in places we are familiar with, comfortable in, so happy just to be there.

Other dreams take us farther away, and if we are lucky, we get to go back home, once we catch our star.

Sometimes, we are not so lucky.

Then, Before We Knew

I was your friend before you knew
I was, before you knew you
needed one, before I knew it, too.

I sat on the wall outside of Gittinger,
having a last smoke before three hours
of research and three more hours of
creative writing.

I watched your sad, dark face while
you chained up your bike and sidled
into the front vestibule, disappearing
into the waves of bodies

coming from class,
going to class.

The red-bound books in the front office
are a constant reminder, even now,
of the hopes and dreams of so many
of us there, where we spilled our word-drenched
blood on the black and white linoleum,

and if you look in the corners, you can see
it is still there, a small piece of
each of us that will never leave this alleyway
of the University.

The days when we could and did
talk about the things that mattered to us,
what drove us to be here in the
first place, each alone and friendless, each
wanting more and interesting readings and
all the knowledge.
All the knowledge.

I was your friend before you knew
you needed one, and I remain that way
until forever.
What was it we lit in the dark, crying halls
of that now dilapidated building, where
we ate our fill of words and broken dreams?

My baptismal dive into Oklahoma came after passing through Joplin, Missouri, heading south along Interstate 44, on what I thought was an incredibly hot summer day. I learned quickly that living in air conditioning 24/7 was normal and that nobody opened their window blinds between March and November. But as I crossed over the border after an interminably long 289 miles through the hilly Ozark part of Missouri, the first thing that hit me (beyond the heat) was the signage: "Do Not Drive Into Smoke," which frightened me, and "Vasectomy Reversals" with a number to call, which terrified me. But later that evening, long past a stunning Tulsa sunset, I stood outside and watched the stars.

Beyond the cities are the vast open spaces of this state, and far from the incandescent lighting along each street, in the black of the night, one can see as if forever, past the millions of stars, each one watching over us, guiding our steps, as we make our way from one town to another. One day at a time, we really are fine.

All Is Well

In the cool of midnight,
the highway center lines
staccato their way from
back there to home;

> along a stretch of
> two-lane macadam so
> black behind and
> beside us, if I look
> upward and squint,
> I can pretend I see
> all the stars.

From Arkansas to Tulsa
by way of the Cherokee
Turnpike, we all
grew older and decided
we'd be just fine.

I learned why I should not drive through smoke, though not through firsthand experience, and I learned that the advertised vasectomy reversals were done in Texas, not Oklahoma. I had so much to learn, not only every day as a doctoral student, but in learning as well the ways of the "Sooner born and Sooner bred," and the vagaries of the weather.

Coming from the Northeast, I had seen many different types of storms: a few hurricanes and many blizzards, including the infamous blizzard of '78. With both hurricanes and blizzards, we were warned (often overly warned by zealous local weather forecasters) and had plenty of time to board up, head for higher ground, or just stock up on food and wait till the snow stopped and the big digging out could happen. But nothing in my many years of storms prepared me for springtime in Oklahoma, and after twenty-two years, I'm still terrified.

Incoming

People hold their breath waiting for the sound of sirens.
Curiously shaped clouds rumble closer from the horizon.
Lawn chairs fold and silently sleep through everything.
Chaos waits around the corner, knowing its time is coming.
Dark winds shriek over rooftops, reaching for anything in sight.
There are times it is too fearsome to open our eyes.

I spent the afternoon and evening of May 3, 1999, in Norman, Oklahoma, watching the events unfold with a horrified fascination that I had never experienced before. Before dark, I was looking out onto the windless street when I suddenly saw people on both sides of the street leave their houses, get into their cars, and sit there, with the cars running. I realized the reason shortly after: we had finally lost power and, without television, the car radio was one of the few ways to follow the EF-5 tornado as it made its way north from Chickasha.

Norman, for the most part, was untouched, but I had students from Moore who asked for extensions on their take-home finals because they had no home where they could work on them. Safe in my little duplex on Arkansas Street, I felt the severity of tornadoes come home to roost in a very personal way. I know many people who will still go outside and look up when the sirens go off, but I am not one of them. No amount of time spent in Oklahoma can inure me to the panic I feel each spring. As I child, I loved spring storms, sitting out back with my dad and watching the dark clouds and the lightning approaching from the west. Not anymore. Not when those storms can bring wrapped-up tornadoes in them.

After all this time, while I may have watched the devastation on television, often while it is occurring in real time, and while I have spent more hours than I care to recall in the basement of the Will Rogers Auditorium on the RSU campus in Claremore, I have never seen one up close and personal. And that's just fine with me. There are too many other, beautiful things I can observe, without even leaving my office.

Where the Canada Geese Walk

Below my office window, where the Canada geese walk
early mornings, the many pairs bring their babies
as they search for breakfast in the still, wet grass;
they disappear, to the pond, long before noon.

Early mornings, the many pairs bring their babies
and I watch them, softly from the shadows;
they disappear to the pond long before noon;
It's like their custom, ritual, for each day,

and I watch them, softly from the shadows
because they remind me of autumns and fiery trees in
    Massachusetts.
It's like their custom, ritual, for each day
and I know I'd miss them if they didn't appear—

Because they remind me of autumns and fiery trees in
    Massachusetts,
their beauty catches tears in my tight throat,
and I know I'll miss them when they don't appear,
so I stand quiet in wonder, simply watching—

Their beauty catches tears in my tight throat
as they search for breakfast in the still, wet grass.
So I stand quiet in wonder, simply watching,
below my office window, where the Canada geese walk.

I've always enjoyed watching Canada geese, and perhaps it's the connection I make that I find soothing—that they were up north, for me, to wave goodbye to in the fall as they headed for warmer places to spend their winters, and that they are here, hatching their eggs and raising their babies, right outside the building in which I work.

It's the nighttimes that are often the toughest for me, being 1,700 miles away from the rest of my family, and I've grown used to all the different night sounds I can hear lying awake at night. I am close enough to State Highway 20 that I can hear the Claremore Police siren pass on the way to perhaps another accident on Keetonville Hill, and I can hear also the ceaseless song of the summer crickets who come back to their favorite camping ground outside my bedroom window year after year. And in the dead of night, if something has woken me so I cannot return to whatever dream was floating in my half-asleep head, I can hear from a mile away a plethora of trains that cut through this small town, in an unending progression, each one louder than the one before it, horns blaring even at 3.00 A.M.

There's been a lot to get used to and understand, and some of it I've been able to appreciate. Most of the time.

Here, by the Verdigris

I rarely hear the trains
in the depth of summer, when
the weight of the air makes
moving painful, the shimmer of
light like waves in the desert, inviting
one to hallucinate, or go quietly mad
with the labor of it all.

That is to say, the noise is
muffled, cocooned in cotton-wrapped
high temperatures, so even the harshest
blasting engineer cannot penetrate
the August curtain, to reach me,
one short mile away.

I'm pleased with the not-hearing
of the trains, though, because in
the heavy silence I can close my
eyes and pretend I'm upstairs in a
house in Massachusetts, instead of
marking time in foreign territory.

I really do like trains, but no one
    believes me.

I really do like much of Oklahoma, though no one believes me, most of the time.

Uncertain Ground

JANICE WILLSON

I am human, and I think that nothing of that which is human is alien to me.
—Publius Terentius Afer (195–159 B.C.E.)

I'M NOT FROM HERE: TULSA, 1974–1993

When I moved to Oklahoma at the end of my fourth-grade year, I knew for sure where I was from: New England. Before then, my family moved often, jumping from New Hampshire to Massachusetts to Colorado, then back to Massachusetts, and eventually Colorado again. It seemed as if states were just boulders scattered across a stream, offering dry land to hop onto as we made our way to the opposite side of some cosmic river. So Tulsa, Oklahoma, just seemed like another brief stop on the way to some other place I would someday call home.

Our frequent moves made me think that we wouldn't be in Oklahoma long, either, so I didn't mind being different in Oklahoma. My differences confirmed my identity as an outsider. Although I was not aware of the connections between language, culture, and identity, something told me to cling to my heritage. I was sure we would move on to the next rock at any moment, and I was happy to continue saying "mum" instead of "mom" and "aunt" instead of "ant." Everything in Oklahoma was exotic to me, and I was an outsider, observing the lives of the locals. Tornadoes? Exciting! Floods? Newsworthy! The accents sounded charming to me, but they were not my own. When I walked into a convenience store and someone called me "honey," it was surprising and endearing, but still alien.

At some point it became clear that I was not a tourist about to leave for a new destination. The expected move never came, and being different was no longer fun. When I reached junior high school, my classmates began to point out my accent. As a typical young teenager, I didn't want to be singled out as an oddity. And so I determined to become a local, too. I had a live Amy Grant album, and her accent sounded Tulsan to me. I would listen to her saying "Thay-ank yew" and mimic her in my young teen voice: "Thay. Ank. Yee. Ooo." I couldn't tell where she was from, but I thought it was close enough to let me fit in.

Growing up and building memories in a place changes your sense of self. Now I was no longer an alien. I had spent evenings watching the stars along the riverwalk at Ft. Gibson Lake, pretending I was at the beach, and I had toured the city's most well-known Christmas light displays. I experienced all the usual rites of passage as a Tulsan—getting braces, getting a job, getting an apartment, going to college—and I was at home in Oklahoma. The license plates at the time carried the slogan, "Oklahoma is OK," and I came to think that was about right. I was a New Englander who had decided that Oklahoma was, indeed, OK.

Years after arriving in Oklahoma, I had become a local. Nobody thought to ask me where I was from because nobody could see I was different. Yet I thought of myself as a transplanted Oklahoman. If someone had asked where I was from, I would have said "Massachusetts."

NONE OF US ARE FROM HERE: CHANGCHUN, 1993–1996

Ever felt so confident that you ventured off into the unknown? This was my situation when I decided to move again, as an adult, to China. It was just for fun! For a year! I'll be right back! That's what I thought, anyway. I thought of this as just another move, no different from any other. I did not think of this as a life-changing decision. So I was not prepared for the challenges of living in a new country. And I certainly wasn't prepared for the question "Where are you from?"

What could I say? The Chinese concept of a hometown, with all your family living together in your birthplace, didn't apply to my situation. Clearly my hometown wasn't New England. I had few memories from there, and most of my relatives were scattered across the United States. I realized that I should say I was from Oklahoma, but that wasn't my birthplace. The best answer was the United States. And thus my new identity was born the moment I stepped onto foreign soil. Like it or not, I was a representative for my whole country and, unexpectedly, a new member of a community of expats.

Many of my early experiences in China seemed to underscore the separation between Chinese and non-Chinese. We were given separate living quarters, were restricted from visiting certain parts of the country, and were often stared at in the streets. We had our own parties, our own holidays, our own church, and even our own currency, known as Foreign Exchange Currency. Entrance to parks and museums cost more for us than for Chinese citizens, and we were not allowed to use public swimming pools or the secret back room of the foreign language bookstore, where pirated copies of western books were sold.

Our attempts to fit in fell flat, too. Chinese dumplings, called *jiaozi*, were not like American dumplings. They were made of pork in a wonton wrapper and cooked in bamboo steamers. We tried to westernize them by stuffing the wonton wrappers with Velveeta and broccoli. It'd be just like ravioli! Chinese-American ravioli, how wonderful! But it wasn't. We tried to recreate Thanksgiving with chicken instead of turkey and apple crisp instead of apple pie. We bought saws and cut down trees, trying to create some sort of Christmas celebration in a world where there was no Christmas. None of these attempts worked; in fact, they underscored the undeniable truth that we were different.

And so all of us expats formed our own community. If we saw someone on the street that was not Chinese, we learned who they were. We invited them to join us. I became close friends with people from Mali, Benin, England, Spain, Germany, Lithuania, and Australia. We adopted one another's habits and learned about other countries and customs. We came to speak our own special language, using Chinese phrases in our English sentences, often without noticing. At other times, we would play with the language, speaking Chinese with a "George Bush" accent. Learning the food, language, and culture of China became an endeavor that involved a close-knit group of adventurers. We were all united in being not-Chinese.

Sure, there were times that were hard, but we were sharing them together in our little community. There may have been no KFC, McDonald's, cheese, or bread, and sometimes no heat, hot water, or telephone, but we were in this together. Sometimes I asked myself if I was crazy to stay in Changchun. One day I decided I was, especially when there was a metropolis south of me with everything I needed. Off I went to Beijing, which seemed like a land of opportunity to me.

WE'RE ALL FROM EVERYWHERE: BEIJING, 1996–2012

Walking down the streets of Beijing, I was a little lost. There were other expats all around, but they were ignoring me. Where was the ready-made community of adventurers I had enjoyed in Changchun? The Chinese people didn't seem to be excluding me, either. Nobody was staring at me, and Chinese and foreigners mingled everywhere. My identity as a member of the isolated expat community was no longer solid ground for me. It seemed that working out my identity would be a continuing struggle. I was now in a city full of displaced individuals. Chinese migrants from the countryside were building roads, students from other provinces were studying in Beijing's universities, and people around me—both expats and Chinese—were redefining themselves. This search for identity was evident throughout the city. One day I went to the gym and started chatting with another gym member. When I asked him where he was from, he said, "I was born in Guatemala, but my dad is from Columbia and my mom is Canadian. I have an American passport, but I grew up in Hong Kong. I went to a British school." I thought, "Dude! Just pick a place and say you're from there! It's just a conversation-starter."

His long answer to my casual question reminded me of that sense of being cut adrift that happens during some of life's milestones. Clearly the man in the gym was adjusting to another move and struggling to define himself. I recognized this as a common situation that happens when we leave some part of our identity behind, and our future is uncertain. Familiar labels such as straight-A student, or first-chair violinist disappear when the goal is reached, and there is some sense of loss accompanied by the need to find a new sense of identity. And so I again was on uncertain ground, a lone American in China, without a community. As I began to make new friends in this more diverse community, I found myself needing to define myself yet again. It didn't help that I had begun to feel disconnected from my homeland.

Questioning My Connections

International disasters like 9/11 emphasized how far I felt from my home. When the attacks occurred, it was late in the evening in Beijing, and I was asleep. My phone was ringing off the hook, but I ignored it. When I got up later in the middle of the night, I listened to my messages and learned that some of my friends in Beijing were getting together at a friend's apartment to watch CNN coverage of some big disaster that had happened. I logged on to the Internet, got a glimpse of the towers falling, and thought, "Whoa." Then I thought that there was nothing I could do from here, and I'd learn all about it later. I went back to sleep. In the morning, I discovered that the long-term expats had, like me, gone back to bed after learning about the attacks, but those who had stayed up to watch CNN all night had only been in China a short time.

I always felt strange when things happened in the States and I wasn't there, as if geography could make things less or more important. But now the amount of time I had been away from the United States added to the distance. Although I was still an American, I suppose I didn't feel connected to my country enough to understand what was happening. I didn't realize the impact until years later. Ignoring the endless CNN broadcasts, I had missed the reports that there was something devastating happening on that day. And I had missed the national response of shock and tragedy.

The response to the 9/11 attacks underscored my separation from both Americans and Chinese people in Beijing. What I remember most about that period of time was sadness upon realizing that, while everyone loves an underdog, they seem to blindly loathe the top dog. Some of the Chinese people I encountered seemed gleeful. The guy who worked in my neighborhood copy shop laughed at me and said, "You deserve it, stupid Americans." One time a taxi driver was gloating about what he saw as our downfall, and I was so angry that I tried to get out of his moving taxi in the middle of a highway. He apologized and kept quiet, but it was an awkward ride. During major international events, I started to tell taxi drivers that I was from some neutral country that wasn't involved in the current incident. I was just sick of the job of representing my own country and wasn't even sure I was still qualified to do so.

I also remember having many pleasant taxis drivers. I recall in particular one whom I encountered who was quite nice. He said that all those innocent people on their way to work should not have been killed, and only a horribly bad man (referring to Osama bin Laden) would do that. I remember thinking that this taxi driver was a man who was so in tune with our common humanity that he was not swayed by political divisions.

I wondered what kind of person I was and how these events were shaping me. Did I react like all the other people around me, or could I be the one person who held to basic truths, as that taxi driver did? Do I have the ability to see people more as people, or did I see them as divided into nationalities and creeds?

Seeking Connection

As I spent more time in Beijing, I slowly began a transformation from expat to resident. I became more comfortable with my new identity. I was now just another Beijinger. When I talked about being home, I meant China, not the United States. I even began to feel that there was little difference between my own country and China. I thought *jiaozi* (dumplings) were as satisfying as pizza. I noticed that, although everyone gave mooncakes as gifts during the Mid-Autumn Festival, nobody ate them. I began to think of mooncakes as the cultural equivalent of the Christmas fruitcakes that everyone gives as gifts but nobody seems to eat. And I thought Chinese superstitions were similar to some of our own in America.

At midnight on Chinese New Year, people set off fireworks all over town. One year I went out at midnight to enjoy the noisy, smoky festival. I saw a man get out of a taxi, hang a string of firecrackers on a tree, and set them off. He did this a couple of times, and then zoomed off in his waiting taxi, presumably to continue doing this in various locations through the city. I knew that Chinese mythology includes tales of an evil spirit called *Nian* who would terrorize villages at the beginning of the New Year. The tradition of setting off firecrackers was to scare away this evil spirit with noise and fire. So when I saw this man choosing specific places to light his fireworks, I thought, "Oh, how superstitious! The man is doing a taxi tour of Beijing, ridding specific spots of evil spirits."

Then I remembered something similar that had happened in the early 1990s with some foreigners in Beijing. I was visiting from Changchun, and my friend was going to a top-secret prayer meeting in someone's apartment. I wasn't allowed to go, so I was waiting in an apartment on a lower floor, and I could still hear them praying upstairs. I was standing on the balcony looking at the trees, and watching the apartment keeper hanging laundry in the yard below. Suddenly, from the apartment above me, something came splashing down and landed on the clean laundry. I saw the apartment keeper look up and shout, shaking her fists like a cartoon character. It was all quite baffling at the time.

Years later, I found out that the group members were symbolically sanctifying Beijing by sprinkling red Kool-Aid, which represented the blood of Jesus, on the ground below. I met the leaders of this movement a decade later, and they had come to see their own actions as bizarre, and described them as a sort of break with reality. But during this break with reality, they also got into taxis and targeted other parts of Beijing. They decided that the imperial dragon and phoenix, which decorate every piece of furniture, every dish, and most graphics in China, were evil. They smashed dishes that had dragon patterns, declaring the dragon to be a representation of the Beast from the Book of Revelation. Phoenixes fared no better, as they were designated the Whore of Babylon. This exclusive, secret group traveled across Beijing, anointing ancient cultural sites with oil. One member, a friend of mine, lamented having spilled oil on her Italian designer shoes at the pagoda at Beihai Park. Others broke chopsticks with dragons on them and threw them into the canal that surrounds Second Ring Road. "We banish you to the depths of hell, Satan!" my friend shouted, and then zoomed off in the waiting taxi.

I couldn't help but think that the Chinese man setting off fireworks was not alone in his quest to rid Beijing of demons. In fact almost everything that used to seem foreign to me in China now had become natural and easy to understand. I could connect with almost everything around me, and I finally understood the quotation from Publius Terentius Afer ("Terence"), a freed Berber slave and classical Roman playwright: "Nothing human is alien to me."

FINDING CONNECTION

I finally reached the point, after I had been in Beijing for many years, that I no longer thought about my identity. The transformation from expat to resident was complete: Chinese people referred to me as *lao zhong guo tong*—old China hand. Neighbors knew me by name. I could remember when their children were born and which school they attended.

One winter morning I woke up and smelled the familiar smell of coal in the air. That had become the smell of winter to me. I thought it must be from the ancient courtyard homes, those lucky remaining *hutong* dwellers who still burned coal to stay warm. I had been in China long enough for the smell to evoke memories and for me to understand what it meant: winter was coming. And on my bike ride that morning, I saw something that brought back a rush of memories: a little tractor truck piled high with cabbage.

I remembered that, when I first arrived in China, I was puzzled to see huge mountains of cabbages—sometimes two stories high—in front of homes. I learned that this was a tradition in autumn. The trucks would come in from the countryside and stop in every neighborhood, selling cabbage. Families would buy enough cabbage to last the winter, stacking the heads against the walls of every dwelling, and a dangerous slippery carpet of cabbage leaves would coat the streets.

During times of economic crisis or drought, Chinese people in the north would make this cabbage into sauerkraut. I was told of long winters in the past when this had been their only vegetable for months. Even though it had been many years since the markets had run out of vegetables, people told me they still bought the cabbage because *you never know*. But on that morning in Beijing, when I saw a cabbage truck speeding past my apartment, I realized that I had not seen the mountains of cabbage for a long time. Apparently the days when "you never knew" were gone. Now they did know, and they had stopped buying it, at least in Beijing.

So when I saw the cabbage truck, I was hit with a wave of nostalgia, and I wanted to buy everything on the truck and make a cabbage mountain outside my apartment. Even though the truck was not stopping to sell cabbages in my neighborhood, I was sure that if it had stopped, I would have bought some, and the management would have come and told me to move my cabbage. Or who knew? Perhaps they would have helped me buy a big vat and make the cabbage into Chinese sauerkraut. My longing for an earlier time marked a new phase for me. I had officially lived in China long enough to "remember when."

China was changing and developing. The days when anyone could easily come to China and find work were almost at an end. Visas were only available to those with advanced degrees now, and the age limitations for work visas were beginning to be enforced. Just when it seemed I was fully at home in Beijing, I felt the ground beginning to shift under my feet. Long-term expats were starting to talk about the difficulty of staying, and some of my friends were beginning to leave. When a job offer from Tulsa came my way, it seemed like an offer I couldn't refuse.

I'M FROM THE HEARTLAND: TULSA, 2012–2017

When I told my friends in Beijing that I was going back to Oklahoma, they all started singing songs about Oklahoma. I had no idea there were so many songs, and would never have guessed that people from New Zealand, Australia, and Scotland would be singing them to me: "Living on Tulsa Time," "Proud to Be an Okie from Muskogee," and of course the song about the wind sweeping down the plain. It seemed that I had a solid identity now, as an Oklahoman returning home.

I was not quite prepared for the reverse culture shock I was about to experience. I was lost again, even though I should have felt at home. I had been gone almost two decades, and I had to ask for help with the most basic things. I called my sister the first time I needed to put gas in my car. What's this pay-at-the-pump nonsense, and how do I do it? I tried to mail something and thought the glue on the envelope was the worst-tasting stuff I'd ever licked. It was an adhesive strip. I looked like I fit in, but nothing was familiar.

Working at a small language school, I should have felt at home. After all, I had taught English as a Second Language for years. But this once-familiar setting was also difficult in a new country. I was supposed to be an expert on the culture and language of the United States, but I was just as lost as my students. My English sentences were still sprinkled with Chinese phrases, and I couldn't understand why people wouldn't use chopsticks when they ate spaghetti. When we held an orientation for the newly arrived international students, I should have been one of the teachers helping the new arrivals understand life in the United States. Instead, I found myself on the sidelines, taking notes.

One of the teachers was explaining how to make small talk in the United States, and he asked everyone, "How do you start a conversation in your country?" The answers were numerous: "Who is your father?" "What is your hometown?" "Have you eaten?" Then he asked us all which question to use to start a conversation with someone in the United States. None of the new students knew, and I didn't either. He said the question was "What do you do?" I thought, "Employment must be the foundation of identity for people in the United States." Never mind that I was still hopping from one rock to another, looking for solid ground.

So it seems the question has changed. People are not interested in where I have lived; instead, the focus is on what I have done. No matter where I go, it turns out that the people I've befriended, the knowledge I have gained, and the experiences that have shaped me have come together to make me who I am. It is not about where I live, but about something closer to the heart. What do I do? I copy Amy Grant's accent. I think of *jiaozi* when I'm eating pizza. I look at cabbage and remember autumn in Changchun. I see a person from another country trying to figure out the gas pump and see myself. I finally know the answer to the question, and I don't have to worry about where I fit with the people around me. I know where my heart is now. Just don't ask me where I'm from.

Advocating

Speaking Truth to Power

PAM KINGFISHER, Cherokee, Born to the Bird Clan

Born and raised in the shadow and secrecy of nuclear power and bomb building, I didn't realize that asking questions was an act of defiance that would lead me to a very full life as an activist for the rights of Native peoples. My dad moved from Tulsa, Oklahoma, to Richland, Washington, to start working at the Hanford Nuclear Reservation in 1943 (an original site in the Manhattan Project, located in eastern Washington State) during its construction and later became a patrolman and then line worker in the hot boxes. He had already survived a very high dose plutonium spill before I was born; my mom had to take new clothes and go pick him up a few days later. My brother also retired from thirty years in management at one of the nuclear reactors at Hanford. So in my doubly nuclear family, I've always considered myself a "daughter of plutonium."

After moving home to my grandmother's original allotment lands in the Cherokee Nation of Oklahoma, my activism started so innocently—I read a flyer at the health food store about chemical waste injection sites located in the town of Gore, and how some folks were getting together to stop this activity. I attended a meeting sponsored by the group Native Americans for a Clean Environment (NACE). Two years later I became the board chair for NACE, volunteering my free time to the cause. We kept our efforts laser-focused on stopping the contamination at the uranium conversion facility in Gore.

Built and operated by Kerr McGee, the Sequoyah Fuels plant came on the radar when they applied for a deep injection well permit for their sludge waste. This event sparked community concern and led to the creation of a non-profit to follow the company's activities.

Uranium yellowcake was brought to Oklahoma from the Kerr-McGee Quivera uranium mine in New Mexico to be chemically transformed into uranium hexafluoride for nuclear power plant fuel. This fuel was sent to nuclear sites and then returned as "depleted" uranium. Kerr-McGee operated a second plant to convert this "depleted" uranium into uranium tetraflouride, the shelling on armor piercing bullets and tanks.

Later, Kerr-McGee, an Oklahoma-based oil and gas company, collaborated with the Monsanto Company to bring us "raffinate," a fertilizer created out of chemical sludge ponds and sold to farmers. These two corporations experimented on five hundred acres in the middle of nowhere, but with the help of local dairy farmers we found their dead cow pits and documented the impact of these pits on the neighbors' lands, animals, and health. We became a mirror for the press, to show the world the corporations' dirty deeds and accidents, which were ongoing.

Kerr-McGee was a corporation with a large presence in Oklahoma and in the broader nuclear world. On November 13, 1974, twenty-eight-year-old Karen Silkwood died in a "mysterious car accident" in Oklahoma. Silkwood had worked as a technician at a plutonium plant operated by the Kerr-McGee Corporation, and she had been critical of the plant's health and safety procedures, especially regarding orders for her to use ink to fix x-rays that revealed cracks in fuel rods. That fall, shortly before she died, Silkwood officially complained to the Atomic Energy Commission about unsafe conditions at the plant. Two months later she died on her way to a meeting with a union representative and a *New York Times* journalist, reportedly with a folder full of documents proving that Kerr-McGee was acting illegally. Her briefcase was never found in the wrecked car, and that disappearance, along with the trajectory of the accident, lends credence to the theory that someone had forced her off the road to shut her up. The compromised fuel rods about which Karen was whistleblowing were on their way to Hanford nuclear plant in Washington where my dad and brother worked.

Karen's suspicious death hit a nerve in me. I believed her story and began learning about Kerr-McGee's nuclear facilities. Singer-songwriter and activist Holly Near wrote a song for Karen—"Karen, we are doing this work for you, we are doing this work for two"—and I always felt this solidarity in my heart, especially when we called out Karen's name in prayer and at our community meetings.

We hosted many meetings in the community to ask questions of Kerr-McGee and to create a forum for the surrounding neighbors to understand the complicated issues at Sequoyah Fuels. We raised millions of dollars and sued every protective service that we felt was ignoring the human threats, including the Environmental Protection Agency and the Nuclear Regulatory Commission. The Cherokee Nation joined us in many of these lawsuits, and our collaboration gave us broader exposure and credibility. Our lawsuit against the NRC gave us access to every meeting and document we needed for participating at regulatory hearings, as well as for touring the site. The purpose of our community organizing was not to attack our local workers but to expose the bad business of a dirty corporation in a rural community whose residents were dependent on these jobs.

In 1993, the closure of the notoriously contaminated Kerr-McGee plant stopped the production of approximately 23 percent of the world's uranium supply. As of this date, there has not been another uranium conversion plant built since we shut down Sequoyah Fuels—not in the United States nor in the rest of the world.

Later, as a member and, for three years, executive director of the Indigenous Women's Network, I collaborated with other Native women in the United States and globally. In 2001 and 2002, I led a group of eight Native women when we attended the United Nations (UN) conferences in South Africa. There we networked with Indigenous women and men from around the globe to demand rights for Indigenous Peoples—literally getting the "s" in "Peoples" inserted into all UN documents. This took a few years, but we won that battle in 2001.

The second UN meeting in South Africa was about energy, and we learned that "water is the new gold" in the world markets. Native women understand the intersectionality of our work—women's bodies are the first environment; our birth waters of creation make us the mothers of our nations. We understand that water is our first medicine, and have been herbalists, healers, and cultivators since the beginning of time.

My recent work with the Native American Community Board in South Dakota has focused on national policy for Native women. The Indian Health Service (IHS) is the primary resource available to Native women for all health care and is our first responder to instances of sexual assault. We work to hold

IHS accountable to its own policies and laws guaranteeing women's health care, including pregnancy, birth control, and preventive services—not only for Native victims of sexual violence but for all Native women.

In 2016, we celebrated a significant victory in our path toward reproductive justice for Native women by forcing policy changes to provide emergency contraceptives over the counter at IHS. We worked with our allies at the American Civil Liberties Union, Amnesty International, NARAL Pro-Choice America (formerly the National Association for the Repeal of Abortion Laws), and the National Congress of American Indians in applying pressure to compel the IHS to comply with federal guidelines by drafting new EC policies to present to the IHS. We also spoke at the UN in Geneva in 2016 on emergency contraceptives and other issues affecting Native women, as well as to the vice president's staff in the White House. After we presented updated IHS policies to the U.S. Secretary of Health and Human Services, which included providing emergency contraceptives over the counter, we obtained a "verbal directive," but it needed to be in writing.

In October 2015, due to our advocacy and hard work, IHS issued written policies confirming improved access for Native women to Emergency Contraception (EC, known commercially as Plan B®) at IHS facilities. These written policies supersede a previous verbal directive which was easily ignored and inconsistently applied. Now I am working to ensure full compliance with this directive and ensure that Native women are aware of EC (what it is, what it is not) and their right to access it.

Even more recently, in January 2017, we released an "ABC Workbook" called "What to Do When You're Raped" for Native girls. This publication opened up a dialogue about the "dirty little secret" of sexual assault, which no one would talk about. Women wanted to talk openly about it, but were just too ashamed. They were, and still to some extent are, afraid of community retaliation, the perpetrator and his family, and the general shame and stigma sexual assault brings. This workbook has broken down that barrier of shame and opened up the floodgates for women to disclose their assault stories, whether stories of rape, incest or domestic violence. This outpouring of "telling" prepares women to testify and discuss these issues in mixed company.

As the conversation spreads within the community, local police forces start to perk up and listen; the IHS begins to hear more about the situation and receive more inquiries for EC or other support; and tribal courts begin to think differently about how to handle the increase in abuse cases. This is how social change happens in a Native community: people become aware of a shift happening in the community conversation, and they begin to see the effect on the community of telling their stories, telling their truth, and speaking up to support others. We have created that wave with our actions and resources, and we see it changing the way tribal communities confront sexual violence and rape.

The responses of Native women to this ABC Workbook have created impromptu talking circles—the kind of kitchen-table talks that slowly open the doors of silence and lead to broader discussions. Women disclosing their stories of sexual assault in public meetings, in hallways at conferences, and at the dining-room table at home creates systemic change. These one-on-one testimonies build momentum and increase our resources, and this communication strategy has elevated the conversation to a movement.

Native women also are particularly vulnerable to sex trafficking, due in no small part to "man camps" (temporary housing compounds that are host to oil workers and that are giving rise to increased violence against women and families and increased sex trafficking) and to the proliferation of methamphetamine use in Native communities (and in many communities throughout the country). Native American women comprise 40 percent of sex trafficking victims in South Dakota, according to Kevin Koliner, the assistant U.S. attorney for South Dakota, in a 2013 article appearing in the South Dakota newspaper *Capital Journal* ("Officials Say Human Trafficking Occurs in SD," www.capjournal.com/news/officials-say-human-trafficking-occurs-in-sd /article_6f03bba6-f812-11e2-98ce-001a4bcf887a.html). Comparatively, only 8.8 percent of South Dakota's population is American Indian/Alaska Native, according to the 2010 U.S. Census.

"Crime in Oklahoma 2016," a study conducted by the Oklahoma State Bureau of Investigation (OSBI), provides a summary analysis of rape in the state, with law enforcement recording "2,134 forcible and attempted rapes in 2016, representing 12.1% of all violent crimes and 1.6% of index crimes. Law enforcement cleared 643 rapes by arrest or exceptional means, resulting in a clearance rate of 30.1%. Of the 226 offenders arrested for rape, 36.3% were under the age of 25; 66.8% were white, 26.5% black, 4.9% American Indian, 1.3% Asian, and 0.4% Hawaiian/Pacific Islander." These 2016 statistics lift the rug on sex trafficking in Oklahoma, a serious problem in other freeway states as well. The Oklahoma Commission on the Status of Women's "Human Trafficking" information page lists three factors as key in Oklahoma's failures in this area.

Factor number 1: Oklahoma has the highest incarceration rate of women in the United States and the world, and according to statistics, children without mothers in the household are six times more likely to follow the dark side than other children. Factor number 2: Oklahoma is second in teen pregnancy and homeless children, therefore creating a "stable" of children. Factor number 3: the FBI reports a well-known belief among truck drivers: "If you want good bar-b-que go to Kansas City, if you want young girls, go to Oklahoma City." (See https://ok.gov/ocsw/_Summit_Issues/2014_Human_Trafficking_/index.html.)

In 2016, my work with sex trafficking merged with environmental concerns and Indigenous beliefs about the environment. The issue of water rights and oil pipelines came to the forefront in the wind-blown northern plains at Standing Rock, North Dakota. Native lands hold most of our country's remaining accessible raw energy materials. About 75 percent of the nation's uranium supply is located on Indian land, primarily in South Dakota and Arizona. Oil and tar sands are abundant on Native lands in North and South Dakota, and Oklahoma.

My client, the Native American Community Board, is based on the Yankton Sioux Reservation. The Yankton Sioux are a river tribe along the Missouri River. The tribe filed an injunction to stop the Dakota Access Pipeline from going under the river, due to the likelihood of the pipeline rupturing and contaminating the water, not only for the twenty-six tribes that live along the river but for the 16 million people that make up America's breadbasket region. My role was to amplify the voices of Standing Rock on social media, and we routinely reached between 500,000 and 1 million people per month that year with our urgent coverage of Standing Rock.

The intersection of Native women's rights, energy extraction, and human health has been the heartbeat of my life's work. As of this writing, the company leading the superfund cleanup of Sequoyah Fuels is requesting to store all of the waste on-site, which would create a uranium mine where there was no uranium. As I sort seeds for my organic garden and tend my bees and chickens, I continue to monitor and report these assaults on our bodies and our mother. Resist and look to the future.

Marriage Equality and the Courage of Our Convictions

SHARON BISHOP-BALDWIN

On November 3, 2004, the woman who is now my wife, Mary Bishop-Baldwin, and I, along with another lesbian couple, Sue Barton and Gay Phillips, sued the State of Oklahoma and the United States of America. Mary and I wanted to be married in Oklahoma, and Sue and Gay wanted their existing union to be legally recognized in Oklahoma, but the state banned same-sex marriages, even those solemnized in other jurisdictions. It took nine years, two months, one week, and four days before a federal judge in Tulsa ruled that we could marry. And beyond that, it took eight months, three weeks, and one day more before Mary and I were actually married on the steps outside the Tulsa County Courthouse.

When I think about some of the central lessons of my life, specifically about courage—what it is, what it isn't, where it comes from, what you can do with it—the fight for marriage equality in Oklahoma is at the heart of everything I know.

One of the greatest things about early dalliances with courage is that you don't realize just how frightened you occasionally should be. We filed our lawsuit on a Wednesday, less than twenty-four hours after a fraction of Oklahoma voters—the "superminority" who bothered going to the polls that day—decided to enshrine an existing statutory ban on same-sex marriage in the Oklahoma Constitution. That day, we felt a lot of emotions, but courage wasn't really among them. Certainly none of the emotions we experienced overrode the defiance that was welling up in our hearts. We would show the bastards. "Think you needed to pass a constitutional amendment to remind us that we're second-class citizens? Well, how's this for a shot across the bow to show you that we're not going *anywhere?*"

Sure, we had had some conversations about what the immediate response to our lawsuit might be, but those worst-case scenarios were theoretical and hypothetical. Now the very real possibility of them was looming large. Would we awaken the following day, as news of the lawsuit found its way to the masses, to find masses of protesters on our lawn? Would someone, indeed, throw a Molotov cocktail into our house, which held our beloved cats? Would we be stalked? The answers, thankfully, were no, no, and no. But because we dodged those bullets (metaphorically, but who knows—perhaps literally, too), we quickly put fear out of our minds.

So is courage the absence of fear? Yes and no. Sometimes courage is about overcoming fear in the midst of truly frightening circumstances. But sometimes courage is just about doing the right thing, no matter how alone you feel, no matter how uncertain everyone *else* is about what you're doing, because you know with every cell in your body that what you're doing *is* the right thing. It is this second type of courage that we four plaintiffs, I believe, exhibited.

From the earliest days of our lawsuit, few people were marching in our parade. At best, friends and relatives believed that we were gutsy and right, we suspect, but they also knew that you can be gutsy and right and still lose. On the other end of the spectrum, some people told us that we would ultimately lose and "set the movement back twenty years." Worse, they said, we might win, and then Congress would be spurred to attempt to pass the Federal Marriage Amendment, which would write a ban on same-sex marriage into the U.S. Constitution. If those last two criticisms of our stand sound bad, wait until you hear who the critics were: the national LGBTQ advocacy groups. Yes, that's right. People who ostensibly were fighting for the same legal protections we wanted, people who were being harmed and treated as lesser-than by the same unconstitutional laws we were challenging, these were the ones telling us to drop our lawsuit and go sit down.

Courage is saying: "No, we won't. We have as much right to our rights as you do and as much right to fight this battle."

Five years after we filed our lawsuit, our original lawyer had a personal health crisis that carried over into the operation of her law firm, and she dropped all her federal cases, including ours. When you're the plaintiffs in a then-five-year-old federal civil-rights lawsuit that you fervently believe will end up at the Supreme Court one day, you don't ring up the local bar association and tell them to send someone over to pick up the pieces. Our options for finding a new lawyer were shockingly limited. And with a great deal of desperation, and having swallowed a great deal of pride, we called some of the leaders of those same national LGBTQ advocacy groups and asked for help. They said no. They hadn't supported us before, and nothing had changed in their minds.

Courage is saying, "We didn't come this far to die with a whimper now." And courage is believing that a miracle will happen.

One did.

Don Holladay, a successful oil and gas attorney in Oklahoma City who, with his wife, Kay, has among their three children a gay son, called our then-lawyer to offer his help with the case. We four plaintiffs met with Don within a week and hired him on the spot—"hired" being a euphemism for "agreed to let him work countless hours on our behalf for half a decade for no money except the occasional filing fees or mailing expenses."

Four years, six months, and about five days later, in early 2014, all that work paid off. Tulsa-based U.S. District Judge Terence Kern ruled in our favor, agreeing that the Oklahoma Constitution's ban on same-sex marriage violated the U.S. Constitution's Equal Protection Clause. And although we had been literally begging for a ruling for half a year—since June 26, 2013, when the Supreme Court ruled in *United States v. Windsor* that the federal Defense of Marriage Act was unconstitutional, thereby drawing a road map for multitudes of plaintiffs and judges across the country to follow in knocking down the remaining vestiges of marriage inequality—we knew that his ruling had taken courage.

Six months and four days later, the Tenth U.S. Circuit Court of Appeals affirmed Judge Kern's ruling. We then learned formally that Tulsa County would appeal that decision to the U.S. Supreme Court, where we had always believed our case would end. In Oklahoma, conservatives don't cede ground to liberals. Ever. And we would never have given up if we had lost preliminary rounds. Still, as the victors, we could have told the high court: "Don't take our case. Two federal courts have sided with us; just let us get married and be on our way." So it took a bit of courage to say to the justices instead: "Yes, we won. But we want you to take our case, anyway, because a patchwork quilt of marriage equality, such as the one that exists across this nation today, is insufficient. We believe so strongly that we are right that we are willing to risk an unthinkable ruling from you that says we are wrong, all in the hope of erasing the haphazard equality of the present."

And when the Supreme Court declined to take our case, it took courage for us to stand before throngs of journalists and supporters and say: "Yes, this is our wedding day, and we are joyous, but our joy is muted, because the Supreme Court did us no favor by allowing states without marriage equality to continue discriminating against us even as it let stand the two judicial rulings in our case that said such discrimination was unconstitutional."

And, finally, even after the Supreme Court made marriage equality the law of the land in 2015 with *Obergefell v. Hodges*, we had to summon courage to tell our fellow LGBTQ Oklahomans that we weren't done yet—that although we could now be married on a Saturday, we could still be fired on a Monday and evicted on a Tuesday just because of our sexual orientation, gender identity, or gender expression.

By then, though, we had come to see courage not so much as something you *do* but as something you *are*. Courage is not the armaments you don to head into battle. Courage is the armor that each battle forges and strengthens to protect you as you continue to stand for justice, equality, and righteousness.

In a decade of fighting for marriage equality, we saw so much courage, courage that has strengthened our armor. And that is good, because there is much work still to be done.

What Is a Girl Like You Doing in a Place Like This?

KALYN FREE

There are plenty of obstacles in your path, don't allow yourself to become one of them.
—Ralph Marston, "Boldly Forward,"
The Daily Motivator, June 11, 2001

I was 20 years old when I graduated from college with two degrees. I was 23 when I graduated from law school and began working at the U.S. Department of Justice (DOJ) as the youngest lawyer ever hired. For more than ten years at the DOJ, I prosecuted corporations for polluting our air, water, and land in federal courts across America. At 34, I was the first woman elected district attorney (DA) in Oklahoma's Pittsburg and Haskell Counties. At 40, I was a candidate for the United States Congress. At 41, I started a political organization that, over a six-year period, helped elect 63 American Indians to state and local offices across America. Just two months shy of my 46th birthday, I got married. At 46, I successfully settled a five-year lawsuit against a Taiwanese corporation for more than $10 million dollars. A year and a half later, I led a campaign that successfully elected a new chief of the largest American Indian tribe in America. I've climbed Mt. Fuji in Japan, run 3 marathons and completed 14 half marathons in 14 months. I've traveled to all 50 states, most of the Indian reservations in the lower 48, and several foreign countries.

"But, I am not what I have done; I am what I have overcome." For a lot of people that's just a saying from one of those "quote of the day" inspirational calendars. For me, it's a continuous reminder that life is not a linear collection of experiences. Life is defined by our ability to control our own reaction to the dynamic circumstances that confront us.

So, how did a girl like me, from Red Oak, Oklahoma, a rural town of about six hundred people, accomplish all of the above? And, what happened to me along the way?

None of us are blessed with crystal balls, so we have no clue what our lives will hold for us. When I left Red Oak at seventeen, bound for college in Durant, my singular goal was to graduate from college and go to law school. I never dreamt beyond that. Not having that crystal ball was a good thing, as I did not know the difficulties I would face during college and in life beyond school.

The first challenge was simply enrolling in college. I managed to find my way to a school counselor who helped me select my courses only to find out that I couldn't enroll because I could not pay tuition immediately. I remember sitting on the steps of the Administration Building at Southeastern Oklahoma State University and thinking, "I wonder who's in charge of this place." I found a directory on the wall inside that building and saw "President Leon Hibbs" listed, and went to his office. After a short wait, I met with President Hibbs and told him I wanted to attend his college but that I didn't have the money to pay tuition. He asked where I was living and I told him with my cousin off campus. He admonished me that all freshmen were required to live in the dormitories. I told him I would be delighted to live in a dorm, if he could arrange that. He asked me how I intended to pay my tuition. I told him I was working the night shift from 11:00 P.M. to 7:00 A.M. five nights a week, earning the minimum wage of $3.35 an hour at a convenience store and that I would make payments every time I received a paycheck, which was every two weeks. He gave me a note to take to the Bursar's Office that allowed me to "temporarily enroll."

That very night, about midnight, I was shocked to see President Hibbs walk into the convenience store. I asked him how I could help him, and he said he was "just there to check on me" and told me to come back to his office the next day. When I arrived for the meeting the next day, he gave me further guidance on loans and work study opportunities, and helped arrange a job for me on campus so that if I were able to pay tuition for my first semester, I could quit my convenience store clerk job the next semester and work on campus.

During this time I didn't have my own vehicle, so I walked to my convenience store job and to campus. The clerks on the night shift had the hardest jobs at the store because we had to clean the toilets, sweep the parking lot, stock all the shelves and coolers, and make all the donuts and sandwiches for the next-day shift. One of my primary duties was making the donuts—standing over boiling grease and sticky icing for hours every night. Because I got off work at 7:00 A.M. and my first class was at 8:30 A.M., I had just enough time to get home, take a shower, and get to class. I will always remember that one day when my relief showed up late to work and I had to go straight to class. I was so embarrassed when a classmate said she smelled donuts. I was terrified they would find out the smell was just coming from me. I prayed the class would never realize I was the girl that smelled like donuts.

I remember how happy I was when, just a few weeks before the end of the first semester, I made my final tuition payment. Because President Hibbs had allowed me to "temporarily enroll," I was not listed on any of my teacher's class rolls and my name had never been called. I was essentially a "ghost student." It wasn't just the relief of having paid my way in to college that gave me such great satisfaction. It was the pride I felt in having my name added to the rolls. For most students, answering the roll call is a meaningless administrative reflex. For me, hearing my name on the roll filled me with immense gratitude. Being able to simply say "present" made me feel like I actually belonged in college.

I would like to say that the first semester of college working nights making donuts and going to school during the day was the most trying time of my life, but there were many, many more. For several months after I graduated from the University of Oklahoma College of Law, I lived in a trailer with no running water several miles outside of McAlester because I had no money for better lodging. Yes, I did *that* in the woods. After my morning daily shower at a KOA campground in McAlester, I donned a suit and went to work at the District Attorney's Office in the county courthouse. Although I was proud of my job, I was ashamed of the circumstances I was living in and strived to keep them a secret. I simply refused to let my financial situation prevent me from engaging in the challenging and rewarding work of the DA's Office.

It can be a hard lesson to learn, but you have to fight like hell to arrive in life. Then you have to work even harder just to keep yourself there.

I wanted to pursue environmental law because protecting the environment was important to me. So I moved to our nation's capital, Washington, D.C., and accepted a position with the Department of Justice. For an attorney aspiring to always wear the "white hat," meaning to always be on the side of the environment, there was no more prestigious place to work than the DOJ as it was the best training ground for environmental litigators. Often times I was simply overwhelmed. The first couple of years were tough. I was subsisting on the meager salary of a public servant while dealing with staggering student loans. I often borrowed money from a colleague to buy food and pay rent. But

I persisted and I adapted, and it certainly wasn't the last time I had to struggle to make ends meet.

Ten years later, I left my job at the DOJ, returned to Oklahoma, and campaigned full-time for the position of district attorney. In 2004, I resigned as DA and was again a full-time candidate for U.S. Congress.

During both campaigns, I liquidated my federal retirement account to keep a roof over my head and pay my bills. After my unsuccessful bid for Congress, I found myself as lead counsel on an air pollution case against a Taiwanese corporation charged with polluting the lands of the Ponca Tribe. I had to find the financial resources to hire expert witnesses and fund the case. Through sheer ingenuity I crafted a plan to borrow well over $1 million from an out-of-state foundation and another Indian tribe to sustain our case. I believed in my client and the righteousness of its claims, and was determined that this corporation be held accountable for its deplorable practices that had caused such sickness and degradation of homes and the surrounding environment.

There were hundreds of times when my co-counsel and I worked all night preparing for depositions and appearances in court simply because we didn't have the financial resources to hire support staff. I often said, "You know why we are going to win? Because right now, the other side is sleeping." My paralegal and I spent months on end doubled up in a fleabag motel room in Ponca City to save costs. But in the end, our tenacity and hard work paid off for our client and for us—and we were able to pay back those loans.

Everyone has to overcome something, and for some of us, those obstacles are larger than others. These were some of my struggles. I know countless women have had a much harder row to hoe than I, but we all carry varying burdens and respond in the way we best can.

What gave me the determination and fortitude to overcome my personal barriers?

Few people in rural Oklahoma have an easy time of it. We all know that. We are no strangers to hard work. I watched my depression-era parents eke out a better way of life for my four sisters and me than what they had experienced. I watched my mother drive sixty miles round-trip every day to work at Jones Academy Indian Boarding School while being so grateful for her job. I watched my dad work night and day in the oil and gas fields, then come home and work the cattle and plow, plant, and harvest a garden to feed our family.

Looking back now, I am confident that I was more inspired to keep going by those who told me I would never amount to anything, than by those who told me I could do anything I wanted to do. I learned early on that only I controlled my destiny, that what I made of my life would be the result of my choices and how hard I was willing to work. I never stopped believing in myself, and I had faith that I could overcome any obstacle that was placed in my path.

As women in Oklahoma, we know that our values come from within us. We know that too many girls and women live in households where they are not respected, where they are not nurtured, where they do not have self-worth, where they can't even dream of overcoming the obstacles that block their paths to a better life. And, as bitter as it is to admit it, too often those roadblocks are placed in front of us not only by men, but sadly, by other women.

Why do we incarcerate more women than any other state? Why do we have such a dearth of women representing us in the state legislature and in statewide offices? How did Oklahoma, once such a populist state, become a breeding ground for contempt of women? How did a state that has such a rich and diverse history, that is home to thirty-eight distinct sovereign Indian nations, each with its own culture and language, become so bigoted and intolerant of others?

While answering these questions is challenging, it is also a necessary exercise. I believe we must change our own thinking and simultaneously chart a course to change our communities. We must instill in girls and young women faith in themselves, tenacity and perseverance, while teaching boys and young men that their sisters are equal to them.

We must resist and speak up and speak out against gender socialization. Equal pay and equal professional opportunities are rights that must be achieved, and getting there starts with simple acts. We must shun statements that diminish and demean girls. When we chastise boys for "crying like a girl" or "playing like a girl," we must realize what we are teaching the boys and girls who are listening. It may sound frivolous, but when we use those simple colloquialisms, we are establishing an expectation that girls are weak and boys are superior and dominant. And this sets up a cycle for the rest of their lives. We must encourage and be proud of girls that show interest in math and science and engineering. We must applaud leadership skills in girls and not stifle them by calling them "bossy." We must not perpetuate stereotypical games that encourage girls to be good mommies and boys to be engineers and doctors and senators and presidents.

Little girls cannot be what they cannot see. And in Oklahoma in 2018 there are only twenty women serving in the Senate and House. With women making up only 14 percent of total House Representatives, we rank forty-eighth in the nation for female state representation, barely beating out Wyoming and Mississippi, according to "Women in State Legislatures for 2016," a study conducted by the National Conference of State Legislatures. Why is it important that we elect more women to public office? Because women bring unique values and mores—distinct from men's—to the legislative process. And having that diversity of thought makes for a more enlightened and forward-thinking body politic.

But should we strive only for gender parity? U.S. Supreme Court Justice Ruth Bader Ginsberg certainly opened my eyes through her response when asked in 2015 on PBS NewsHour about when she thought there would be enough women on the nine-member Supreme Court. She answered "nine." There were nine men for more than two centuries and not once has anyone asked how many men should serve on the highest court in the land.

While most boys are taught growing up that they are fully entitled to serve in elected office and that they should be aggressive in defense of their beliefs, girls seldom are taught to have the same view of themselves, or that they can dare challenge a man's point of view on how the world should work. Women must be asked, encouraged, prodded, and often literally begged to run for office.

And what happens when they do run? They are marginalized, dismissed, and rarely supported by their respective party apparatus, often being told to "wait your turn." The same donor that routinely writes substantially sized donations to male candidates gives women candidates only minimal financial support. Why? Because donors give money to candidates they believe will win, and too often those that follow politics—men and women—don't believe voters (including largely women voters) will vote to put women in the high offices of power. And, for women of color candidates, the hurdles are even higher and more plentiful. The social networking that opens doors for donors is largely still off-limits to women.

So what can we do? We must have each other's back. We must encourage our mothers, our sisters, our daughters, our nieces to run for office. We must do more than simply give them lip service when they do run. We must give them the training and financial resources they need to run professional campaigns, we must volunteer on their campaigns, we must write them checks regardless of size, and we must defend them when we hear the usual nonsense about why they are not the best candidate for the position. We must talk about their platforms and their issues, not their hemlines, husbands, or hairstyles. We must not yield to the double standard that is imposed on women; we must stand up for them and stand with them, in every way, on every day.

We must hold our current elected leaders accountable when they write laws that threaten a woman's health, safety, and life. We must demand criminal justice reform, and we must revise laws that lock up addicts who need substance and alcohol abuse treatment. When we re-examine the "lock them up and throw away the key" mentality, we will realize that warehousing people who are not dangerous to society is bankrupting our state and ripping out the very heart of our families.

We must understand that children of parents who are incarcerated not only face stigma in school and society at large, but are more likely to be jailed in the future as well. We must realize that grandparents raising grandchildren as a direct result of our state's love affair with private prisons is creating a perpetual pipeline for the "prison industrial complex." Prison is not an effective solution for drug and alcohol addiction, poverty, or mental illness.

We must not allow ourselves to be limited by our society's restrictions, especially as women. For me, that means donuts be damned. We must find that inner strength to not back down when every logical reason is laid out for us to give up. We must keep working, because the other side is sleeping.

We must show up, speak up, stand out, and stand up. Our children's future, for both our sons and our daughters, depends on what we do today and tomorrow.

Roots or Wings

PRIYA DESAI

My name is Priya Desai, and I am of East Indian descent. I am a first-generation Asian American. I have lived in Oklahoma my entire life. I graduated from college in 2010 and hold a bachelor's and master's degree from the University of Oklahoma in Social Work with a concentration in Administration and Community Practice. I work in one of the Oklahoma State Systems of Higher Education. Much of my experience is grounded in grassroots nonprofit work, advocacy, and social justice, and comes from the perspective of a woman of color.

My personal relationship to "success" has evolved over time. I used to think being successful meant attaining visible, external indicators like awards, fame, money, and public recognition. As I have grown, I have learned that success is multifaceted and ever-changing. My vision of success is less reward-driven and more focused on connection, involvement, and impact on the people and community I work with and for. The interesting thing, however, is that I have always struggled with internalizing my success and accomplishments. This is not unique to me. For all of us women, there is a high likelihood that we will experience impostor syndrome at some point in our lives. This can be especially true for women of color because we are always made to feel like the accomplishments we achieve are undeserved. Women are socialized to be humble and quiet, all while being gaslighted, underestimated, and downplayed by society's archaic standards of how women should behave. In my mind, it feels like women, especially women of color, have to be exceptional for people to recognize their humanity; otherwise they are considered throwaways and worthless. This is doubly compounded by living in a red state that is hostile to minorities.

I have a love-hate relationship with Oklahoma. I have lived here my entire life. There is so much that I love about the state, but being a nonwhite woman here can be difficult. The political environment here has taken a toll on me. After receiving my master's degree in Oklahoma, I was hell-bent on getting out, so I took a shot in the dark and on a whim applied for a postgraduate certificate in international law at Australian National University. In March 2015 I was actually accepted into the program. The only thing I needed was a scholarship, and this university was the only institution to offer one for which I even qualified. I had to place all my eggs in this basket. For weeks I patiently waited for the results. I was positive that my scholarship application was top-notch and would be seriously considered. When I got the notice that I didn't get the scholarship, I cried. I spent the following weeks analyzing what I could have done better. I was angry, and the rejection really stung. I was so close to getting out of Oklahoma that I could taste it. After having several heart-to-heart conversations with colleagues, friends, and family, I eventually came to understand that it was simply not the right time and that it was not in the cards. Maybe I was not as qualified as I thought I was. Maybe I still had some learning to do before moving on to such a big adventure. So I did what I have learned is most effective for moving through disappointment, be it with myself, my government, or my state: I threw myself full swing back into nonprofit work as a way of distracting myself from my feelings.

In 2016, I came across a leadership development organization called the Global Health Corps that focused on health equity. I saw that it offered fellowships, but only for people age thirty and under. I was twenty-nine at the time, so clearly there was an urgency to apply. Global health, especially sexual and reproductive health rights of women and girls, has always been a passion of mine. It is one of the reasons I joined the United Nations Association of Oklahoma City and the Oklahoma Call for Reproductive Justice. I really liked what the Global Health Corps fellowships offered, and I thought the organization would be a good platform to further my knowledge and practice. I spent weeks working on my application essays and perfecting my resume. I was a nervous wreck while I waited for a response, only to find out I didn't make the cut. I really believed this was my second shot at getting out, so I was crushed to find out the result. There was no anger this time. Just unbelievable sadness. This disappointment dealt a blow to my self-confidence and belief in myself and my accomplishments. Again I felt like I wasn't good enough.

My internal dialogue tends to say that most of my successes were because of dumb luck, coincidence, timing, or some other magical interference, not due to the hours I spent planning, organizing, and executing programs and projects, or to the due diligence I have put forward. I have come to understand that such thinking is compounded by societal and cultural influences, expectations, and rules surrounding the idea of women and success. Often I feel that my worth is overlooked, dismissed, or doubted not only because am I woman but because I am a person of color. When I make a mistake, I feel that it is doubly scrutinized. It is really frustrating at times because people cannot get past my gender and race. Even now, as a high-achieving adult woman of color, I feel that I have to work twice as hard to get the same recognition as others for the same job.

With the help of my friends, I had a light bulb moment when I realized I enjoyed doing local work. It was—and still is—where I have the most impact. My friends, family, and life are rooted in Oklahoma. Here is where the fight is. Here is where I'm needed. Experiencing local success as a teacher and advocate has been important to me because it helps me to see how I have grown over time. By nature I am not a competitive person; in fact, I strongly dislike having to contend for anything, so for me success is not equivalent to winning or being better than anyone else. I am successful because I am constantly trying to be better than I was before. This inclination has been a source of strength for me in that it has allowed me to reflect and align myself toward people, situations, and opportunities that encourage me to achieve my goals. For example, in surrounding myself with other reproductive rights advocates, I have been able to gain a better understanding of the field while orienting myself to fellowship and advocacy opportunities that expand my skills and knowledge base.

I attribute much of my success in Oklahoma to my friends, family, and the organizations that I work with. They have continually invested in me by nurturing my talent and passion. I have had some amazing mentors who have guided me along the way. Without their support, I don't know where I would be. They have all had a profound impact on me, inspiring me to be a better person at every turn and supporting me even when I was deep in the throes of imposter syndrome. They were there for me when I faced failure and rejection and continually encouraged me to keep trying, to never give up on my goals and dreams. My real supporters knew I was likely to cloak or ignore my fears of inadequacy to the point of repression. They would ask me how I was *really* doing. After a little poking and prodding from them in individual settings, I would finally give in and the tears would just flow from my face. They told me if I kept going as if nothing was wrong, then eventually everything would fall apart. If I didn't address the grief that arose from those failures, I would be trapped by it.

Unresolved grief can come back to haunt you. Many of these people actively helped me by forcing me to realize that I have been too hard on myself. One person actually made me sit down and write down all of my accomplishments so I could physically see what I had done. Mentally I knew I had accomplished a lot, but that realization was clouded always by "what-ifs" and "should/could/would–haves." Another person actively sought out opportunities for me based on what I loved and was passionate about. To me, all these gestures were profound. It meant so much to me that someone would take time to help me refocus and regain my footing in a world where I constantly doubted myself and my abilities. Not everyone is fortunate enough to have that kind of support system, so I thank my lucky stars every day for them. I've also learned that you won't always be successful on the first try. The important thing is to keep trying. To be successful you have to have the ambition, grit, and resilience to withstand doubts, questioning, failure, rejection, and criticism. Success is often born from these challenges.

I also firmly believe that success necessitates paying it forward. When you have been given an abundance of opportunities, you have the responsibility and the obligation to open doors for others. It is also important always to remember where you came from because it made you who you are, and you did not get where you are alone. Being successful means acknowledging and thanking those who have helped you reach your full potential by investing in your success. These relationships have been available to me in Oklahoma, even though my home state is not the easiest place for a woman of color.

Because I am career-focused, I am more than my day job. I chose social work because it is more than a job. Social work is a theoretical approach to life; it is a values-based ethical orientation to which my colleagues and I connect on an internal level. This means the work we do is never done. Fortunately, being career-focused in social work means I must focus on opportunities that are bigger than employment. I think it is helpful to mention here that from an early age I knew that getting married and having children were not for me.

Not having to worry about familial obligations and a relationship is a huge relief for me. Without these ties, there is so much freedom to do what I want personally and professionally. I find much joy, pride, and fulfillment in what I am doing. It can be lonely at times, but I am growing to love my own company, which is liberating.

Being career-focused means that I push through the disappointments of missed opportunities. It means that I live the old adage of "think globally, act locally," which encourages me to look at the bigger picture but also focus on incremental, concrete steps with meaning and impact. Much of my success stems from what I have done outside of my forty-hour work week. I work closely with the two aforementioned organizations that are dear to me. The first is the United Nations Association of Oklahoma City, a local chapter of the United Nations Association of the USA, a membership organization dedicated to informing, inspiring, and mobilizing Americans to support the ideals and vital work of the United Nations. The second, for which I am currently serving as co-executive director, is the Oklahoma Call for Reproductive Justice, a coalition of organizations and individuals promoting reproductive health, rights, and justice in Oklahoma through education, empowerment, and advocacy. These two organizations have allowed me to channel my passion for international issues and sexual and reproductive health, rights, and justice, and to make productive changes in the lives of women. Being involved with both these organizations has given me the opportunity to network, meet with new people, cultivate growth opportunities through attending national events and conferences, and to connect with other local organizations for collaborative partnerships. I have grown so much due to working with these organizations. I would encourage everyone to find something they are passionate about and pursue it by working with local organizations.

I tell you my story in the hopes that if you find yourself wanting to leave, that feeling is normal and understandable. There is no shame in either leaving or staying. There is value in both of those things. You have to do what is best for you. Some are born to spread their roots and others to spread their wings. What is important is, wherever you land, find and surround yourself with people who believe in you and support you, even when you don't believe in yourself. They will guide you into finding your passion and purpose.

Action Potential

APOLLONIA PIÑA

When I was growing up, my family regularly discussed politics at home, usually while standing in the kitchen or sitting on the porch. Common themes we discussed were the lesser-told histories of America: the genocidal practices of the U.S. government; the massacres that were allowed, then scrubbed clean, and officially named "battles" (Sand Creek and Wounded Knee come to mind), and the false narrative of American exceptionalism. I was a teenager when I first had hands-on experience with political organizing. When George W. Bush's declaration of a "war on terrorism" after 9/11 was gaining traction, my father and I, along with many others, were opposed to this approach. We made signs and joined fellow Tulsans at the corner of 41st and Yale to demonstrate. Little did I know that this would set the tone for my future involvement in the political process and my desire to tell the full truth about American history.

Books were not censored at home, and I had access to many. P. D. Ouspensky's *In Search of the Miraculous*, Richard Rhodes's *The Making of the Atom Bomb*, and Ira Levin's *This Perfect Day* were books that gave me pause. My father, Valentino, was Xicano and told me about Cesar Chavez, the Brown Power Movement, and Afro-Cuban jazz. My Mvskoke mother, Yvette, was versed in Native American causes prior to becoming an environmental and sustainability activist. In her mind, there was no need for me to stand during the pledge of allegiance. She imprinted in me an awareness of the bias taught in U.S. history:

the strong slant in the story of American expansion and conquest, and the erasure of anyone who didn't fit into the program. It's a story of American imperialism. When we learned in school about "Old Hickory," Andrew Jackson, I spoke up about what he did to my Mvskoke great-grandparents and other families, knowing I had the support of my parents if I were ever sent to the principal's office (which I was). These experiences raised my awareness of the tactical extremes the American government pursues in order to get what it desires. Amid the current politics of globalism (neo-colonialism), trade, and international social-class economics, American imperialism maintains its stronghold to this day.

During my teen years, my relationship with my mom became strained, and I moved out of our house when I was seventeen. This was in the early aughts. I went to live at the Phoenix House, a punk house two blocks down the street from the house where I grew up. The Phoenix House was the third iteration in a lineage of communally lived punk houses that were on Tulsa's Phoenix Street. It was located in what is now known as Crosbie Heights. Back then, prior to downtown revival and gentrification, it was just a nameless neighborhood whose residents were firmly embedded below the poverty line. The house had been around for a while but had gone through several different phases in three different physical locations on Phoenix Street, each location keeping the Phoenix House name. Versions 1 and 3 were a half-block from the Blue Jackalope, a small neighborhood grocery store and part-time venue on Charles Page Boulevard. Version 2 was a block away from the Blue Jackalope; this was the generation that I actively lived in.

The Phoenix House was an all-female punk house, a rarity in any locality, let alone the Mid-South. I lived there with my friend and bandmate Jesska, and Nomi, a fellow Native punk who is Choctaw. Jesska and Nomi were a few years older than me and showed me the ropes through a number of youthful life experiences, some practical, others more mischievous in nature. This is where I learned how to organize a show, feed a mass of people, put up traveling bands, handle belligerent drunk punks, produce and print flyers and zines, and all other shades of hustling in between.

During this time I remember late night talks that stretched into new mornings, jugs of Carlo Rossi wine being passed back and forth (always Paisano), cheap beer, cheaper smokes, shared boyfriends, and writing. The unspoken rule was that anything and everything was up for discussion and deconstruction, no matter the topic. Drugs, trauma, sex, Beat writers, punk writers, boys, menstrual blood, local Klan, San Francisco, local Neo-Nazis, gender, Bob Wills, ethical "sluthood," Branch Davidians, rape, the Tulsa Race Massacre, "Marry, Fuck, Kill," heroin, Hickey, tattoos, BDSM, RE/Search, cats (*lots* of talks revolved around our cats), molestation, race . . . I have stored countless memory files of these conversational topics, some of which I promised to take to the grave with me.

Back then, when promoting the bands we had booked, we used word of mouth, and not so much the Internet. We barely made rent month to month (some months we didn't), and with social media still in its infancy, it was cheaper and faster for us to make paper flyers ourselves. We were strict acolytes to an analog DIY ethos—scissors, glue sticks, staplers, and paper. We'd promote house shows with flyers and by word of mouth—talking to people out at bars or at other shows. We got fancy a few times, printing flyers approximately the size of a cigarette pack to store in the cellophane wrapping. Anytime someone went for a smoke the tiny flyer was a reminder to make it to the show.

Whenever out-of-town bands stayed with us, we had a particular way of treating them. We'd greet them and invite them in, and then we'd feed them a standard dinner of potato burritos and Milwaukee's Best. I remember touring bands telling us on a few occasions that they were not accustomed to being greeted in such a manner when they arrived somewhere. Our hospitality toward them was one of the reasons why they enjoyed playing a dinky house show in Tulsa, Oklahoma. Without a doubt this could in part be chalked up to the gregarious tendencies of Okie women (try as we might to revolt against such midwestern social mores, we still "had company coming over"). We were known as cordial, but within reason—if needed we could turn into mouthy shitheads at the drop of a bottle.

It might seem unrelated, but hosting shows was pertinent to future activism: when the police were called, I often became the de facto person to talk to cops, acting as an intermediary to shut up drunks and bargain with the cops to let us squeeze in a few more songs. My strategy was to put up my beer, then greet them and divert their attention from any shenanigans going on in the periphery. Sometimes they would let their guard down and let a band play two more songs. During these encounters I unintentionally learned mediation tactics, which proved useful later in helping to defray the odds of me or my friends being arrested. I saw the ways conflicts could escalate, especially from observing the experiences of a few reliably antagonistic friends.

Once, when one of these friends was at a park in North Tulsa, a few Tulsa Police Department (TPD) officers approached him. He was by himself working on his van that had broken down. Even though it was still daylight, they asked him what he was doing there and continued to tease and harangue him for some time. A person can only take being provoked by those in authority for so long, and my friend reached his breaking point and punched his van in anger. That was all the TPD officers needed (and were waiting for), and they used this action as justification for jumping him. He was attacked by multiple officers at once, and the next thing he remembered was waking up at night in a pool of blood and vomit. Who do you call in that situation? If he had reported it, could we have really trusted the TPD to investigate one of its own? At the time of this writing in 2018, over a decade later, TPD officer Betty Shelby has been recently acquitted for the shooting of unarmed North Tulsa resident Terence Crutcher. Despite video evidence showing his back turned to her and no evidence of his possessing any weapons, she still walked free, was quickly hired by the neighboring Rogers County Sheriff's Department, and had her records expunged. In fall 2018 she began teaching a class at the Tulsa County Sheriff's Office titled "Surviving the Aftermath of a Critical Incident" along with conducting a national speaking tour of the same name. As Shelby continues to portray herself as the crowned victim in the shooting of Terrence Crutcher's death while simultaneously exploiting him, he remains dead in the ground, unable to disclose his side of the story. Certain Tulsa residents (particularly those that live in north Tulsa or east Tulsa—and double down if they are brown) know the TPD has a lengthy history of shiftiness and protecting its own. Thus, whenever the cops showed up at the Phoenix House, a few people would understandably turn hypervigilant. Who could blame them?

The year 2011 brought the Occupy movement to the streets in a collective grassroots wave not seen in decades. I became involved with Occupy Tulsa and hosted meetings at my house: poster making, planning, and coordinating impromptu learning workshops about such issues as class inequality, police harassment, and the Keystone XL Pipeline. My boyfriend and I also occasionally hosted salons at our house, akin to today's Ted Talks. Some friends had started the Tulsa Secular Fellowship and were holding meetings every Sunday. Each week, someone would give a twenty-minute presentation on all manner of topics, followed by a Q&A, then food. One time my mother gave a talk on water quality and environmental science. Others gave critiques on organized religion or presented on art projects they were undertaking, philosophy, science, or politics.

The Occupy Tulsa movement eventually left a bad taste in my mouth, and I ended up parting ways with it. Within its ranks, a split had opened between

Okie libertarians and the white liberal activists. We Native activists wanted to address issues specific to Oklahoma, such as decolonization* and illegal land grabbing, but were made to feel as if we were infringing on other white liberal agendas. When the tensions came to a head, many Natives felt shoved out of the conversation, and some of the white activists proceeded to file court orders against some of the Native participants. It got ugly. That confrontation was my first experience with 1) how fearful some white liberals are of outspoken brown people, and 2) how dedicated they are in remaining oblivious to their culpability. Privilege is invisible to those that possess it, after all. Eventually Occupy Tulsa ended, largely due, based on my experience, to infighting. This was my first attempt to organize a large group of people, and in the process I saw egos coming to the fore, and people clashing.

My next experience as an activist was at the University of Oklahoma in Norman. It was here that I was able to focus on Native causes and meet like-minded skins. One of those skins was my brother Talon (clan ways), who remains one of my closest confidants to this day. We were in a Native debate club together and cut our teeth every week arguing topics that affected Indian Country. Some of those debates became so heated that people would walk out in anger. Grudges would be held, sometimes for a week, a month, or to this day. This goes with the territory when working with Natives. Intergenerational trauma—the transferred trauma of historical oppression and the negative consequences thereof across generations—plays a role in this kind of activism. It has both positive and negative effects. It arouses a well of anger that can electrify Native people and motivate them to protect their tribes and future generations from the horrors their parents and grandparents survived. We know that we cannot always rely on the American government to hold our best interests in mind. However, this historical trauma also deeply impacts the rapport within our communities because many activists are hurting. Some of them seem to get involved so that they can promote their own cult of personality and try to maintain what they deem as the "right" way to engage in activism. This can take the form of some Native activists publically shaming others they deem not

---

* A few thoughts on the word "decolonization": true decolonization, as in tribal people living as they did pre-contact, is not realistic, given how long they've been in contact with white settlers and influenced by them. Rather, we should take these colonial influences and overlay them with indigenous thoughts and beliefs, thereby indigenizing them. A Native person indigenizing his or her daily life is absolutely obtainable.

radical enough, not adequately "full blood" (the origins of which are colonial), or not traditional in the ways they deem worthy. Some are males (the colloquially coined "macktivists") who get involved as a means to meet women and end up engaging in multiple casual relationships. Usually we make our peace with each other (or keep our distance) because ultimately we know that there are only relatively few of us up against a much larger institutional structure, one concerned with maintaining the ingrained class structure and a groomed American history lesson.

This brings me to purpose, or intention. I like bringing together people who I think would be intellectually compelling for one another. I see myself as acting as a conduit for others, creating spaces that allow people from detached circles to overlap and create. The analogy I use here is neuroscience-based. Imagine neurons, dendrites, terminal buttons, and action potentials—electrical impulses that travel along the axon to other neurons to effect a change by opening and closing millions of ion channels. The action potential has causality, affects a chain reaction, communicates a demand or desire. Once it hits a certain threshold (–55 mV, if anyone cares), the action potential cannot go back; it must complete the process of polarization. Repeating this process dozens, thousands, millions of times has the potential to build a new neural pathway, a sort of cortical remapping. Neurons that fire together wire together. If you are dedicated to repeating a process enough, it can change even the most stubborn of habits.

I've come to understand I am an amalgamation of lived experiences. My parents nurtured a strong moral compass in me at a young age. Later, living communally and taking an active role as an organizer further influenced my values and principles. As I matured and those values and principles crystallized, I learned to align my actions with my convictions. Drawing on my experiences of living at the Phoenix House at a young age has proven invaluable as I later navigated more structured activism within the Occupy Movement, campus organizations, and presently in the Native female-led initiative Matriarch.

Coming from a scientific background, I cannot help but observe how physiological processes are applicable to social behaviors as well, and that much like action potentials, determined, intentional change can rewire habits and affect long-term patterns. This connection gives me the optimism that both my experiences and persistent actions will enable me to affect positive outcomes for fellow Natives and for my community following centuries of historical abuse.

Forging Paths

Do I Belong?

ARIELLE DAVIS

In the fall of 2016, a group of students from Rogers State University, myself included, piled into a white van at 6:30 A.M. heading from Claremore to Oklahoma City for a communications conference. The annual Oklahoma Association of Broadcasters conference invites communications and journalism students to come ask questions and glean knowledge from people who work in the media industry. These professionals share their experiences and serve as real-life examples of the career possibilities these disciplines offer. The event lasted from 8:45 A.M. to 3:30 P.M. Yet during nearly seven hours and five panels, not one person of color was present. Not one. What does that signal to me as a woman of color? Or to the other students of color who traveled to this event? Is there any opportunity for me? For us? If there is, is there less of an opportunity? Do we belong here?

If I were to judge from the panels at that 2016 conference, my reasoning would lead me to believe that either there isn't any opportunity for me in this industry, or if there is any opportunity, it is my job to blaze the trail. But what are trailblazers? Trailblazers do not set trails ablaze to elevate themselves. They set the trail on fire to burn down oppressive structures so that it is easier for those coming along behind them. It is not a burden I want, but it seems to be one I will have to bear.

So where does the pain come in? It should have been every time a new panel sat down to represent the future—a future that left me out of the picture, unless I forcefully inserted myself into it. But these were not the moments that later caused me to swerve over the dashed white lines of the highway on my way home from RSU after being dropped off because I was so distraught, my eyes stinging with pain from the mascara leaking into them as a result of my tears. I screamed at the top of my lungs and pounded my steering wheel with blows of frustration. I arrived home doubled over, unable to get out of the car because the weight of the pain had become too great for that day.

At the end of the conference in Oklahoma City it was revealed to the students and faculty that the organization was proudly and swiftly approaching its sixtieth anniversary. The organizers wanted us to celebrate the legacy of the men who had started it all. To kick off this celebration they showed two videos. Each video displayed the accomplishments of each man who had founded the organization. The second video showed a clip of one of the founders in a blackface clown costume with large painted white lips. It's important to emphasize that this depiction was shown in a video that was intended to invite students to celebrate the legacy of Bill Thrash and his accomplishments on behalf of Oklahoma's public television channel, OETA. It is equally important to emphasize that this organization is TV channel has educational authority in Oklahoma. Remember that I was at a conference that was supposed to inform and educate students about the importance and power of media. So I was obviously immediately shaken by this extremely racist image, enacted by the man we were celebrating and perpetuated by the film we were being shown.

After the film concluded, we began to pack up to leave the conference. My professor gathered my classmates and me toward the front to take a picture. As I was exiting the aisle, she turned to me and asked, "So what did you think?" I responded, "I thought it was good. I wish that people of color had been included on the panels, and I have an issue with Bill Thrash in a minstrel clown costume." She became flustered and defensive, and said, "Well, they had people of color for the panels, but those individuals were unfortunately unable to make it, and you have to consider that that portion of the video was shot because it was the 1920s and 1930s, so everybody was like that at that time," she said. I began to respond, but before I could say anything she interrupted, saying, "This day has been so nice and for you to complain about those sorts of things is just offensive. I mean after everything they have done putting this together for us." My anger began to overwhelm me. How was she offended? What message was her response supposed to send me? That because most people were racist at that time then it was okay for this man to be racist as well? Was she saying that I should be forgiving of these racist images because in the 1920s and '30s racism was prevalent and normal? I was furious. I was humiliated. But I was a student.

It was obvious to all my peers who watched this conversation take place that I was upset, so of course the conversation carried over to the van. Inside the van, I explained to two of my classmates and friends why I was upset about the video clip and the lack of people of color on the panels. I would love to end this story by saying that my friends were empathetic, understanding, and wanted to enlist themselves in helping to do something to make sure instances like these never happened again. Their responses, though, didn't resemble anything that displayed friendship. I explained that clowns in blackface were meant to make fun of black people and their features. I explained that this image was making fun of the way I looked and the way my family looked. The video said to me: your full lips and dark skin are freakish and grotesque. It said that wide noses are circus-worthy and real-world ugly. I suggested that the clip should be removed because it was hurtful to black students.

My friends, all nonblack, didn't understand. One asserted that these images were a part of Bill Thrash's legacy, and suggested that his blackface performance might have been how he had gotten his start. If that's the case, I argued, his legacy is predicated on a racist history that exploits and makes fun of African Americans. The other friend, I think, was closer to reaching for understanding. She suggested that maybe the organization didn't know that the image was historically racist. I responded to her by saying that her claim made this an even bigger issue because this was a channel that was supposed to educate people. If they didn't catch this information, then who would? Their insensitivity was indicative of a larger issue. I also tried to meet my friend in the middle. I told her I couldn't be sure whether or not the organization knew that clip was offensive. However, I suggested that once a black student says, "This is painful for me," then the image should be taken down, unless context is provided for how and why those minstrel clowns were used, and why that usage was offensive. My friends still didn't get it. At some point, another student chimed in to say he understood what I was saying. He said he understood that the responsibility of educators is to educate, and if they didn't call out these issues, who would? At this point my professor, who was driving, had had enough. She told us to stop talking about it. She said, "I am sick of talking about race all the time."

Under no circumstance, in any academic setting, should a professor say to a student of color that she or he is sick of talking about race all the time. It is an insult to my everyday experience. I am myself sick of dealing with racism all the time. So, to say to me that you are tired of the conversation is like spitting in my face after I've told you I am hurting. It is like you are wrapping your hands around my throat and squeezing until I can't speak. It is choking my voice out of me because you can. It is silencing me because you have the authority to. It is telling me and everyone who hears you that my experience makes you uncomfortable; therefore, I need to keep it inside. It is saying that I need to suffer quietly. It is telling me that I need to suffer alone.

But here is why I will not "stop talking about race all the time." And here is what I know. As much as I feel alone, I know that I am not. I know there are students of color all across the country who feel how I feel. They see what I see. They experience what I experience. They hurt like I hurt. More important, there are a multitude of students of color coming up behind me. Students who are eager for education and opportunity. Students who will face a lack of representation. Students who will have their painful experiences dismissed. Students who will have their professors silence their voices and their pain. Students who will feel alienated by their peers. This is why I must do everything I can to make sure that I decrease the chances of this silencing happening again.

I am blessed with the gift of communication. I am articulate. I am expressive. I am strong. I have a voice. I will always use that voice to fight for those who do not have a voice. I will always use that voice to represent the experiences of those who are not present to represent themselves. I will never stop fighting for the generations who are coming up behind me. I will remain on the front lines of academia to ensure that students of all races are treated equally and fairly. I will use my voice to lessen the opposition that they may face.

In case you are wondering who this essay is for, I will make it plain. This is for any student of color who has ever felt alone, overwhelmed, underrepresented, misunderstood, dismissed, or hurt. I am saying to that student: you are not alone. I am with you. I am validating you. And I am fighting for you. I will not stop. I will not be silent because you matter to me. You matter. Your experiences matter. You belong.

Impossible

JENNY YANG CROPP

I was headed down the hall toward class one day in the middle of the spring semester and noticed my phone flashing. It was my aunt calling.

I think I have a nervous tic, a conditioned response whenever my aunt comes up on caller ID, that forces me to answer the phone no matter what I'm doing. During my teenage years, each time my grandfather's heart landed him in the hospital, she would be the one waiting at the house to tell me when I got home. Whenever someone in the family died, she was usually the one to deliver the news. Even though I now know, logically, that when she calls, she's probably just calling to say hello, to see how I'm doing, the moment before she speaks is filled with anxiety, and if I miss her call I panic a little until I can reach her. Phone tag with her is a kind of short-term hell.

I couldn't stop myself from answering the phone even though I was walking through the door into my classroom. There was only a minute before class was supposed to start, and I would not normally take a call in front of my students, but I did.

And sure enough, she was calling to tell me that someone in the family had died, so I kept talking to her instead of telling her that I would call her back after class. To shorthand the family tree, it was my father's cousin's husband who had passed away. I didn't know him very well, which is what I told my aunt, but I did know his nephew, my second cousin Terry, because he and I had gone to the same junior high and high school. We hadn't been close, hadn't shared the same circle of friends, but I had enjoyed seeing his face in the halls and being in the same class with him once. Back then, I felt as if Lawton, Oklahoma, was my home despite leaving from first grade to sixth grade. Returning to Lawton all these years later to teach at Cameron University, I still felt connected to this place because I knew I had a bunch of cousins there, living their lives, and that anywhere I went, I might run into someone related to me.

When my aunt told me it was Terry's uncle who had died, I was sad for him, for all of them. I told her I wouldn't be able to go to the funeral with her because I had to teach class, and then I hung up the phone.

At this point I was standing at the front of the classroom. My students had been sitting quietly, waiting for class to begin, and listening to everything I said. It was a small class, only four students left on the roster at that point. One of them was a middle-aged nurse who usually came to class in her scrubs because she was fitting in classes during her lunch breaks. She was staring at me in a way that I couldn't quite read, and it made me suddenly self-conscious.

"Sorry about that," I said.

"Were you talking about Harold C—— and Terry E——?" she asked.

"Yes."

"Because Harold is my uncle, and Terry is my brother," she said.

I connected the dots slowly and awkwardly. I can imagine how stunned and puzzled I must have looked, my forehead furrowed the same whether I'm angry or I'm just thinking hard about something. "Then you're my cousin," I said.

It was hard to start class after that. I had too many questions. The first and foremost was, "Why didn't you say anything when you knew my last name was Cropp?" It was my grandfather's last name, my father's last name, the maiden name of her own grandmother, and I knew that she had to have known it. She had to have known my grandfather the way I knew her grandmother, whose sweet childhood face—low dark brows over soft eyes, the Cropp chin framed by curls—appears next to his in so many of the family photos from the 1920s and '30s. The only reason I hadn't made the connection was that this student, my cousin, was going by her married name instead of her maiden name. Had it been her maiden name, I would have felt compelled to ask her if she was related to me.

She had thought about it, she said. She did know the name. "But I didn't think it was possible," she said. Something in that phrase struck me, made me speechless and sad and angry and frustrated. I changed the subject. I taught the class, and every class after that until the end of the semester, like normal. But the phrase remains stuck in my head and my heart. What wasn't possible? What about me seems impossible? I have been trying for months to figure this out. I have told this story over and over, to anyone who will listen as well as to myself, puzzling through her response to me.

I was no more than five or six years old when I decided I would always be a Cropp. My grandfather was holding my younger brother, James, in his lap, giving him sips of coffee and chuckling at his little man-in-training. James couldn't have been more than three or four years old. My grandfather was explaining how important my brother was. He was the only grandson who would carry the Cropp name. I wasn't happy with this, so he told me I was special in a different way. I was, after all, a little woman-in-training, being raised to become a wife and mother.

Except I wasn't very good at it. In my family and church community, it was high praise for a young girl to be called a "little mama." She was being lauded for nurturing her siblings. It was high praise for a little girl to be called pretty and sweet. I knew that. But I was a sullen and rather serious little girl. I was thrilled to receive high test scores. I read a lot and kept to myself. I had a hard time making friends. I gained weight easily. By middle school, my grandmother was regularly sitting me down to watch beauty pageants and asking me to try harder so I could be like those girls. By high school, my grandfather was daily commenting that I dressed like I should be pushing a wheelbarrow. I spent most of high school in my room, reading and writing. At one point my grandparents flew me out to California so that one of my aunts could scold me for not spending more time in the living room, watching TV with my grandparents, being social.

When I began college, I had a full scholarship, but it felt as if my family was generally disappointed in how I had turned out. My grandmother was the sweetest woman I have ever known, and I know she thought she was doing the right thing, but every time I let her down she'd say, "It's okay. I won't die until I hold your child in my arms." And I let her down a lot. I lost the scholarship, and after being sexually assaulted my freshman year, I lost just about everything else. Between prescription psychiatric drugs and my own self-medicating, I landed myself in in-patient treatment four times in two years. I kept quitting my jobs. I kept dropping or failing classes. I entered into damaging relationships, self-sabotaged, sank into months-long depressions during which I barely left the house. When I start to list it all out, it becomes overwhelming, even now. All those bad choices combined with the uncontrollable parts of life—the death of my grandfather, the murder of my sister, the extreme side-effects of my medications. These all wore me down.

But I am not a cautionary tale, at least not in the way you might think. I tell my students about my bad grades, how I ended my first year of college with a 1.7 GPA, how it took me ten years to finish, how getting all A;s in my last sixty course hours still meant graduating with a 2.8 GPA. But I don't tell it as a warning. I tell it as a story of hope.

There was no one moment in which it all got easier for me, no sudden epiphany. There is no neat dividing line between the old me and the new me who made better choices and worked harder and found happiness. Change can be excruciatingly slow. It can be so gradual that no one believes you're actually changing, not even you. The myth that we can remake ourselves overnight like people do in movies can make us think we're not doing it right, that we're perpetual failures, but it's not true.

Going back to college after flunking out was hard. I was still self-medicating. I was still struggling to get out of bed. I was still making mistakes. Each time I messed up, though, I told myself I had already lost it all once and survived, so this wasn't the end of the world. And the next day, I tried to start over, to not hold the mistake against myself. Eventually there were more good days than bad, more good choices than poor ones, more A's than F's. One day, years later, I found myself in front of an advisor who was telling me I would have enough credits after that year to graduate. It had taken so long, and so many people had given up on me, that both family and friends had switched from asking when I was going to get married and have kids to asking, "Are you ever going to finish college?"

"No," I told them. "I'm going to stay in college forever." It was my smartass answer, but now that I had figured things out and was on a roll, I wanted to go to graduate school. My parents and grandparents hadn't gone to college. The women in our family got married, and the men went into the military. I was going to get a master's degree. Worse, I wanted to be a writer.

I went to a writer's conference in the fall, about six months after I learned I was an impossible Cropp, and the theme of the conference was "Impossible Possibilities/Possible Impossibilities." I was drawn to it because I still had my cousin's words floating there on the surface of everything I was doing and thinking. At one of the panels on creative nonfiction, a woman read a piece about taking a road trip with her child. She had gotten pregnant in high school. She was a single mom who had been told she wouldn't be able to finish school or go to college, but she did it anyway. She told us that the conference theme had given her the frame she needed to write about her experience. Her success had seemed impossible to others, but it was her particular set of difficulties, her journey through them, that made who she is today possible. She got through it by not listening to the people who said she couldn't do it.

I started to make a list of the not-so-helpful things people told me were or were not possible for me:

1. You're not cut out to be a writer. You should do something else.
2. You're not going to be able to do much with that degree.
3. You're never going to get a husband if you look like that.
4. If this medicine keeps you from writing, you will have to give up writing.
5. You won't be happy until you've lost the weight.
6. You can't get into graduate school with that GPA.
7. You always have good ideas, but nobody believes you'll do anything with them.
8. Are you sure you're cut out to be a mother?
9. You might not make it through grad school if you have a baby.

Spread out over time, viewed in isolation, these seem like the kind of statements we're told we should just ignore. Let them roll off our backs. But list them out like this (and these are just the first ones that came to mind) and what you have is a pattern of naysaying.

Then I started looking for all the examples I could find of people doing the impossible. I teach writing at an open-enrollment university, so I didn't have to go far to find them. Nearly every student here has story after story about all the people, including themselves, who tried to get in the way of their success. Trauma. Abuse. Addiction. Poverty. Prison. So many impossible situations to have faced, but here they were, writing their hearts out.

A week or two before that phone call from my aunt, I had successfully defended my dissertation and become the first member of my family that I know of, immediate or extended, to get a doctorate. My son was born one year before I sat for my exams. I wrote my dissertation while parenting and teaching a full load of five classes per semester with an average of 120 students. During that time, I also published my first book and traveled to give readings and promote it. I did all the things people said I wouldn't be able to do, partly out of spite and a certain rebelliousness that began when I was that five- or six-year-old girl being told who I had to be when I grew up, and partly because of the grit and persistence I learned growing up in Oklahoma. This is, after all, a place where droughts, floods, and tornadoes wipe away entire communities, and we insist on rebuilding every time.

I never asked my cousin in that class what it was about me that she thought was so impossible, but her denial of our connection makes sense to me now, or at least it doesn't bother me so much anymore. I think about all the messages she might have received about what she should or shouldn't do with her life, about what she was or wasn't capable of, and I think she probably said it for the same reason that I tell my students how spectacularly I failed as an undergrad. It does seem hard to believe. While I jokingly suggest they not do what I did, I tell them my story because I want them to know that the impossible happens every single day, that failure isn't the end of the world, and that we can achieve, not in spite of the impossibilities we face, but because of them.

Time

UREKA WILLIAMS

A few years ago, my children and I were at the Tulsa State Fair and I became excited to learn that nineties hip-hop trio Naughty by Nature would perform on the Oklahoma Stage. See, over twenty years ago I would turn up the volume to listen to their socially conscious "Uptown Anthem" and I would confidently raise my arms in the air and move them back and forth to the bass of "Hip Hop Hooray." Now, twenty years later, here they were about to perform at a fair.

After overindulging in curious fair delicacies, I was guided by a sea of thirty-something-looking faces to the back of the fairgrounds where I heard a refreshingly familiar sound. As my children and I got closer to the stage, my then ten-year-old son, with the left side of his lip raised, asked, "Who's Naughty by Nature?" Surprised, I told him with my eyes bucked, "Only one of the best hip hop groups *everrrr...*" He shrugged his shoulders and nodded his head to the right and I shook my head in disbelief, thinking, *How could he not know Naughty by Nature?* As we continued our walk to the stage, there was a jolly Caucasian man walking past us, nodding his head, while mouthing the words to the song, and I told him, "My son doesn't even know who Naughty by Nature is." He flashed a bold smile and said, "These kids today don't know good music."

We stayed at the Oklahoma Stage for just a few minutes, which was all that my son could muster. However, it was at that moment that I realized I truly was getting older, much older than I thought, and that time had finally caught up with me.

I can recall as a tween hearing music from the seventies like Gloria Gaynor's "I Will Survive" and the Commodores' "Brick House," and thinking this music is so old and dated, yet my relatives and other adults seemed to really vibe to it. Now, I was here. At this seemingly unfamiliar moment, the tide had turned on me. I finally understood that the clock's second hand doesn't stop. A present truth is that Father Time does not move aside or disappear for anyone. He holds the mighty banner of reality that includes all the things that we need and enjoy, in addition to a huge mirror.

Another revelation that sucked me into a vacuum of disbelief occurred when one night I was watching Bevy Smith on *Fashion Queens* as she was commenting on a celebrity's gown. She mentioned that it was vintage 1990s. My heart must have skipped a beat because that was all I heard. I could see her on the screen talking with her celebrity guests, but I couldn't hear what she was saying. The only thing that echoed in my ears was *vintage 1990s.* When had I and my era become vintage, dated? When did I start getting old? Yes, the occasional gray hair would sneak in and claim its final territory every now and then, but when did I start getting older? What did aging really mean?

I guess time had finally caught up with me, because I can remember in the late nineties and early two thousands still writing friends and family handwritten letters, even as e-mail was becoming a more popular and feasible form of communication. I can recall physically going to the airport to purchase and pick up hard-copy plane tickets, whereas now the entire transaction is usually completed online. Growing up, I can recall always making sure I kept a little change in my purse, so that I could make a call at a pay phone if needed. I even remember having a membership to Blockbuster Video, so that I could watch the most recent films.

I also grew up as a "Cosby kid." I can't think of a Thursday evening from 1984 to 1992, from 7:00 to 7:30 P.M., when I wasn't sitting in front of the television listening to Cliff Huxtable offer some moral to his children that I would tuck away in my consciousness for later. (However, now after his legal trouble, it seems Mr. Cosby should have memorized his own mantras and kept them close to his vest.) And I would marvel over Clair's presence in the courtroom, her endearing relationship with her husband, and how adored she was by her children, so much so that I even named my daughter after her. No intentional disrespect for television today that seems to be monopolized by "reality TV," but I can't think of any shows that inspire my son, daughter, nieces and nephews, or students to comment that they want to mirror the characters represented. Oh, but they do remark on their opulent means.

I suppose what I've really figured out as time passes is that I can't expect my (or anybody else's) children to be familiar with older musicians, dated clothing styles, or what we "used to say," if we don't take the time to teach them. Yes, I've officially become an elder, and I have accepted this responsibility. I must teach my children like my immediate family and village family taught me. I am charged with bringing "back in the day" to the present.

I have to share with my daughter that Kadeem Hardison, who plays K.C. Undercover's dad in *K.C. Undercover*, became popular in the nineties for playing a flip-top-wearing math genius on *A Different World*, which greatly influenced my decision to attend a historically black college for my undergraduate education. I also have to share with my son that before actor Will Smith became an A-list celebrity featured in films that included *Independence Day* and *Enemy of the State*, he was equally as popular in the late eighties and early nineties for performing such songs as "Parents Just Don't Understand" and "Summertime," and for playing, for six years, a precocious nephew in the popular TV sitcom *The Fresh Prince of Bel-Air*.

Children have to understand that what they have now was built on a process of trial, error, defeat, and eventual success by fearless trailblazers from years ago. Just as I know that I may exercise my right to vote thanks to women like Fannie Lou Hamer, my daughter will one day know the same. My son, who is kindled by all things pop culture, must, too, be reminded that many of the songs he enjoys today echo lyrics and beats from when I was not much older than he is now; so, in essence, we really do enjoy the same music.

Better yet, what I really want my children and their generation to know is that the artists they listen to today—Rhianna, Drake, Beyoncé—likely won't be who their two-year-old cousin and her generation listen to; and that they, too, will not only be charged with sharing what happened in terms of entertainment, but with sharing a legacy that's been left for them. They must pass down the knowledge that their maternal great-grandfather played in the professional Negro Baseball League; that their paternal grandfather served the United States in the Korean War; and that their father, a dentist, has brothers who have served our country having earned the distinguished titles of U.S. attorney and Secret Service agent. Essentially what they need to understand is that they must continue to build on a foundation that has been left for them. They need to understand that hard work is not the exception but the expectation. With my guidance, they will fully grasp all of this, in their own time.

Letter to My Grandkids

SPRING HOUGHTON

Dear Readers,

I have imagined in the following piece that my dad—who died in the year 1999 before he even knew grandchildren would come—could have written some words to my own kids from wherever his soul is now. I found out I was pregnant with my first child six months after he died. My second didn't come until sixteen years later—so, I write to you now with an infant and a sixteen-year-old, and without my own dad. I don't believe in heaven or hell, but I also don't believe souls just die. So in my imagination the following letter is completely possible in some realm. As if I am a medium through which my dad can speak to my kids, I'm conjuring his voice like the witch that I may be. In a very literal, suburban sense, I mean, if he raised me and I caught a bunch of the ideas and lessons he tossed my way, then it makes sense to me that I can pass those ideas to my kids, right? Why not through a piece of writing where I assume his voice? Thank you for reading and for bearing with me as I take on this male voice, in a necessary and lovely collection of women's voices.

Blurring binaries forever and yours truly,
Spring Houghton

I was born in 1945—the year World War II ended and the year FDR began his fourth term—into a two-parent household where my mom worked and my father swindled and lied and stole. I watched as my mom carried and bore five more children, and my father came home to take what he could and then run away again. She was an angel and he was a thorn in the finger, a nail in the tire, a kidney stone. Nothing good could come of him, I thought. She worked two or more jobs as long as I could remember, while he forged his way into a seminary outside of Dallas, Texas, and then embezzled money from those godly people and was sent to jail. I knew early on I wanted to be just like her: hard-working, kind to children, passionately loyal. I was not always successful at loyalty. I managed to be enough like her, though, that I was not much like him, and for that I am grateful from the grave.

My little brother Mark died of measles—I'm not sure if we were too poor to get a vaccine or if the vaccine wasn't widely available yet. But I never forgot watching his immune system slowly lose. I came home from school and stood by his crib every day, even after we buried him. The house we rented had two bedrooms, one for my mom and one for all the kids, three boys at the time. Mom cooked every meal; we always had something sweet; the house often smelled like bread, and I made peanut butter and banana sandwiches. I probably prayed, but not as hard as my mom because she trusted God and Jesus more than anyone else realistically could. And this was when my faith in the Divine was critically damaged. Even the abuse from my father I could chalk up to him just being bad, but I could not comprehend a god who would let an innocent baby suffer. My saint of a mother was still loyal to both, and I couldn't understand that either.

When I was a junior in high school, I had a quarter every day for lunch. I had a job and helped Mom pay bills as much as I could. My mom, working at this point a pretty good job at the nearby GM plant, could afford for me to spend 25 cents a day to eat at school. Well, I was saving my money because I wanted something or other new. Probably clothes, shoes. So I skipped lunch every day for 95 days and saved up $19. The usual routine was to study or go to the field house over the lunch break to keep myself occupied and fly under other people's radar. Even in the early 1960s, teens were assholes to other teens, especially to poor boys like me. I made all A's and played on the football team, but kept to myself. I did not want trouble, or necessarily to be noticed in any way other than for my hard work. And so the secreting away to do more "work" worked for me. Every day, I put the newly earned quarter in a sock in my top drawer. And then one day my father returned.

He had been gone for a while but that was nothing new. My mom, bless her heart, used to say he'd come home long enough to get her pregnant and then leave again. I don't remember how long he stayed, but it was just long enough for him to find my sock full of savings while I was at school. I came home to put my quarter away with the others and found them all gone. The anger that came up in me that day stayed with me until the day my dad died. I don't recommend holding on to anger for forty years, but then again, if you have something that makes you that angry, let it be fuel for good. Good trouble, good work, good action, good creations, good love. You'll be okay. People say don't be angry and let it go, but I say let it be. Use it. It's energy. It's being given lemons and marching your ass to get sugar and water so you can make the most delicious lemonade possible. It's enjoying that lemonade on your hardest day and sharing it with your favorite person, or with no one if your favorite person is you on that day. It's okay if this lemonade metaphor is tired—if it is honest and true, child, you'll remember it.

I grew up and married your grandmother in 1965, and went on to become the first person in my family to go to college and graduate. I became a chiropractor and started a health food store, and then went to medical school and became a doctor. Your grandmother and I had your mom in 1980, and five years later we opened a medical clinic in a small town in rural Oklahoma. Here is where I began to wonder if people try so hard to believe in God that they have given up believing in each other. I'm afraid I passed this suspicion on to your mother. She's really unsure about God. She thinks about the possibility quite a bit, but she's still unsure. I'd bet she always will be because she is very like me in many ways.

The thing is I believe in loving and providing care for people, especially vulnerable people, especially children. I believe in wheeling my patients to their cars after a procedure, and calling people to hear how their broken ankles are healing. I've provided stitches at my home for simple fishing accidents, given money to a high school sophomore for an abortion she desperately needed, and rushed my daughter and son to get care that I couldn't provide. I believe in constantly learning. I believe that the division between healer and patient is a big lie, like the lie about the line between God and humans. I believe that, sometimes, my dad bubbled up in me even when I tried to do my best. People think that we are just made good and bad, like I thought my dad was the bad stuff in life and my mom was all the good. But the truth is that we are all capable of both good and bad, and you'll have to pick which one you're going to try to be every day of your life. I wrote to your mom once, "Be strong, be honest, and always be true." And here is what I meant: have enough solid faith in your fellow humans that you know they can see your soul—they know if you're bullshitting them—and work to get your motivations right with your own god. Don't bullshit others, not only because they will pick up on it, but because you will not be proud of yourself for it. You will feel false and phony, as Holden Caulfield would say. You can't save everybody from falling off a cliff, but you can save your own soul.

Anyway, a few last things I want to tell you.

Don't be afraid to be smart. Even if other people make fun of you for it. But don't be a dick about it. It's in your blood so you might not be able to escape it anyway. I started clipping and saving pieces from the newspaper and from magazines and sending them to your mom when she went to college. I would send her interesting scientific discoveries, riddles, and short stories from the *New Yorker*, mostly. I annotated them and highlighted and underlined segments that stood out to me, but of course also because I wanted to show her how to focus and really take in the reading, how to always be a learner, a student. I don't know how much she kept, but I enjoyed the giving.

I want you to try to be patient with yourself. Hard times will come. Let the crisis happen, and trust me that every pain will pass. It might come back, but no pain is permanent *and* constant. Two months is a significant marker. Two months after his father's death, Hamlet breaks down over what he sees as his mother's lack of appropriate, widowly grief; that's where we get the famous "frailty thy name is woman" line. Funny how he's calling his mother frail, she who bore him, while he's the one crying about being a prince. I won't spoil it for you—it's a fine play. Read it yourself. Anyway. Every time I moved to a new house, it took right about two months for me to get used to the new doorknobs and halls and placement of the light switches. Your grandmother, usually a stoic woman, much more stoic than I ever was, broke down emotionally two months postpartum. I don't know what it is about two moons, but love yourself over that hump and you'll be okay.

I wish I could have seen your mother give birth to you. I wish I could have met you and taught you things and given you donuts on a Saturday morning and watched you enjoy jumping on a trampoline. But I did all those things with your mother, and I know she will do all those things with you. And she will be the best at it.

Lastly, remember that we are connected. We never got to meet in person—in body. But we are still tied together. Beyond all our very different bodies—a brand-new baby one, a healthy teenaged one, your mom's having just given birth, mine ashes in a cookie jar. We come from the same. We'll end up the same.

My Love is a promise to keep connections. With Love.

Your grandpa,

Michael A. Houghton, M.D.

Notes on Humiliation, Compassion, and Oklahoma, My Home

LEANNE HOWE

I'll begin with humiliation: airport mayonnaise in the twenty-first century.

Ingredients: Soybean oil, water, egg yolks, high fructose corn syrup, vinegar salt spice (who knows what this is), Calcium disodium EDTA (a preservative so it can be eaten after the second coming of Christ). Contains eggs.

This humiliation might pass for something edible if the consumer were a zombie. It's sugar-water-greasy, unfit for, *well*, for all animals on the planet—even those trafficking in fast foods at 6:45 A.M. at World Rogers World Airport in Oklahoma City.

During holidays, Okies like me return to our beloved homeland by flying in and out of this, *ahem*, world-class airport where there are no less than four condiment counters offering free packets of airport mayo, those little packets verily strewn on the bathroom floors of this one-terminal wonder.

I've written many times about my life as a Native eighteen-year-old waitress working at the Will Rogers World Airport Sky Chefs restaurant. In 2009, I did a one-woman show at the Krannert Center for the Performing Arts at the University of Illinois in Urbana-Champaign about my experiences as an airport waitress.

As I retrace my steps back to 1969, I remember the waitresses, cooks, and dishwashers at Sky Chefs very clearly. Mary was one of the first waitresses I met. She had soft brown eyes and smoked while she ate. I'd never seen anyone swallow a heaping spoonful of ham hocks and beans, and then pull a drag from a Camel cigarette while reading the newspaper. I had to look away if we were on break together. The only thing Mary seemed to care about was smoking, cooking German food, and her six-year-old son. Her hair was blonde with dark brown roots, she was short and muscular, and young, but at the time I thought she was old. Probably thirty.

She taught me how to "close" the restaurant at the end of our midnight shift. We had to wipe down the aluminum refrigerators, sterilize all food surfaces, clean and wash out the soft drink fountain. Clean and refill each of the thirty-six condiment containers with Duke's Mayonnaise. We had to count the cash register, and if we were off by less than a dollar, one of us would use our tip money to balance the drawer.

Mary was also the first person to coax me into putting a dollop of Duke's Mayonnaise on hot French fries.

"That's how they do it in Europe," she said. "It's delicious and so much better than ketchup."

And she was right.

Once while swallowing a mouthful of food and blowing smoke out through her nostrils, Mary said, "I made potato beer soup last night." I admitted I'd never heard of cooking with German beer, so she gave me the recipe.

Obviously the era made an indelible impression on me: the people were unusual, and the politics of our German Jewish supervisors, who flew in from New York once a month, were new to me. In a way they were like history teachers explaining what it is was like living in Germany, or Russia during World War II before immigrating to America. I inhaled all the political discussions around the coffee bar. Until I worked as a waitress, I'd never even heard the term "Axis Powers." When our shop went union I became a union steward.

The earliest nonfiction book I read from that period in my life was *Toil and Trouble: A History of American Labor*, by Thomas Brooks (1971). An AFL-CIO organizer suggested it to me as I served him coffee, and I'll never forget his advice: "People can be a force for good if we work together for the benefit of all." It was more than good advice; my early experiences of working at the airport restaurant are the reasons I became a Democrat, and, much later in life, a writer and teacher.

The year 1969 was one of the most tumultuous periods in U.S. history. Consider the draft lottery of 1969 for military service in the Vietnam War, the civil rights marches for equality, and the takeover and occupation by eighty-nine Indians of the abandoned facilities on Alcatraz Island. They called themselves the "Indians of All Tribes." The Indian activists used the 1868 Treaty of Fort Laramie to argue that because the Alcatraz penitentiary was closed on March 21, 1963, and declared surplus federal property the following year, the island qualified for reclamation by American Indians.

While the Alcatraz Island occupation only lasted for nineteen months, from November 20, 1969, to June 11, 1971 (the Nixon administration forcibly ended it), the takeover had a powerful effect on American Indians in Oklahoma. It sparked activism in the Native community in Oklahoma City. Just imagine—only eighty-nine American Indians occupied Alcatraz Island and one of their demands was that a university be built for them. They wanted to be educated by Native faculty with a Native studies curriculum.

Other things were happening in 1969. In Oklahoma City the sanitation workers went on strike and called their protest movement "Black Friday." They cited low wages, poor treatment, and lousy working conditions. No one had to school me on low wages; I was making $1.15 an hour as a night-shift waitress at Sky Chefs.

The airport restaurant was always busy during the day. Late-night delayed flights made the night shift worthwhile for waitresses relying on tips. But business slowed after 10:00 P.M. until closing at midnight. American Airlines, our parent company, owned Sky Chefs, and we received roughly the same benefits as the baggage handlers and flight attendants (stewardesses in 1969). After completing a year with the company, Sky Chefs employees could fly anywhere that American Airlines flew for the cost of flight taxes. We could also take one international flight a year with an international carrier, again only paying taxes.

Jeani Sparks, a coworker, and I decided we would fly to San Francisco for two nights and three days. We'd been friends since grade school, and she had helped get the job at Sky Chefs. The flight tax to San Francisco was something like $2.69 one way, and would be deducted from our paychecks. We stayed in the Hotel David on Geary Street in San Francisco for $5.00 a night. American Airlines pilots and flight attendants overnighted at Hotel David and we were afforded the same rates. We walked all over San Francisco, trekking up and down Nob Hill, then walked to Fisherman's Wharf and Chinatown. We rode a cable car for the ridiculously low price of a quarter each. My first flight from Oklahoma City to San Francisco would instill in me a brash sense of adventure, of hurrying into a new landscape without a map, and talking to strangers on busy street corners. On that final afternoon in San Francisco, I prayed for a rainstorm that would delay my return to Oklahoma, like forever.

The dining rooms at the airport restaurant in Oklahoma City in 1969 could hold close to 130 people, plus snack bar seating. During the last years of the Vietnam War, the nightshift crew would serve an average of 120 draftees before they were flown out of Oklahoma to Fort Benning, or Fort Bragg, or Fort Bliss. Every Monday through Friday around 5:00 P.M. they would arrive, and four waitresses, including me, were assigned to serve them their last meal as civilians before they left for boot camp.

Each night was the same. Young draftees would tumble into the airport dining room. They were always quiet, trying to come to terms with the realization that they were about to be plunged into the biggest drama of their lives. Warfare. Most were my age. Take a moment and consider their numbers. On average we served dinner to 500 eighteen-year-olds a week, 2,000 draftees a month, 24,000 Oklahomans in a single year. We served fresh vegetables, salad, Salisbury steak, mashed potatoes, and chocolate Jell-O pudding for dessert. The meals were generally the same each day. If a draftee was twenty-one, had his own money, and wanted a beer, we'd sell him a 3.2 Coors on tap.

As a Choctaw woman from southeastern Oklahoma, I'd never heard of some of the dishes on the menu. A New York Reuben sandwich with authentic corned beef was completely foreign to me. The corned beef was flown in weekly from a deli on 7th Street in New York City. I'd also never seen strawberries that grew the size of baby red potatoes. They were also flown in from New York. My grandfather grew strawberries in Ada, but they were the size of the end of my little finger. Very sweet. The New York strawberries didn't have much taste, but they looked good in a pie. All Sky Chefs waitresses, including me, would learn to make strawberry pies at the beginning of our shifts by mixing a sweet gooey red filling with New York strawberries. We poured the mixture into a prebaked graham-cracker crust. Strawberry pie was a Sky Chefs specialty, served cold with a generous topping of whipped cream. Delicious, but expensive, something like $2.50 a slice. (I had to work for two hours to pay for one slice.)

I'd also never seen anyone make real mayonnaise from scratch. It's French in origin and not a condiment my family bought. Too expensive. We ate yellow mustard. But our professional night cook, Selma (not her real name), whipped up a bowl of real mayonnaise one evening. She used egg yolks, light oil, and a pinch of salt. Amazing, when I think about it. I learned how to make fresh mayonnaise from scratch at the Will Rogers World Airport in Oklahoma City. The recipe has stayed with me all these years. Sadly, there are no professional cooks at most of the nation's airport "restaurants." Today in Oklahoma City's airport there are fast-food fries and fake watery mayo in shitty tubes while some guy wearing a black hairnet yells, "Don't blame me for no ketchup. Sonic's going out of business at the airport. It's all we got!"

The problem with losing myself in these little daydreams and memories is that I'm making the past sound so much better than it was. 1969 wasn't better, just different.

One night around 9:00 P.M., Delia, the tall, black-haired night manager, rushed downstairs to find Jeani and me. We were cleaning out the restaurant's walk-in freezer. Delia's hands were shaking. She'd just gotten a call from a girlfriend who was in trouble.

"I've got to leave and find a doctor."

"Are you sick?" Jeani asked.

"No," said Delia, "but my friend Cathy's gonna bleed to death if we can't find a doctor, quick. Maybe I'll call Elsie at Cattlemen's. There's a guy I know, he eats there all the time. Drinks too much, but I think he's a doctor."

Here's where I was a little slow on the uptake. "Why would you call Cattlemen's Steakhouse in the Stockyards to find a doctor?"

Delia looked at me, the pupils of her bright blue eyes contracted to needlepoints. "I gotta go!" She ran upstairs and we followed her like a pair of ducklings behind a mother hen. She grabbed her purse from behind the cash register and ran out the glass doors. "You two are in charge until I get back."

I called after her, "Take her to the emergency room at St. Anthony's."

Jeani punched my arm.

"What?"

"You don't know anything!"

"That's right, I'm an Indian. Tell me, Kemosabe."

"Three words: Coat hanger abortion."

I'd never heard of such a thing. At this point in my memory Jeani was frowning. She took her pencil and ticket book out of her uniform pocket. She drew three little scenes in stick figures. The stick woman with loopy curls was supposed to be Cathy poking a coat hanger between her legs.

"That's terrible," I said, sucking in my breath. "Tear that up."

Jeani's face looked ashen. We walked side by side back down the faded yellow tiled stairs and resumed scrubbing the walls of the walk-in freezer. We didn't speak. I couldn't think of what to say, but I was suddenly very weary. When I went to the women's bathroom and looked at myself in the mirror, I realized I'd been crying as I cleaned the freezer. I didn't even know Cathy, but I felt no woman should have to endure a self-induced abortion with a coat hanger. I played out an imaginary conversation between Delia and Cathy—if she lived.

"He'll never desert me. Never."

"How can you know that?" Delia would say.

"I just know it."

"Goddam it, Cathy, you almost died!" Then I imagined Delia would soften her voice the way she does when she scolds me at work. "Forget him honey, he's married."

―――――

For those who don't know what a coat hanger abortion is, here's the scoop. The wire is bent into a crude instrument for erasing a growing mistake. A woman carefully shoves the curved wire up inside herself. The wire's job is to get through the pregnant cervix safely and excavate the mass. *I know what you're thinking. Sounds horrible. It is.* Another reason I'm pro-choice is that no woman should have to mutilate herself if she has an unwanted pregnancy. If a woman isn't careful with the coat hanger, it can go right through her cervix and through sidewalls of the uterus. When this happens she can easily bleed to death before she gets to a doctor.

I'd never heard of a coat hanger abortion until that night at the Oklahoma City airport. Jeani said her mom had told her what it was. But I was out of the loop. I would have to ask my Cherokee grandmother about it. I felt sure she would know what to do if an Indian woman found herself in this situation. On my next trip to Ada, I'd ask Grandmother for advice, what I should have done that night at the restaurant, or how I could have been help in some way. I felt terrible for this woman, a stranger I'd never met.

When I was little, my grandmother and my great-grandmother Callie were always making poultices and teas out of the plants that grew around their houses or in nearby fields. Making medicines could be a scary business. I was told these recipes had been passed down from mother to daughter for generations. If you could not find the right ingredient, your remedy might fail.

Often my grandmother and I would sit side by side on the couch in her living room. She'd talk in a low voice and say things like, "Too much man is bad." I knew she was trying to warn me about unscrupulous men and what could happen to me. Now she was two hours away, and I longed to be with her in Ada. It would be many days before I could lay my head on her shoulder and tell her what happened.

Around midnight, just as we were closing out the cash register drawer, Delia returned. She'd had a big to-go cup of whiskey. I know this because she told us what she was drinking. Delia had found a doctor; he saved Cathy's life, but she would never be able to have children. She was on sulfa tablets and bed rest for two weeks. Delia hesitated, then said, "He sewed her up, something he could lose his license for."

I can still see the way Delia would light a Virginia Slims cigarette, pulling tobacco smoke deeply into her lungs. She was a sexy, professional woman. A powerhouse manager. And I admired her. In 1969 Virginia Slims began marketing their cigarettes to young professional women with the slogan, "You've come a long way, baby."

What none of us could have known that night was that a legal case would eventually be filed by Norma McCorvey, identified in the court documents as Jane Roe, against Henry Wade, the district attorney of Dallas County. *Roe v. Wade* was working its way up to the Supreme Court. The decision would change the lives of thousands of women around the country who found themselves in Cathy's situation. In 1973, the Supreme Court held that a woman's right to an abortion fell within the right to privacy (recognized in *Griswold v. Connecticut*) and was protected by the Fourteenth Amendment. None of this had happened yet. But I made a commitment that night. I would always support a woman's right to choose how she lived her life, including whether to have an abortion or not given her circumstances. I never want another woman to have to resort to using a wire coat hanger. Ever.

Yet I'm very aware that in Oklahoma in 2018 the story I'm telling may be considered profane. Abortion is something most women in Oklahoma never talk about in public. Instead of showing compassion and understanding, some right-wing zealots and evangelical Christians in Oklahoma call for ignoring the rule of law. Oklahoma Republican 2018 gubernatorial candidate Dan Fisher has said that the courts should ignore *Roe v. Wade*. Fisher has repeatedly called for abolishing abortion in Oklahoma; so where does that leave Oklahoma women? The answer cannot be a homemade remedy with nasty coat hanger.

So here's another imagined conversation. The remnants.

"Did she?"

"How?"

"Could she?"

"Where?"

"Could they?"

"When?"

"They did!"

"What?"

"Sacrilege!"

"Bereft."

"Bereaved."

"Aggrieved."

"Blasphemy."

"Sleeps with a machete?"

Okay, the last line came out of nowhere. I have no idea whether Cathy sleeps with a machete, or even if she's still alive. Delia and her friends were a decade or so older than Jeani and me. I long to know what happened to the many people I once worked with at the Will Rogers World Airport restaurant. The job was my first education, and the travel benefits helped me learn about the world outside of Oklahoma. For that I am grateful. While working at the airport I was exposed to new foods, odd coworkers, beloved co-workers, and union organizers. When the AFL-CIO Union came to Sky Chefs I jumped onboard the union train and received a nickel an hour pay raise—to $1.20.

About six months after the incident with Cathy, I had a chance encounter with the U.S. Speaker of the House Carl Albert as he walked through the airport terminal. He was a hero to my family. I'd seen pictures of him on the nightly news. On the afternoon I saw him walking down a corridor toward his gate, he was alone: no Secret Service or aids were with him. I rushed out the door of the restaurant so I could shake his hand. (I was always a Democratic sycophant.) I remember I said my family was very proud of all he was doing for Oklahoma, and I hoped he would keep fighting the Nixon administration. Ever since Nixon's inauguration, the news at that time had been full of reports about the president's alleged criminal activities. My cousin Gary and I would spend hours talking about Nixon, and John Mitchell, H. R. Haldeman, and John D. Ehrlichman. Gary would say, "The country's going to hell in a hand-basket." As troubled by the Nixon administration as we were, we didn't know the depth of the president's corruption. In speaking with Speaker Albert that day, I hope I didn't use the word "tyranny," but I might have.

"Thank you, we do what we can," he said.

Here, picture me grinning like a Cheshire cat with a black hairnet on my head as I faced Speaker Albert. I was growing more and more embarrassed because I didn't know what else to say. So I stood up tall and straight-backed, and smoothed the white apron against my pear-yellow waitress uniform.

Speaker Albert broke the awkward silence. "Where is your family from?"

"Ada and McAlester, sir. But now I live in Oklahoma City."

"I was born in McAlester," he said. "My family moved to Bug Tussle, where I was raised." As he talked about his hometown, I remember thinking that we were about the same height. Five feet, four inches. His nickname was the "Little Giant from Little Dixie." I knew that from watching Walter Cronkite on the CBS evening news. In 1931, Carl Albert studied at Oxford University on a *Rhodes scholarship*. My family valued education and bragged on Oklahomans with good educations. Both my grandparents only finished the ninth grade, yet they both wrote poetry in the margins of the books they owned.

Speaker Albert still had tuffs of bright red hair, lingering freckles. He was the son of a poor farmer from our area of state, yet he presided over one of the most turbulent periods in U.S. history. During his tenure in Congress he witnessed the resignations of Vice President Spiro Agnew and President Nixon, and as a member of Congress he would oversee the end of the Vietnam War. Carl Albert rose to the highest government post of any Oklahoman in the state's history.

I wish I could say that after shaking his hand I immediately went out and enrolled in college. It would make a great ending for the story. But it wouldn't be true. College would come later, a benefit of the AFL-CIO Union that paid for my first college course at the University of Oklahoma's Outreach Program designed for working adults.

I began this essay by writing about something very frivolous: terrible airport mayonnaise in shitty tubes. I'll end with compassion—something else I learned from my three years at the Will Rogers World Airport restaurant. Here's Selma's homemade mayonnaise recipe. It takes about ten minutes to make and is well worth the effort.

Ingredients:
Two large eggs, at room temperature. Separate the eggs. Use the egg
   whites for something else. Or discard.

Fresh-squeezed lemon juice. 2 teaspoons. (Do not use the junk in the fake squeeze bottle.)

1 cup of lite vegetable oil. Olive oil may be too heavy.

Add sea salt to taste, but use just a tiny pinch.

In a medium-sized bowl, mix the egg yolks and lemon juice. Whip with a strong whisk. Slowly dribble a stream of oil into the bowl until the mayonnaise begins to thicken. Keep whisking. Once it has started to thicken you can pour the oil in a little faster. Add the sea salt to the mayonnaise but very sparingly. Salty mayonnaise tastes terrible. Finish with the freshly squeezed lemon juice.

Voilà. That's French, you know, but it's also Okie. We say it when we mean "well done."

Incarceration and Liberation

Poetic Justice

ELLEN STACKABLE

Ariel has just finished reading her poem "What It's Like to Be a Cutter," and there is a stunned silence in the room. The honesty and raw vulnerability of it has swept through twenty-five women who are dressed all alike in gray pants and gray tops; the only other color in their uniforms is the white name tag sewn on the front—name and number—and the black letters—INMATE—stenciled on the back of their shirts. I look at the three other volunteers with me and they too are speechless, all of us afraid to open our mouths and speak, lest we say the wrong thing. Ariel has described her struggle to cope with being in prison by cutting herself:

"It's dancing ballet with pain and then falling in love with the asphyxiation of your agony."

"It's knowing you're being reduced to scar tissue and believing the lie that pain will always be beauty because it's the only thing that stays the same."

Finally, Tina, whose short hair is punked up with toothpaste gel, the only hair product available in prison, looks at Ariel with eyes full of tears and says, "That was just amazing. You wrote about something that we all struggle with. Your words are beautiful, and thank you, thank you for sharing them." Tina's words are like a champagne bottle just uncorked. The room explodes with cheers and applause, and everyone close to Ariel reaches out to hug her.

And like this, every Tuesday evening, we all sit together in this small room, in a small chapel, in a large prison, in the middle of Oklahoma. This is the Poetic Justice class, and we are at Mabel Bassett Correctional Center, which is home to more than 1,400 medium/maximum-security incarcerated women.

The whole world compresses in this room, and for the two hours we have together every week, something miraculous happens. Here in the middle of the most unsafe, unfree place, there is safety and freedom. Words become more than just words as they are written, erased, and written again. They become life and power and truth.

We are no longer volunteers, who come in from the outside, and they are no longer prisoners, who can never leave. We are all sisters, poet warriors sharing our struggles, pain, joy, and laughter. And it is love and freedom in the deepest way.

These are women of courage, wisdom, and wit who desperately want to make sense of their lives, who want the sum of their lives to amount to more than just being "an inmate," "an offender," "a prisoner." Nearly all of them have come from backgrounds of abuse, and sometimes I marvel that they endure. Bea told us one night that she had been born in prison, and now, she said with a laugh, "Forty years later, here I am again!" Her mother had been pregnant when she was incarcerated, so Bea was a prison baby.

Our Poetic Justice course lasts eight weeks, and in that time a fierce love and loyalty binds us together. Some of the women in our classes will never leave prison—those who are in their sixties are serving life sentences. And Lisa, who was sentenced when she was 18 years old is now 42—life without parole, and she knows she will never leave. As these women who know they will never leave prison write, they confront their past, make sense of their present, and even look forward to their future. Sharon, who is 63, told me that because of her long sentence, she knows she will never leave, but she wants to write to leave a legacy to her grandson. She wants to be remembered for the stories she writes, the beautiful poetry, not just as the grandma that was always dressed in gray and who lived in a prison in the middle of nowhere.

The ones who are preparing to re-enter society after years of prison are scared and nervous and excited. They don't want to ever come back to prison, but they are well aware of how hard it will be to do this. Writing becomes therapy and a chronicle of change. The words they write empower them, give them hope, and a voice—and no one can take this away. Angelina writes about her time in prison, "You will become fluent in listening, empathy, and diplomacy.

You will cease looking in life's rearview mirror and start, instead, to hone in on the horizon." She tells us she can't wait to volunteer with Poetic Justice.

So, every week, not only at Mabel Bassett but also at the Tulsa County Jail, you will find me and a host of volunteers sharing life, sharing healing, sharing hope as we write together with women in prison and in jail. And every week I know that for one brief span of time, I am absolutely certain I am exactly where I am supposed to be. In those two hours, ambushed by eloquence, we become part of each other's lives. Poetry invites us in, and there we stay.

On graduation night, I read this poem I wrote:

*To the poet warriors at Mabel Bassett Correctional Center
and the Tulsa County Jail*

They think that they know you, but they don't.
They see gray and they see orange.
Not wise-old-owl gray or tangerine orange,
But bland, cement gray and harsh hunter-safety orange.
They think that they know you, but they don't.
They see screw-up, mess-up, dumb, ignorant, hardened, hopeless.
Broken—broken down, broken apart, broken in pieces.

They don't know the day you ran through the grass barefoot,
Just to feel the softness between your toes.
The time you sat outside, late at night, talking to friends and looking at the starry night.
They don't know that you love to watch the fireflies when they come early in summer,
Or the time you watched the snow come down, and the time you played in it,
Even when you were so cold you couldn't feel your fingers.
They don't know the books you read, the letters you write, the times you cry,
The nights of prayer, your joys, your sorrows, your losses, your victories.
And they sure don't know all the nights you stayed up 'cause your baby was sick.
The times you watched and cheered your kids, and watched and cheered,
Until they won.

You are strong.
You are brave.
You are overcomers.
You are writers and you are poets.
You are becoming free—right here—right now—you are free.

They see gray.
I see freedom.
They see orange.
I see life.
They see gray and orange.
I see beauty.
I see courage.
I see hope.

Driven

RHONDA BEAR

I am driven by a desire to reduce incarceration in Oklahoma, to see women succeed, and to see children restored to their mothers.

I am assured my history has become my herstory. Romans 8:28 says we can be sure that every detail in our lives of love for God is worked into something good. I am confident God has pursued me my entire life. I am thankful for my roots and for the privilege of learning about Jesus at a young age. My first recollections as a small child include my grandmother rocking me and singing to me, "Are you washed in the blood of the lamb?" At the age of five, I went to kindergarten and learned the hymn "How Great Thou Art," which is still one of my favorites, and I memorized my first scripture, Psalms 23:7: "Surely your goodness and mercy will follow me all the days of my life and I will dwell in your house Oh Lord, forever." Little did I know as a child how that scripture would be so prophetic in my life, but God's mercy and grace has followed me all my days so far and still does.

I grew up in southern Louisiana until my parents divorced when I was nine years old. The divorce came quickly after my dad announced he was in love with my babysitter. My mom's and my sister's and my lives were turned upside down very quickly. Though my dad's behavior was crazy, my sisters and I, and even my mom, were crazy for him. I loved my dad.

My mom moved us to Pittsburg, Texas, the day after my dad's announcement, and we started over. I was so broken-hearted, I swore I would never let anyone get close to me again. My mom and dad fought a lot after their separation, especially during the divorce procedures, and my mom declared we would not see our dad anymore because he would not pay child support. We lived in poverty until my mom married Al, a former high school sweetheart of hers. Mom said Al was rich; he would be taking care of us. I resented Al for taking my dad's place so immediately. We were off to a rough start. I thought of Al as an idiot; he got drunk every night and at times become so violent we had to run for our lives. This was nothing too new, for my dad had done the same thing to us.

Al moved us to Mesquite, another city in Texas. There I began to play soccer. I did not like soccer too much. I did not feel I was aggressive enough and did not want to be aggressive. I had been a majorette in Louisiana. I loved marching in parades and twirling at football games. That is who I thought I was. But Al said I had to play soccer, for he wasn't going to let me have too much time on my hands; I would just get into trouble that way. As I started ninth grade, my first year in high school, I began to ride to school with my friends and co-soccer players. There I was first introduced to marijuana. At first I didn't really like it, but it seemed like the thing to do, since that's what my friends were doing. One night during a state championship playoff game for soccer, I was very nervous. My team was great but I wasn't that great and I dreaded the pressure, so my soccer coach offered me a little pill, a Valium to help my nerves. I played the best game I had ever played that night. I felt the best I had ever felt, and I made a promise to myself that I would never lose that feeling. And there my addiction to Valium began.

Valium was only the beginning, though. My addiction grew to all types of barbiturates and sedatives. They didn't knock me out but only made me numb, and I loved it. Soon I went from being a straight-A student to getting straight F's, and it took me approximately twenty-eight years to completely escape that tailspin. Now you see where my drug addiction started. It led me down a path of regrets and shame. I say this often: close your eyes and envision what you think the worst drug addict looks like, and I can fit into that picture. Drug addiction cost me everything: my self-respect, my integrity, my freedom, and most of all my children.

I am the mom who missed Christmas with her children. I am the mom who missed birthdays and special occasions at school. I am the mom that put drugs and unhealthy relationships before her children. Year after year I continued to be the no-show mom. Though I lost custody of my children and though I failed to see them, in my poor judgment I thought methamphetamine would be my answer. I put my hopes in a drug and another drug addict. I thought if the drug deal went down like it was supposed to, I would make enough money, bribe the judge, and gain custody of my children. The more I put my trust in the drugs and relationships, the further away I got from my children.

Now I will tell you how it ended. November 22, 2000, Thanksgiving eve, I was Christmas shopping for my children with a friend. After shopping, my friend and I went to a casino. While in the casino, I noticed security watching me, so I quickly exited the building and ran into a field. I dove into a brush pile and crawled to the very bottom of the pile. Soon the field was surrounded by officers and drug dogs. The weather turned from pleasantly warm to pouring down rain that soon turned to freezing rain. I was scared to crawl out of the brush pile. I began to breathe with my shirt around my face in order to keep a little warmth on me. I waited for hours until the coast was clear to crawl out of my hiding place. As I exited the brush pile, I tried to stand. My legs collapsed. I could not stand, and I could barely crawl. In the distance I saw a man in a long black trench coat standing behind a bar smoking. I made my way across the field crawling. As I approached him, I told him I had been hiding in a ditch from an abusive boyfriend. I told him I had money, but I needed his help to get to a hotel room. He picked me up and hid me under his jacket, and proceeded to get me a hotel room. He ran me a hot bath and proceeded to undress me. He said I was going into shock due to prolonged exposure to the cold and that he had to get me into hot water and get my body temperature up. He took my clothes to the hotel dryer then he helped me and left. Soon I called a friend, who came and got me.

The days that followed were traumatic. I was paranoid and completely unclear about which direction to take. For several days I took a large Hefty trash bag and filled it with folded laundry, then set the bag by the door, crawled in the bag, and sat and listened for cops coming up the walkway. One day I said to my friend, "I need help to go to a detox center. If I don't make it to the detox center, I am going to kill you and kill myself." As I recall this memory, I know this was a very possible option.

I made it to detox. From the detox center in Tulsa, I called the District Attorney's Office in Sequoyah County and told the DA I was going to turn myself in. I had warrants in six counties in both Oklahoma and Arkansas. I hadn't earned any favors, but that did not stop me from requesting the DA to put all my charges together; I assured him I would plead guilty and accept my sentencing. I also requested to see my children and begged not be arrested in front of them. The DA agreed. On December 7, 2000, I left detox. On December 8, I said good-bye to my children and told them I was sorry for being the mom I had been, for they deserved so much more. I knew I was going to prison, but I did not know for how long. But I had a plan. I was coming back to get them and I was coming back a different person.

On that same day, December 8, I turned myself in. I received a 10-year sentence with a stipulation that I would complete a 12-month drug program before I was ever to walk out of prison. The judge put the ball in my court: I could go into prison and act out, or I could go into prison, get focused, get into a program, and, upon completion of the drug program, have 10 years on probation outside of prison. I was told if I messed up during the 10 years on probation, I would be given a maximum sentence. These terms were the best gift anyone could have given me.

Prison saved my life. I did not receive an excessive sentence but a fair sentence. I participated in both the Kairos Prison Ministry and the twelve-month drug program. It was a life journey of change. On June 22, 2002, I walked out of prison. I came to Tulsa, where everyone I knew was a part of prison ministry. I was accepted into the Exodus House, a transition program, and then accepted into a program called Stand in The Gap Ministries. Both of these programs played a huge role in my success. Stand in The Gap Ministries connected me with multiple couples who made the commitment to "walk beside me" for twenty-four months. They modeled healthy behaviors for me, prayed for me, and taught me to be a good mother and a good wife. They taught me the word "accountability," and though at first I did not like it, today I love the word.

It took me approximately four painful years to restore relationships with my children. There was much healing that needed to be accomplished. My children needed to forgive me, not because I deserved it but because they deserved it. Un-forgiveness is a heavy negative weight that holds a person back.

Today I celebrate relationships with two great sons, an amazing daughter, and six precious grandchildren. Today I am a good mom and a really good grandmother. Thanks to my mentors I learned to trust and live a life that can be trusted, and with all of that came an amazing gift—the man I call husband.

With all I gained, I decided to pay it forward. Three years after being out of prison, I became a volunteer for the Oklahoma Department of Corrections.

Today my service impacts thousands in the prison system. On May 31, 2007, I opened a transition home in Claremore, Oklahoma, with the intent of helping women after their release from the local county jail. My vision grew and my thought abounded. I thought, "If I can save a mom, I can save a child." My organization, called His House Outreach Ministries, gained its not-for-profit status, and now it owns four houses, rents three houses, and has a house donated for our use. We currently serve approximately twenty-four women and multiple children yearly.

In November 2012, we created Saving Our Daughters with the intent of forming a non-profit that would provide job training experience for the women in His House Outreach Ministries. Unfortunately, the Internal Revenue Service shot down our request for nonprofit status. Nevertheless, I continued with the vision. With $300, faith, and a neighbor's help, She Brews Coffee House was the first entity created under Saving Our Daughters. We rented a flea-market booth, and with crock pots for making hot chocolate and wassail, a coffee maker, and vision, She Brews Coffee House began. The first year was extremely tough, and I reached a point where I conceded to the thought that it was a bad idea. I made a plan to close the booth and chalk it up to experience. Then, out of the blue, five women came into my life, caught the vision, offered me support, and would not let me close the doors. We raised money, rented a new location, began to collect proper equipment, and hit the ground running. We recently expanded our current location.

Since our opening, She Brews has been the starting point for many women who would otherwise not have employment opportunities due to their criminal past. The partnership between She Brews Coffee House and His House Outreach Ministries has produced college students and entrepreneurs who have branched out to start their own business, and on average we restore twenty-five children a year to their mothers. Some look upon my program and see success. Here I must brag on my community. The community of Claremore has reached out and provided every type of support imaginable. It is a partnership that is changing generations.

Walk a Mile in My Heart

RUTH ASKEW BRELSFORD

I get up at 4:30 A.M. My alarm is set for 5, but I can't sleep. If something happens and I don't make it by 9:15, they will close the yard for count and I will just be hanging around in the middle of nowhere 'til count clears. It has happened before. I just hate it. He is pacing in his cell, and I am pacing the parking lot. Best to allow plenty of time for what usually takes three-and-a-half hours. I slip out of bed so that I won't disturb my husband and creep down the stairs for a couple of cups of strong coffee. The dogs cuddle with me as I sip my coffee, check my bag of quarters, and make sure I have his DOC number and my tag number (forgot the tag number last time and had to go back out to that steaming-hot gravel parking lot to stand behind my car and write the number down on my palm since no pen or paper is allowed inside).

    I ponder what I will wear to visit my young friend, Vet, who is incarcerated at a medium-security facility in the heartland. I'm sixty-seven years old and my costume is not the first thing I normally think about when I get up in the mornings, but it is on Visitation Day. I try to avoid all hassles and all reasons to hold up the line: no zippers on my pants, shoes that are easy to slip off and have no buckles or heels that might appear to conceal contraband, no underwire in my bra. No scooped necklines, no T-shirts announcing my liberal politics, no open-toed shoes or sandals, no cute little hat to camouflage the fact that I need a haircut. Some of the rules are written; some are not.

I don't want to do anything that will hold up the line. We've all got to get in there before the yard closes. There's a regimented timeline in this strange place where men are doing time and time drags on and on. Face-to-face time is special and monitored and limited in prison.

I close the door of our house quietly and slip out to my car, and drive slowly down the gravel road as the sun comes up over the mountains. I am joining hundreds of women all over the state on the way to visit our loved ones in prison in Oklahoma. Many of us have kids in our car, sleepy kids in car seats or grumpy teenagers slumped in back seats with headphones on their nodding heads. These are our kids we are taking to see their daddies. Sometimes they are our grandchildren we are taking to visit their moms. There are lots of grandmothers my age raising their daughters' children and making the weekly, or sometimes monthly, trip to visit Mom.

I'm alone. No kids in my car. No brothers or sisters. I am not visiting a family member. I am visiting a friend, a former student, a young man I believe in and try to encourage named Vet Colbert. I send him books through Amazon, and he reads them and then we discuss issues during our monthly visits. We pray, too. And hold hands, sometimes, and laugh and joke and sometimes cry. Well, I do. He would never let them see him cry. "Them" he defines differently depending on circumstances in this crazy subculture we call prison. "Them" can mean corrections officers, can mean other inmates, can mean the state, can mean a society that considers my young friend expendable: a young black man with faded gang tattoos on his body and a twenty-year sentence stretching out in front of him into what feels like eternity.

I drive along and sing and pray and watch the dawn and marvel at how beautiful my state is. My part of the state in the southeastern corner in the mountains. By the time I get to the plains of north-central Oklahoma 165 miles away, the sun will be well up and the early morning just as beautiful, though different, where the sky meets the grasslands stretching for miles in every direction. Why are most of Oklahoma's twenty-three prison facilities in rural areas? I actually enjoy the three-hour drive, but it is so hard on most families.

I head north and west, pushing the speed limit, just a bit, because, as I said, I have a deadline. As we families and friends, preachers and teachers, and children and mamas park our cars, grab our clear plastic bags of quarters, and hurry to the gate of the Dick Conner Correctional Center in Hominy, I look at us and marvel at how representative of America we are. We are black, white, American Indian, Latino, Asian. Some of the women are wearing hijabs. Many are carrying single diapers and clear baby bottles with powdered formula that will be inspected and then mixed with water so that Daddy can feed the baby. None of us have the ubiquitous purses that women carry as second nature. Of course not. Not in prison.

In one way, however, we do not represent society at large. As I look around, I realize that we are disproportionately female. There are men, of course: prison ministers, older fathers looking uncomfortable, teenage boys shuffling along with low-slung pants barely scraping the sidewalk, hard-working men with farmer's tans and squinting eyes because they had to leave their John Deere caps in the truck. Yes, there are men making their way to the barbed-wire fence, but mostly there are women. Women with babies or women whose "babies" will not be coming home with them tonight. Women all dressed up and looking as sexy as they can for their men. Women who can barely afford to make the trip. Women with heavy Ziplocs full of quarters because it takes a lot of quarters to feed a family from vending machines. We joke that there is more than one thief in this visiting room where a bag of chips costs two bucks and a stale sandwich will cost upwards of four dollars. A little prison humor...

We are young, we are old, we are short, tall, thin, and not so thin. Some of us are comfortable; we do this every weekend and have for years. Some of us look tired, worn, and weary. Like the three women who drove to this small town from Indiana and found that their son/brother/boyfriend, who had just been "shipped to this yard" and was in prison for the first time, had not filled out the paperwork properly, so their names were not on his approved list. I thought for sure the mother, close to my age, was going to cry. The CO (Correctional Officer) was competent, professional, and kind. She made a phone call and they were approved for a one-time first visit. I could have hugged that CO! But, of course, that kind of thing is not allowed. I did smile and compliment her. She smiled quietly back and kept the line moving. Remember: we have a deadline. Everybody she doesn't get through check-in will just hang around her waiting room 'til count clears because there is literally nowhere else to go.

Oklahomans often boast that we are the heartland of America, centered as we are in the middle of the nation. We claim to symbolize the very soul of our country in our dedication to family and hard work, patriotism, and Christian values. Though we have a higher percentage of Native Americans than most states, we generally represent current American demographics: predominantly white, with a typical percentage of African Americans and a growing Hispanic population. We are educated, but not too educated. Protestant, Republican, working-class.

I would say that we represent the heart of America in another way, too. A heart that is breaking. In a nation that incarcerates a higher percentage of our citizens than any other nation on earth, Oklahoma incarcerates more women than any other state in the union and, therefore, the world. We are the second-highest state in incarcerating men. According to E. Ann Carson's U.S. Bureau of Justice Statistics *Prisoners in 2014* report, we incarcerate 700 inmates per 100,000 population. The national rate is 471. Oklahoma's incarceration rate is 79 percent higher than the national average! Are we 79 percent meaner than everybody else? Or just 79 percent poorer and more addicted? I keep asking myself, Why are so many of us in prison?

The answer is not simple. The failed war on drugs; high poverty rate; failing schools; high rates of divorce, child abuse, and teenage pregnancy; punitive long sentences that target minorities and poor people, a shrinking state budget that doesn't provide basic services to our citizens, DAs who stay in office because they are "tough on crime"—all these are contributing factors. I don't know that there is any one specific cause, but I do know that hearts are breaking in the heartland.

Most of the incarcerated, particularly women, are in prison for nonviolent crimes, like writing hot checks, receiving stolen property, trying to pawn something that doesn't belong to them, and the ever-present scourge of people who live in poverty: drugs. Usually possession, sometimes intent to distribute. These women are not raising their children. Their mothers are. The fathers of their children are not visiting them on Saturdays. Their mothers are. Children in tow. The men in prison are not raising their children either. Or paying child support. Or taxes.

I muse about this cycle of poverty and imprisonment and how ineffective it all is as I stand in line. The family in front of me is laughing and talking. Sometimes in English. Sometimes in Spanish. I gather that the tall, handsome boys of the family haven't done this very often. One has forgotten his ID and has to run back to the car to get it. The matriarch scolds him for holding up the line and smiles a weak apology at those of us behind her, glancing at the clock. It is inching toward 9:00.

The family in front of them—a single mom with four sons—is one I see every month. Her stair-step boys giggle as they take off their shoes and prepare to walk through the full-body scanner. They squirm as the CO uses the wand to "search" their little bodies. This pretty mom has her hands full. I remember how last month, when I was sharing the last of my quarters with her, I asked her husband when he was going to be released and admonished him to "get out, get straight, and help this lady raise these boys." Absolutely none of my business, of course. But you start to feel like a community when you are locked up together for several hours, rain or shine, visiting the men you love. The boys' mother laughs and her pretty eyes sparkle as she watches her children's daddy roughhouse with them. She is supposed to sit on her side of the table, and he is supposed to sit on his side; however, the kids can run and play freely. So the three little boys crawl all over the daddy they resemble so closely, while the sullen preteen sits by his mom, cutting his eyes around the room. I wondered as I watched him if he realizes he is in danger of becoming a statistic? Biracial son of an incarcerated parent living at or below the poverty line. I wonder if Mom knows the odds are against all of her boys?

That's one thing I was surprised about the first couple of visits: no one is yelling at their kids. No one is yelling at each other. No one is pouting. No one is scolding. Everybody is happy. The noise is deafening. Laughter, card-playing, board games, flirting, praying, Bible reading. And I think about that every month: what if the rest of my state could see these families? Could see these men with their loved ones? They aren't monsters. They are men who made mistakes. Addicted men. They are men who tried to make an easy buck. They are men who got caught. They are men who should have been home with their wives and kids on the night they did whatever they did that landed them in prison. They didn't know that then; however, a lot of them do know it now.

Behind me in line is a lady about my age. Tight, deeply lined face; freckled, blue-veined hands twisting her bag of quarters nervously. Her daughter-in-law whispers, "I think you can go to the bathroom now. Don't wait. Because you will have to go back through the metal detector, and we won't make it in time." Again, it is none of my business, but I turn to her and say, "Just ask the CO. She's real nice. Not all of them are, but she is."

The lady's tired eyes peer into mine for just a short moment as she whispers, "They need to be nice to us. Some of us have never done this before."

"I know," I whisper, "it is so hard." She looks at me again with such pain in her faded gray eyes and then she looks down at her shoes quickly.

"Beyond hard," I say. "Excruciating." More to myself than to her.

We make it! Everybody in line fills out the roster, hands our car keys and IDs to the CO, and gets a token with a number on it for retrieval at the end of the visit. We take off our shoes, empty our pockets, walk through the scanner, and stand spread-eagle for the wand and the officer's hand just making sure we aren't bringing in drugs or cell phones. We all get our shoes on and go through two locked doors in groups of no more than six and, finally, are in the Visitation Room before the yard closes for the morning count.

    I have a wonderful visit with my young friend, and after he has eaten his fill of "junk" from the vending machines, and after we have laughed and argued and discussed and prayed and I get ready to make my way back to southeastern Oklahoma, we stand. I'm allowed to give him a hug as long as it doesn't last too long. I turn my back and go to the door that will have to be unlocked from the other side. I turn around and blow him a kiss. I whisper a prayer that he will be safe again tonight. One thing I've learned since starting to work in prisons ten years ago is the true meaning of the motto "one day at a time." What did Vet tell me he used to pray when he was in solitary years ago? "Lord, don't let me go crazy this day. Lord, keep me sane this day." In prison, you can't look too far ahead. My friend taught me that. He smiles, pats his hand on his chest, over his heart, turns, and signs out. Without a backward glance, he goes back to his cell. Only five more years. If we're lucky.

    As I turn in my token and get my key, a large lady with pale skin and pale eyes and a middle-school-aged boy who looks just like her are standing in line for afternoon visitation. "Excuse me, ma'am," she says. "Do you think they will let me take my money in if I don't have a Ziploc bag?" She clutches two rolls of quarters that I know will not buy much in that vending hell. "I forgot my plastic bag." She attempts a chuckle. The boy looks away.

    "No," I say. "I don't think they will let you take them in like that. Here take my bag; I'm through with it for another month!" I, too, offer an awkward chuckle.

    I hand her the bag and she says, "Oh, thank you. But take your quarters. I just need the bag."

    "Oh, keep 'em!" I say. "Not that many and you gotta feed a couple of growing boys!"

    Staring out the window, the boy blushes. Poor kid, I think. What a way to spend a Saturday afternoon. Her eyes fill with tears as she thanks me. She hugs me and I say, "Better hurry! You want to get in there before they close the yard for afternoon count!"

    I go to my car, planning where I will stop to get something to eat that will taste better and cost less than what everybody else had for lunch. I laugh because Vet always accuses me of being "uppity" about food. I don't think he realizes that I want him to have all the Orange Crush and Skittles and stale pulled pork sandwiches he can eat because it will be another month before he can "feast" again.

Everybody is walking slower as we make our ways back to the parking lot, sun starting its descent. There was energy and anticipation this morning, but sadness and longing now. We are all leaving our hearts behind. Half of us is not going home tonight. Quiet voices drift away on the late afternoon breeze as each mother/wife/lover/friend gets in her car and heads home, leaving someone she loves behind locked gates and barbed wire. In the heartland...

Pilgrim
SHAUNTE GORDON

At eighteen years old I was in the Oklahoma County jail, on my knees, pleading, "God, if you have a plan for my life, let me know with a ten-year sentence. But if my life is going to be the same misery it has always been, you will let me know with a life sentence." Instantly fear overtook me at what I was asking God to do. I despaired. I could never be different. My charge was murder. How could my life ever change? I was doomed.

I was born on July 27, 1978, in Holdenville, Oklahoma. My first experience of trauma occurred when I was three years old. My mother and sister and I were hiding in a shelter for abused women and children. My mom was a victim of domestic violence, and the reality terrified me. Then my mother was incarcerated, and, from ages four through twelve, my only sister and I were both victims of sexual and physical abuse. Later, while in foster care at the age of thirteen, I gave birth to a baby girl. She was automatically born into the system. I would get to keep her with me for only a short time.

By age eleven, I was already exposed to and intrigued by the street life of Tulsa. In the sixth grade I would walk to school and see women and young girls working the streets as prostitutes. Some had pimps and boyfriends, and some even lived with us at times. The behavior was not discouraged in my home, and I began to look up to some of the girls. They were tough and could take care of themselves, while I mostly lived in fear. Yet I was curious. I had a friend at school whose mom and sister worked as strip dancers. They flashed lots of money, counting it, and had men who gave them a lot of attention. The care, attention, and financial independence appealed to my naïve, young mind.

While living in Tulsa's Department of Human Services shelter at the age of twelve, I started smoking marijuana and cigarettes, and drinking alcohol. After being placed in long-term foster care, I began running away and doing drugs every day. The hard part was that I had come into state custody pregnant and was separated from my sister. Being away from my mom and sister made me depressed, and I suffered nightmares constantly. I would blame myself and had so much guilt. Though my foster mother was trained as a specialist in taking in very troubled young women, I was struggling. After the birth of my daughter, my foster mother and I became close. I longed for my mother, but my foster mother was with me through the birth of my baby, and from that day forward I called her Mom.

My behavior issues escalated. One day I came home after school and found my social worker. My infant daughter was removed from my custody until I could complete a treatment plan. Devastated by yet another loss, I gave up hope. I ran away, over and over again, back to the streets of Tulsa.

Around this time my paternal grandmother searched for and found us. She wanted to win custody of me, my sister, and my daughter. Even though it had been years since seeing anyone from that side of the family, I had fond memories of her affection for us. My grandmother lived in Wewoka, Oklahoma. Immediately after being placed with her and moving there, I began to get into gang trouble. I was jumped by a group of teenagers from a different gang in front of my little sister and infant daughter. My drug use escalated under the influence of older cousins, eventually leading me to a crack cocaine addiction.

Even though I wanted to be with my family, the street life of Tulsa lured me back. The pain of my life was drowned out by drug use and survival on those streets. I had one purpose for using drugs: to be numb to the shame of my life and temporarily forget. The result was rage and helplessness. I became a drug-addicted prostitute. I found myself at the mercy of dangerous strangers. My mother found me in Tulsa. My health and appearance were shocking. We rode on a Greyhound bus to Oklahoma City. Among my minimal possessions was a handgun I concealed in a purse. The rules of my mother's halfway house did not allow me to stay with her, but I sneaked in a couple of nights and slept there to be close to her. When she had left us, I had been only eleven years old, and now I was a fifteen-year-old crack-addicted prostitute.

In Oklahoma City my choices were no better. My mom did not want me to be homeless, so she rented me a cheap, weekly apartment downtown. My life was so chaotic and my thinking so addled at that time, and right and wrong had no relevance for me. I decided that I was just going to shoot the next john who picked me up and scare him enough into giving me his money. I shot the man but did not realize that I had killed him until the man did not respond to my demand to give me money but only stared back at me. I came into full reality after taking his belongings. Within fifteen hours I had shot another man who had picked me up. I murdered two human beings.

I was arrested shortly after these shootings and placed in the Oklahoma Juvenile Detention Center. As I went to court dates for the next two and a half years, I would see people who were free, and I wished I could be any other person than myself. If only I could have been born another person. I had now done these horrible, irreversible things and was trapped in my misery. The state worked out with my attorney an agreement that would send me to Lloyd E. Raider, a juvenile diagnostic center, where I would stay as a juvenile until I was nineteen, then I'd go back to court for adult certification and sentencing on the remaining charge, which carried ten years to life. In all my environments gang violence was a common occurrence, and my participation in gang activity was part of my court record. This behavior resulted in my being sent from Raider to Oklahoma County Jail before my nineteenth birthday. It was that morning—the day I was sent to the new jail—when I got down on my knees and asked God to please reveal to me the plan He had for my life. In front of Oklahoma judge Charles Owens, I signed a blind plea at the recommendation of my lawyer, who had explained to me what the sentence could be: ten years to life.

Judge Owens wanted to hear the circumstances of my upbringing and the steps that led to living on the streets. He took my story into consideration and sentenced me to twenty-five years, all to be suspended except the first ten. I could not believe he had given me a ten-year sentence. This meant that God had responded to my prayer in a hopeful way. In my mind I believed that I needed to change for God, and I decided that I was going to be good and stop doing destructive things. However, I was helpless to stop making harmful choices. This was a huge disappointment. How could I let God down like this?

Soon I'd pushed these thoughts to the back of my mind as I was just trying to survive prison. I prepared physically by exercising. I found out that due to my lengthy incarceration my parental rights were terminated. I had no idea the legal impact of my crimes. I counted the years in my mind—how old I would be when I saw my child. As hard as life was, it never quite broke my spirit. But I went to prison with no comprehension of how the system operated. I became one of the worst disciplinary problems at Mabel Basset Correctional Center. Almost twenty-seven when I was released, I went immediately back to the streets and everything I knew, including drugs. One day working the streets I recalled the answered prayer to God. Here I was walking free from the jail and prison . . . but why was my life still the same? Blowing it off, I thought to myself that my life could never be different. I still had fifteen years of probation, had been arrested a few different times, and was trying to put off going back to prison by prolonging hearings for revocation of probation. I kept sinking lower as my shame increased. There was so much fear and condemnation that I could not help but feel dread.

When one of the girls I knew well was found dead, I remember the panic from feeling alone and in great danger. The unknown was beginning to torment me. I used drugs nonstop in great amounts. My mom and sister were afraid for me. I felt sorry for myself and blamed my behavior on my dysfunctional upbringing, never taking responsibility. When I became pregnant again, my family became outraged at my continued addiction. I gave birth to a little girl with multiple drugs in her system. I made feeble attempts to keep from losing this baby to the state by trying to make my court dates. I failed miserably and with each failure became more hopeless and condemned. I sensed I was coming to something terrible, and the truth was, I deserved whatever was coming. I began plotting suicide. But first, just one more high.

I was at the lowest of lows. My biggest fear was that I would finally be tested for diseases I recklessly exposed myself to daily. At prison I would be tested. I believed I would be better off dead than going back to the rules and scrutiny of the institution.

One day while I was pregnant and alone in my mother's home, a couple from the neighborhood came knocking on our door. They attended a local church and were seeing if there was anything they could do to help. I told them about some of my struggle with drug abuse. My mother came home, and this sweet couple prayed for us both. I will never forget them and their interest in me.

Before my mother married, when we were still small children, we had gone to a church in Oklahoma City. This is where I saw a live Christmas pageant. There was a real donkey and huge palm leaves. I had heard of the God of John 3:16. When my mother would allow us to go to church on the Sunday School bus or when the family we were staying with attended church, I learned enough to have fond memories later on. I was pondering in my heart, "Wow, God loves the whole world so much HE wants to spend forever with us." Something about Him sending His only son and the words "that whosoever believes in Him would be saved" seemed awesome and just to me. I could believe. Almost always I had some knowledge of God, and I never believed there was any other one besides the God of the Bible.

My genuine encounter with Jesus Christ came on January 3, 2008. I was fighting with a guy and had him drop me off at my mother's house. I had no fear of being in jail even though I had a warrant out for my arrest. As I was preparing to leave my mother's house, suddenly I was being handcuffed and placed in the backseat of a police car. It was in that moment that I was broken. Sobbing, I asked Jesus to please save and forgive me. I encountered the Prince of Peace. The chaos seemed to be sucked out of the atmosphere of my life, and even the officers seemed to relax. I was booked and my bond was set at $100,000.00.

For days I kept fighting the returning anxiety and torment of being trapped. Recurring images of my rebellion played over and again in my mind. At one point when I was left in the cell by myself I started to read the Bible. I was discovering the God who so loved the world. The God who split the Red Sea in half to help His people. The God who was so true He would not even leave His son in the grave longer than three days but brought Him back from death to life. My response was to act on my belief, and this time I started to change. "Change isn't change until it's changed," Pastor Jesse Bufford told us at the prison once.

By the time I left jail to start serving the remaining fifteen years of my twenty-five-year prison sentence, I did not do drugs, cuss, smoke, or disrespect staff anymore. Some of the guards wanted to know what had happened to me. I told them I had accepted Jesus Christ and this was the result. They skeptically waited to see if my change was real. A miracle followed me from the county jail to the prison. I continued to seek God through worshipping and attending chapel services. I became friends with one of the volunteers, Gayliss. One day she prayed with me about the diseases I had exposed myself to, and she anointed me with oil and read James 5:16. I believed I would one day test positive for an STD. But I tested nonreactive to the entire range of sexually transmitted and infectious diseases. Eight years later I am still negative.

During the next six years of my incarceration, I took educational and career courses and remained under Pastor Bufford's teaching and direction. He preached the unadulterated word of God. The question that kept coming to my mind as I got closer to being released was about making it on the outside.

One day after I had started working in the Chaplain's Office during a Kairos retreat, some people let me know that someone was looking for me. She had come in as a Kairos volunteer and was passing out cookies to all the women on the yard. I recognized her immediately. Her name now was Rhonda Poteet (now Rhonda Bear). She had been there with me the first time I entered prison as a fellow inmate. Now here she was, free, and coming back in to serve. I knew her to be a very godly person, soft-spoken, humble, and brave. I was definitely not a godly person back then, but we had become unlikely friends during that time. Now I know that, in God's wisdom, He was preparing the way for me to make it in society. I told her about the change in my life, and she replied "About time."

Over time, as my friend continued to come back in, she told me about the work she was doing. She had opened up transitional living in Claremore through her organization His House Outreach Ministries, and she gave me an invitation to live in one of their houses. One day she looked me in the eye and told me, "You are going to make it. You're going to work at the coffee house She Brews, and we are going to surround you with a team of mentors." I knew it was the truth. On April 2, 2014, I was released and everything happened just the way she told me. She paired me with a Stand in the Gap family who stood with me through that first year. We experienced answered prayers and sweet community. There were so many gaps in my broken life: they taught me to drive, helped me connect closely to my mother at a critical time, and drove with me to meet my own daughter for the first time in twenty-one years after she unexpectedly contacted me one day. Also, they helped me accomplish my dream of starting a business, She Does Odd Jobs With Integrity, doing personal and subcontract work. I have now hired my first payroll employee.

I am blessed to be in the community of Claremore. Members of the First Baptist Church held a fundraiser auction for She Brews Coffee House (no ordinary coffee shop) that hires women transitioning from prison to the community. Their love melted my heart. The community God let me live in is truly a safe one that does indeed give second chances and is led by many successful community leaders. One example is a man who walked into She Brews recently and asked for an iced tea. We regularly have the opportunity to share our testimonies with customers. After I told him a little of my story, he stopped me short and wanted to know what college classes I was taking. I told him "none" and that I was busy with working and starting my own business. He asked me what kind of business and asked for my card. The next time he came in, we visited more. Before we ended our conversation, he asked what I did to go to prison. I reluctantly told him, and he told me, "I'm going to give you a chance anyway." I found out he was a former state senator and now practiced law. He gave me employment and friendship.

Countless men and women have responded similarly in this community. Relationships have been formed here that restore lost and stolen innocence. Now I know for sure I'm going to run and endure the good race. It is one of success, and the best is still to come. In the end, even after enduring so much loss, I am a pilgrim of hope.

Weathering Trauma

One Lightning Second

EDEN HEMMING

The first time I saw a midwestern storm, I was ten years old. My family was at a reunion in Minnesota, staying in cabins by a lake for a week. It came up in the night, loud and intense. I had never heard such cracks of thunder, splitting the air like a whip. I wasn't scared; I was fascinated. I pressed my face to the glass of the cabin window, watching as the whole world lit up for one lightning second before going black again.

I could feel the lightning. And then the storm was gone.

For a kid who'd only ever known the lazy drizzles and rare, distant, languid thunder of the Pacific Northwest, it was magic.

I'm writing this for you, Anna, in the hopes that someday you'll read it and understand. You're only three. You can't understand, not now. When I whisper to you that I'll be gone tomorrow night and may not see you before you go to bed, I can't yet explain that I'm doing this for you, that this is hard for you and for me but that I'm driven to it. When you wrap your arms around me and tell me that you'll miss me, I can't yet tell you that my politics are driven by that animal protection instinct that rises up when I think of your future. I can't yet explain that I feel divinity in the combined power of humankind, which crackles in my limbs like a midwestern storm.

My father was a narcissist. His will was exacting. He never hit me in the early years, but that threat was frequent enough that I grew to fear and avoid his wrath. His anger would come as quickly and unpredictably as that Minnesota tempest, but rather than run to it, I shrank away. I shrank and shrank and shrank until years later, when one of my first boyfriends raised his hand to hit me. He didn't, but I saw that spark in his eyes, felt my hair stand prickly. By the time he lowered his hand without following through on its threat, I had grown back into someone almost person-sized again. I vowed never to let a blow stop me.

There's a picture of me in a Seattle newspaper from a few years later that you can still find easily if you search online. I have bleached hair and black tape over my mouth. I am sitting on the sidewalk, protesting an ordinance that specified fines for sitting on the sidewalk but was only ever used against the homeless. At the time I was hanging out with homeless kids a lot. I had sought out other shipwreck survivors, ones who had seen worse things. I told myself that I was doing something good for them by treating them like human beings. In hindsight, they provided me a context for my life. I wanted to help them because I wanted to help that part of me that had been through similar things, no matter how much less severe my experiences may have been. I still bear the marks of those survivors, just beneath my skin, in ink and in heart.

The best place to witness one of these storms is under the shelter of an overhanging building. First, everything gets still. Then a tree *shushes* with a violent wind and soon all the trees join the chorus. The sky sometimes turns dark in warning, with stained, inky clouds. A fat drop falls, loudly, then another, then the rain increases exponentially until it is coming down in buckets. It rushes into the gutters as the first full roar of the storm sounds. The beast is here. The air has turned in moments from moist and warm to dry chill. The clouds rend themselves. The lowest shreds may be swirling or maybe that's just your imagination. A lightning bolt cracks nearby. You can almost hear it sizzle, it's so close. You are poised and tense with the indecision of intertwined awe and self-preservation, but you are part of this world. You are part of this storm, so small as to be insignificant, so powerless as to be inconsequential, and yet your heart is tied into it and you feel as though it will all stop happening if you leave and then . . . and then the world will be a little less amazing.

On the night of the 2016 presidential election, I watched the results come in at the Oklahoma Democratic Watch Party in the company of friends. It wasn't until I left the building and the warm cocoon of like minds to walk in the cold and dark to my car that it hit me. Our country had elected a man who would not represent us. They had elected a man who resembled my father in almost every way, from the vague, fractured speech full of impossible promises to the gross sexualization of his own daughter. I knew this man, intimately, and I knew he would shred the whole world in service to his ego if he could.

But I didn't let the despair carry me. I followed the path that had brought me out from my father's shadow—led by anger subverted into action. I grieved, but I didn't lose my head. At 3:00 A.M., I awoke in a panic but soothed myself back into sleep. I let the excess rage spill out but held the rest close, eventually mixing it with joy in the hopes that the successive alchemical reaction would create gold.

To my astonishment, though, it wasn't just me. The election sparked my survivor instinct, but it sparked something in others too. I joined community groups to find ways to direct my anger; those community groups burgeoned as more and more members took the same action. Friends formed groups, and groups formed out of new friends who had never seen a reason to discuss politics before but couldn't resist the impulse now. It wasn't just me and my friends and a few other activists forming rallies anymore; the rallies were full of faces I'd never seen, so many that I couldn't even begin to count them. There was an air, and a statement in speeches, that we were there not for glory or fame or ego but for each other. There was an air, and a statement in speeches, that we were not divided by the lines that people often arbitrarily draw but united by our shared humanity. There was an air that shared humanity was enough.

It took some time for me to learn how to talk about the weather. It was a phenomenon I had heard about in stories, but growing up where I did, there wasn't much to say. It was either raining or about to rain, as the joke in Seattle went. But in my new home here in Tulsa, new things were happening in the atmosphere all the time. Rain, hail, snow, sleet, ice; colder cold and hotter heat; tornadoes, blizzards, snownadoes and thundersnow. I had never known that the sky could turn green naturally or that the midday sun could temporarily turn into midnight for only an hour as a violent hailstorm passed through. I had never heard the beginning of wind before, nor the end. Each new phenomenon was revealed to me like a secret, and I was spellbound by its magic until I, too, could talk about the weather with a stranger.

———

Giving birth to you was a catalytic event in my life. You came with a trickle turned to a torrent. Life in Oklahoma hadn't prepared me enough. I was suddenly a whole new person. The clouds rolled in fast and dark. I struggled to feed you, to care for you, to care for me, to love you. The responsibility became a beast that ate me whole. The long darkness didn't begin to lift until you were already a year old.

But then there you were, a beam of sunshine in the broad and ravaged world. In the almost three years now that have passed since I finally found your beauty, I have changed so much—because of you and for you. I wrestled with all those dark demons curled up in my soul, named them one by one, and cast them out. I did it for you, so that you would never lose the wholeness that you were born with, so that you would grow and continue to grow like the happy little weed you are, tended by my adoration rather than my fear. You have blossomed so beautifully. So often now, I find that you glisten and glow like the rain has just passed through.

———

It took some time for me to learn how to talk about you. It was a phenomenon I had heard about in stories, but having never done it before, there was so much to learn. There were so many competing feelings and thoughts in the beginning, and so many experiences that I had never had, let alone had words for. Words were so inadequate for the awe, the terror, the certainty, the confusion, the jumble of every feeling all at once or the moments unfolding one after the other with no time even to breathe in between. New things were happening all the time and at lightning speed, it seemed. Each new moment was a surprise, and I was drowning in that flood until I could find something familiar to cling to.

But I learned, with the help of a group of other moms. These women, my friends, scattered across the country, so perfectly encapsulated the exultant frustrations and deceitful joys of motherhood. They said the things that I was feeling when I didn't know how to say them. They posted thoughts that were only fleeting to me but that were key to mastering yet another conundrum of parenthood. Before long, I let them lead me down paths I had never seen, paths lined by different sensibilities and ideas but a mutual respect for the ultimate goal of raising well-loved and cared-for children while still nurturing the humanity in ourselves.

This was a world I had never seen before. This was Minnesota with my face pressed to the glass, awe shaking my body. But this time, I could find myself in the lightning. In fact, there was no glass, and there was no atmospheric storm. There was me, a spark in the night sky, and all the other sparks that lived there. They welcomed me into the clouds; they showed me that I was part of the clouds too. They watched me take my fumbling first steps and encouraged me to keep going. We stepped together into this world so new to me, and felt the electricity bursting through our chests together. We lassoed each other and others with light and heat, close but not restricted, and lifted our voices together to laugh like thunder, joyfully.

Call to Compassion

KATIE RAIN HILL

To write for this anthology, I had to look within myself—to analyze and digest old, and new, memories and tribulations—rediscovering insecurities, buried regrets, and unanswered questions. I had to recollect and contemplate the challenges that I had faced and what I did to overcome them. And even though I found the activity encumbering and exhausting, in the end I found this experience to be incredibly therapeutic and rewarding.

Growing up, I looked everywhere for hope. I didn't have a role model to look up to, supportive parents to confide in, a religious or spiritual faith, or friends that I could talk to. My father was a devout Mormon and a lieutenant colonel in the Marine Corps, my mother a Southern Baptist. Both possessed headstrong values and opinions. In church I was taught that the wicked were damned and punished and the good were blessed and rewarded; the world was separated into two distinct groups of people, the good and the bad; there was little to no room for nuanced thinking. I began to interpret my shortcomings and traumatic experiences as acts of God. For some reason, despite avidly striving to be compassionate, kind, faithful, and good, I became a target for God's cruelty and punishment.

I learned the hard way at a very young age that the dynamics of the world are far more complicated than what our quixotic teachings would suggest. I realized that reality is not governed by merit or virtue, despite what many claim. Life is harsh and often unfair. Our sexual frustrations, bodily insecurities, failing relationships, and philosophical ideologies are summarized and simplified on the covers of magazines and billboards, and demonized within the pages of our holy scripts. All of these portray suffering as being a deviant interruption to our lives needing to be treated immediately with the guidance and assistance of a faceless expert. In my short lifetime, I have experienced beatings, discrimination, verbal and physical harassment, multiple assaults, public ridicule, and many other tribulations that I haven't addressed and recovered from yet.

I was only able to survive because I learned to understand myself and others. Every day I strove to develop my capacities for compassion and understanding, the abilities to recognize the complexities of myself and other people, and to appropriately analyze my issues and how they relate to the rest of the world. These skills might seem obvious, or simple, but they all require considerable amounts of dedicated study, concentration, and reflection. I learned that dilemmas are often tailored to the individual and they can be surprisingly dynamic and complicated. We lose family and friends; we become sick; we lack money or access to primary needs. We suffer from more invisible, abstract issues such as the contemplation of our futures, what we consider important in life, if we are truly in love with someone, and if we are a good person. Common issues like job-hunting, domestic upkeep, and maintaining our relationships can, and will, elicit incredible amounts of complex emotions and anxieties.

I know now that my struggles, all my struggles, even the minor ones, mattered; without them I would not be the person that I am today. Countless other people as well have learned through their struggles to understand multiple aspects of themselves and their loved ones. I was changed from a scared, beaten child into someone who is worthy of self-love and pride. I could do this because I ignored the people who defined me as a monster and an abomination; instead I chose to define myself based on my actions and how I chose to understand myself and my dilemmas. I learned that it was not the people I confided in or the advice I was given that helped me overcome my tribulations. It was me; it was how I calmed the tempest of thoughts in my head late at night when it was time to sleep, how I interpreted my hardships, and, most important, how I responded to and recovered from them.

We've all been there, when the demented voices in the back of our heads tell us that we're worthless, that we're imposters, outcasts, or that we're not fit or suitable for the affection of another person. Perhaps you haven't felt this way, but no doubt you completely understand how it feels to be in pain. For a lot of you (myself included) there have probably been times when you've looked at the people around you, or the celebrities that are plastered on the fronts of magazines and billboards, or who have large followings on social media, and thought to yourself: "Why can't I be like that? Why can't that be me?" It always seems like everyone else has it all figured out. And maybe you keep telling yourself that you'll be happy once you get that one thing that's missing from your life. When you kiss that friend, buy that house, get that degree, get that job, marry that lover, or become well known by millions, then you'll be happy. Of course it is never that simple. We all hide our true feelings and thoughts because it's easier to lie to everyone and say you're fine—to put up a facade so everyone will think that you're one of the people who has it all together, fully capable of taking care of yourself. Even though it often feels like you're as fragile as glass. Everyone in the world knows what it feels like to be in a room full of people—and yet feel so alone.

Truthfully, until very recently, I was once again going through a very tough time. I lost my job, lived out of my car, and was bombarded by the concerns and disappointments of my loved ones. All of this left me feeling like a hopeless failure. At times I felt as if I was losing my mind, succumbing in an instant to overwhelming familiar feelings of anxiety, anger, depression, and stress. I would lash out with irrational outbursts toward my loved ones and continuously make poor choices. I often felt remote and disconnected, unable to properly empathize with others or even plan the next few weeks of my life, let alone the following years. Regardless of whatever mood I was in, whether blissful after a long night's sleep, or a big tasty meal, or after being embraced by a lover, if anyone were to ask me "Are you doing okay?" with even the slightest hint of a genuinely concerned tone, I would start to cry. All I had to do was stand inside an empty room and I could feel my knees bend and weaken. I could sit beside a therapist in a quiet room and immediately want to grab the nearest box of tissues and scream, for what often felt like no good reason.

It was difficult to pivot my thoughts from this position. I reminded myself daily that I was not being unfairly punished by a deity, not deserving of suffering because of my sins and wrongdoings, and not a victim of a terrible combination of coincidences. I refused to allow my suffering to turn me completely bitter and cold, into a naïve wounded creature that would claim to understand the world better than others because of its gnarly scars. I couldn't accept such a shallow interpretation of reality, one that was dictated by savage coincidences.

Learning to understand oneself is far easier than understanding the foreign complexities of other people. The person we generally understand the most is ourself. Other people are unpredictable and often disagreeable; their intentions and thoughts are completely hidden from us. They are the ones who harm us and are often the cause, or the victims, of our hardships and shortcomings. Yet somehow we all naturally develop amazing abilities to understanding and interpreting other people. We begin to understand empathy, literally feeling the pain of others. We learn to pity, and we learn how to censor our own thoughts and feelings for the sake of others. And we eventually learn to anticipate their wants and needs. I expanded on these abilities, learning to recognize how fundamentally complicated and flawed other people are, how easy it is for them to make a mistake, to miscommunicate or misinterpret, even with their parents or their most cherished friends and intimate partners. Instead of perceiving others as external enigmas—obstacles and targets of my gratification—I started thinking of them as complicated individuals who have dreams, fears, ambitions, and equally complicated thoughts and ideals, all of them astoundingly unique.

I believe that many of our societies and people within them fail to recognize an essential law of human nature: we all suffer, and we suffer differently. When our suffering and victories are objectively framed, we compare ourselves to others. Our accomplishments seem to pale in comparison to those of celebrities, and our ideas and levels of intelligence seem insignificant when compared to renowned intellectuals. Sometimes we intentionally degrade and devalue our struggles with humble rationality. Phrases such as "It could always be worse" or "There are people who have it worse" are usually intended by others to frame our perspective—to help us realize our accomplishments, be grateful for our privileges, and be thankful that we have the life that we have. However, such phrases often dismiss our feelings and promote shame, bitterness, and anger deep within us.

For a while I believed that many of my simple or abstract dilemmas were trivial and unimportant to the overall health and trajectory of my life. I felt that by being upset about these types of problems I was being immature, weak, or begging for attention—they were only distractions from the true issues in my life. After all, it doesn't make sense that I was able to recover from a brutal rape, or to juggle a full-time career and college, yet sometimes was unable to pay for bills, maintain relationships, or plan my future with equal amounts of poise. Truthfully, it was often difficult to allow myself to be upset about the more typical issues in my life when compared to the more atypical that I had conquered with far more success.

I am a white woman in America; I live in a nice Oklahoma neighborhood; and I have a job and a place of my own, a pantry full of food, and friends and family. So, because I have these wonderful things, should I convince myself that my problems are trivial in comparison to those who are suffering just as much, if not more? Beneath the face-value analysis, I am an individual who has indeed suffered in ways that are often impossible to articulate. I am constantly struck by overwhelming feelings of exulansis—the inability to properly articulate one's reasons and feelings—when I try to convince friends or strangers that I objectively experienced noteworthy sufferings at a young age. I want to say that I have somehow learned something that is worthy of being shared with others to acknowledge without being dismissed or labeled as an overly dramatic, crazy, stupid, or naïve woman.

We must learn to adopt a more nuanced view of fellow humans—our rivals, our parents, our leaders, and our romantic partners—to understand that we will not always get along with our best friends, disagree with our enemies, or be satisfied by our lovers and spouses. Perhaps by adopting a new perspective, we will be able to dissolve much of the fear and hate we harbor for our fellow men and women.

We must accept that there are differences between people, even if sometimes the differences are so immense that conflict is arguably inevitable. By delicately dissecting every emotion and initial reaction to find flaws in our reasoning, by taking great effort to analyze every solution, and, of course, by doing our best to understand the feelings and perspectives of everyone involved, we can become better, more compassionate individuals and build more humane societies.

Salvation

DEBORAH J. HUNTER

When people talk about the South they rarely, if ever, include the state of Oklahoma. Yet in personality and politics, Oklahoma behaves as a southern state. I was born "colored" in 1950 in Tulsa, Oklahoma, under Jim Crow laws that made racial segregation legal and mandatory. All my grandparents were survivors of the 1921 Greenwood Invasion, traditionally called a "riot." Today, Tulsa continues to be ranked consistently as one of the most segregated cities in the nation.

I have no idea how difficult it must have been for my grandparents, parents, and other adults living in Tulsa who had to work outside of the African American community. As a child I was insulated from racial bigotry by our forced segregation. I lived in an all-"Negro" community and attended all-black schools and churches. Recently, Linda, my friend of more than fifty years, observed, "White people were on TV—not in our lives." This was certainly true. White people were as peripheral to our young lives as black people were to the white community at large. I write about race in this essay because of who I am and where I came from. But this is not an essay *on* race. It is about writing and poetry and how they saved me.

I spent most of my childhood days at my grandmother's house. I lived with my parents and siblings across the street from her. When I wasn't reading, I was filling my time with imaginary alternate lives. At the end of my grandmother's driveway was an elm tree. It's where I had my picnics. I would spread out a blanket, set up a tea set and dolls that I had gotten for Christmas or a birthday and, complete with British accent and extended pinkie, pretend I was having tea with the Queen of England or one of my favorite movie stars. Or I would sit in Gran's garden on the warm, dry earth amid the rows of vegetables and imagine I was in the desert. I'd poke sticks at horned toads and watch them puff up before deflating and scurrying off into the grass at the edge of the row. Or I would sneak across the railroad tracks into the tiny, shady glen on the other side and cross the creek, where I became Robin Hood or Peter Pan. Never Maid Marian or Wendy. I made a bow and arrows from twigs and string. I climbed my favorite tree and hid in the top branches, camouflaged by the foliage. Sometimes I just leaned back against the trunk and listened to the creek water run over the rocks. Other times I took off my shoes and danced on the soft, green, cool moss that covered the ground. I was invisible and safe.

I adored my father. He was away from home a lot working one of his jobs. He also played on the local Negro League baseball team, T-Town Clowns. Daddy had seven children; three with his first wife and four with my mother. I'm the oldest of the second group. In August of 1960, when I was nine years old, my father died from gunshot wounds. A man he barely knew shot him over a card game. I was teased about his death when school started in the fall. Murders were so uncommon at that time that everyone knew about it. I was starting fifth grade. I don't remember much about the year following his death. We tend to treat children as if the tragedy that invades their lives is of little consequence to them because children are "resilient." The trauma of losing my father impacted not only me but my siblings and my cousin (who thought of my father as hers) for the rest of our lives.

I learned to read at a young age. Books were my vehicles into other worlds. After Daddy died, I started writing stories, poems, and character portraits. My mother didn't allow the outward expression of emotions. If I exhibited sorrow—or joy—she said I was being dramatic. But as long as I could escape into a book and release my grief and aloneness through my pen onto paper, I was able to survive.

One of my favorite early memories was seeing my mother and father all dressed up in semiformal wear. Mama was beautiful in "After Five" apparel and jewelry. Daddy was so handsome in his tux, white shirt, and cuff links. They often went to the Big Ten concert and dance hall. It was one of the stops on the "Chitlin' Circuit." The Chitlin' Circuit consisted of venues across the country where black artists were allowed to perform. Concert-goers had to take their liquor with them, BYOB—Bring Your Own Bottle. People had to purchase their "set up"—ice and mixes—at the venue because liquor by the drink was illegal.

I couldn't wait until I was old enough to get dressed up and go out too. However, after my father's death, my mother's social drinking escalated to alcoholism. She already had an explosive temper, and her outbursts became more unpredictable and violent with drinking. Corporal punishment often went beyond a spanking or a "whipping." She was overly controlling and verbally abusive, even when sober, and she kept me close to home. As the oldest I was responsible for running the household while she worked. I rebelled by joining any group or organization that would get me out of the house. I was in speech, drama, and choir at school. I was in the youth Bible study group and choir at church. I was an active Y-Teen through the YWCA and, for a short period, I sang in a community choir. I know. Tame. But these activities were rebellion for me because they gave me the opportunity to be away from home for many hours every week.

My mother died in 1974. Colon cancer. I was twenty-three. She was forty.

I married young—one month before my eighteenth birthday. My husband had enlisted in the Air Force before our high school graduation. This was during the Vietnam War. We were stationed in Wichita, Kansas. I stopped writing during that time. I felt that writing was part of my childhood and now, as a married woman, my focus needed to be on my family. We had three beautiful daughters and a German Shepherd–Elk Hound mix named Basil. We had the perfect picture-book life. Or so it seemed. When our youngest was a year old and after we had just purchased our "forever" house, my husband told me he wanted a divorce.

I slipped into a deep depression complete with anxiety attacks and suicidal impulses. I started writing again. Eventually I found a great therapist. When I was well into my therapeutic recovery, I asked my therapist if I would still be able to write when I was no longer depressed. Everything I had written up until that time had grown out of loss, anger, and sorrow. My brilliant therapist said, "Yes. And your writing will be better." She was right. With writing and what I learned in therapy, my relentless suicidal impulses ended.

In 1984, I moved back to Tulsa. I continued writing and tried unsuccessfully to publish my poems. I joined a writer's group in the early nineties and started reading my poetry in coffee shops at open mic nights. I drew a following. I read regularly at Living Arts of Tulsa and other locations, some that no longer exist, like Gold Coast and Snooty Fox. I finally started having poems published in literary journals. At some point I stopped submitting poems for publication, except on rare occasions. I had become addicted to the immediate gratification of live audience acceptance and praise. I was presented with ample opportunities to perform. Locally, I became well known and accepted as a spoken word artist. I signed up as a teaching artist through multiple arts programs and taught in schools and at community sites all over northeastern Oklahoma.

I was happy in my own skin, as the saying goes. I couldn't imagine that anything could cause me as much pain as I'd experienced years ago on the morning I woke up to discover my husband had packed and left during the night, leaving a note on the fireplace with a phone number telling me where he could be reached. I was wrong. In 1996, my youngest daughter was stricken with a mental illness. Paranoid schizophrenia. Her bizarre behaviors were difficult to live with, and her diagnosis was devastating. My writing shifted focus. I started writing poems about my experience with my daughter at the onset of her illness and a separate collection in the voices of homeless women I had encountered during my years of working as a case manager at the Day Center for the Homeless. In the 1980s I had seen the play *for colored girls who have considered suicide / when the rainbow is enuf* by Ntozake Shange and always wanted to act in it. In 2000, Theatre North produced it, and I was Lady in Yellow. Inspired by that experience, I decided to turn my collection of poems into a play.

The result was *Amazons, Gypsies and Wandering Minstrels*, a performance piece comprised of monologues in the voices of women who have survived mental illness, abuse, addiction, and homelessness. Tulsa's Theatre North showcased it as part of a reader's theater of excerpts from plays by black playwrights. However, I wasn't satisfied with the way the characters were portrayed by other actors. They didn't look onstage the way I saw them in my head. Living Arts of Tulsa presented an arts festival every year called New Genre. I was particularly interested in performance artists who introduced poetry and spoken word into their performances. That started me thinking of *Amazons* as a one-woman performance piece.

Amazons, Gypsies and Wandering Minstrels, entertaining as a work of art, had an educational and emotional impact on audiences. It gave people permission to talk about their own experiences with mental illness and homelessness or other things related to the topics of the performance they may have gone through with their loved ones. I have been called to perform the mother-daughter portion of this performance piece dozens of times since the first production as a training tool for law enforcement, mental health providers, and prison staff. People who might have ignored lecturers and guest speakers on mental illness were moved by the story in *Amazons.*

Because of my anger and the sense of loss I felt—and still feel—about my daughter's illness, I became an advocate in the mental health community. In the beginning I was driven by my maternal need to "fix" her. I had a deep belief that if I researched enough I could find the answers to the mysteries that had invaded her brain. I became more knowledgeable than some of the professionals who treated her. I was able to argue in her behalf and get treatment for her where other parents had been unsuccessful. But no matter what I did, how hard I worked, who I educated, I was not able to fix her. To this day, twenty years later, she still believes that I am not her mother and that she was born in another country.

The books I read and digested, the events and incidents I experienced, and the ability to transform those experiences and emotions into art have given me as much as I have given my audiences. Writing opens places that we have closed to protect ourselves. By opening and cleansing the wounds of past trauma, we allow ourselves to heal. We never forget what we went through, what we overcame, but we can use what we learned as a tool to help others. I have used poetry to enlighten, trigger compassion, or evoke emotion. I have given people poetry as a tool they can use to begin their own self-healing. Poetry shows us the world in ways we may not have seen before. Creative writing in all its many forms can be healing and spiritual, but it was poetry that saved me.

Excerpt from the Mother-Daughter Monologues in *Amazons, Gypsies and Wandering Minstrels*—One-Woman Performance Piece by Deborah J. Hunter

Mother

In the middle of the night
a sob awakens me, pulls me
straight up out of my pillows
and I realize I am the one who is sobbing
I realize there is no voice
until tears run like the Nile
and cries resound like the wail of the loon
and the body heaves like the Earth

when she vomits with the pain of
a fissure in her skin bleeding fire
with terrors so deep that no volcano
can cauterize it

then there's the rocking
the rocking
the rocking
for comfort
but nothing can ease
this outrage
this anguish
this gaping raw hole
that was my heart
ripped out while I watched
impotent, moaning, rocking,
sobbing rivers
of fire
of lava
a flood

and she walks
she walks
in the heat
the cold
the wet

when she does not walk
she rocks
she rocks
she wants to run but
she knows she will drop
to the ground
on her knees
on her face
smashing her teeth
crushing her nose
piercing her eyes

and sometimes this is what she wants
this outside pain to shroud the inside pain
the pain that never goes away
but ebbs and flows
until the next explosion
of fire
of lava
a flood
of sobs
of wails
and rocking
and rocking
the earthquake in her body
an eruption
of lava
of fire
and she rocks
to comfort herself
but she can't
no one can
no one could
no one could have prepared her for this

I had to sign an affidavit
get a judge's signature
have the sheriff ordered
... to pick her up ...
take her to the hospital
and the last time she called me "Mama"
was from the backseat of a deputy's car
hands cuffed
face masked by mesh
tears sliding down
pleading,
"Mama!
I'll be good.
Just let me stay."

From This Side

NANCY MICHNO

I am almost sure that, in the summer of 2007 when I decided to stay in Oklahoma, I brought the flood with me to Bartlesville. I was born and raised in Mar del Plata, Argentina, where coastal winds are strong and storms move through often and quick. Flooding was so common in Mar del Plata that when I was little, on rainy days, my main entertainment was to place paper boats on my street to see how long they lasted without sinking. So it makes sense to believe that in the summer of 2007, the rain followed me all the way from Argentina to Eastern Oklahoma, briefly altering the landscape, giving the trees a skirt of water and the streets a Venetian look, without the gondolas and the greatness of the Italian city. That year the rain also brought to Bartlesville intolerable humidity, gigantic mosquitoes, and impassable roads as if my sole presence created some kind of imbalance to the Oklahoman land. Perhaps the nostalgia for my country caused the lakes to overflow. It never rained again like that summer. The following years were a series of blazing hot days and tornados threats, but they all formed the beginning of another life, totally different from the carefree times of my hometown.

Before I lived in the United States, I came every winter to visit my parents who had moved there to work. In Argentina, I was living with my grandparents and my aunt while I was attending university. I was pursuing two careers at the same time: literature and visual arts. Plus, the little time I had left when I wasn't studying I used to frequent film festivals, circles of intellectuals, symposiums, and Thursday night gatherings of wine and literature. However, I always felt I did not belong; I was just a witness to the successful achievements of my friends. I was not happy with my performance in class. I was getting tired of living in the same city, Mar del Plata, and frequenting the same kind of people. I needed a change. Oh, brother, did I get what I was wishing for!

That summer of the flood, I met my husband, a country boy from Copan, Oklahoma, a small town north of Bartlesville. On our first date, we talked about politics. I let him know from day one my strong beliefs about the world. I told him the United States goes to war to fulfill its imperialist ideals: "Fighting for freedom is a tall tale to make the American citizens support the government with its evil plans." The funny thing was, I did not quite speak English at that time. I only had studied English for two years in school. All I really knew how to say was, "Would you like a cup of coffee?" He did not speak Spanish, not even a *"Mi casa es su casa."* I am certain my political ideas did not sound eloquent or provocative to him. He probably thought we were talking about movies, and that might be the reason why we kept seeing each other. I learned to speak English eventually, thanks to his patience and love, as well as my obsession for reading books in their original language.

A year later we had our first daughter, Atenea, named after the Greek goddess of wisdom. I had dreamed her already, with her big blue eyes and her dark hair. I spent my hours looking at the baby, wondering how so much perfection and pure love can fit into such a tiny person. At fifteen months old, she was walking and talking, laughing and loving. Just as the greens and blues of trees brighten and the landscape awaits motionless before a tornado hits the ground to remind us of the ephemeral nature of things. My life was beautiful; everything around me was starting to blossom. But Atenea had to remind me about dualities, that life is not a monochromatic palette, that where there is happiness there is also a profound fear and pain.

That afternoon was cold inside the house, yet Atenea insisted on taking her socks off. She was running around the house, barefoot. I still can hear her feet engraving her tracks on the wooden floor, her little steps of a wizard. This was the beginning of her ceremony of inexorable metamorphosis to reveal to us, her ignorant parents, her rare and complex design. I noticed she started to feel sick. I put her on my lap and took her temperature. I gave her medicine to make the fever go down, but soon it scaled like a wave and no medication could control it. That is when she began to fade away. I placed her in the bathtub believing the healing power of water would cool her down, would bring her back to me. Her blue round eyes were covered by a transparent veil. I did not realized at that moment, but she started to have seizures. When I called her name and she did not respond, I knew it was time to rush to her the emergency room.

There was a nurse—I memorized his face so I could thank him one day—who never left her side. Atenea was unconscious; she forgot how to breathe. He was pumping air into her lungs, keeping her alive while we were waiting to move her to intensive care. They kept me in a corner. My husband had to drive ahead to Tulsa to meet us at Saint Francis Hospital. Here in Bartlesville, the nurses and doctors needed to stabilize her first. I was a powerless witness to her struggle. I, her mom, the protector, was standing there immobile, relying on a group of strangers to lift her back up. I was there, watching how my daughter's heart rate slowed down, threatening to quit. But these people refused to let her go. They were obstinate, and they persevered. They were whispering desperately in her ears to come back, come back. I could see the fear in the paramedics' eyes. I could not do anything about it. I was frozen in time.

For a moment, it was not me standing there and that was not my daughter dying. I was walking with my friends to the beach. I was young, stupid. My only worries were about how Maria was still friends with Manuel after he and I had broken up, about why they were seeing each other behind my back. I was speaking another language. I was riding a bicycle to go to school. I was making pottery. I was going to the bars. I was enameling copper. I had no fear. I had never fallen in love. I must be dreaming about a hospital. I must be dreaming of a little girl dying.

The image of the warrior girl, so small, with little hands and little feet, connected to machines, her chest barely rising, did not go away. I recognized Atenea again, and I was her mother. She was fighting hard to stay, so we could sing songs together, dance, paint, ride horses. I knew she could not miss meeting her little sister.

After a week of being hospitalized, Atenea slowly recovered. She hated the nurses who poked her arm with their giant syringe. She wanted to run free without catheters and cables on her head. We still did not know why the doctors had not explained to us the reasons we still had to be there, and why she had had what they called a status epilepticus, meaning a continuous state of seizure. The only thing they told us was that it was caused by pneumonia. On the day we were going home, a group of doctors finally appeared in our room. They spoke unintelligible words; they pronounced unspeakable terms. They began to label my child, my baby: Tuberous Sclerosis Complex (TSC); Polycystic Kidney Disease (PKD); hypertension; seizures; tumors in the brain, heart, kidneys, gums, skin, eyes. Specialists every three months: neurologist, nephrologist, cardiologist, geneticist, ophthalmologist. MRIs, CT scans, ultrasounds. Kidney transplant. They left us a pamphlet with terrible percentages. The list continued for each organ of the body. But the worst was the sentence that stabbed our hearts: "There is no cure."

I learned that Tuberous Sclerosis Complex is a genetic condition. In my daughter's case, the disease is the result of a spontaneous genetic mutation. The two genes responsible for Tuberous Sclerosis are TSC1 and TSC2. Only one of the genes needs to be affected for the disease to be present. Both TSC1 and TSC2 suppress tumor growth in the body. When one of these genes are defective, cell growth cannot be controlled, and Tuberous Sclerosis results. This is the reason why so many organs are affected. Genetic testing showed Atenea had a deletion mutation of her TSC2 gene. The PKD1 gene lies adjacent to TSC2, causing Polycystic Kidney Disease as well. How lucky she was, two diseases in one! Atenea had tumors in her brain, heart and, of course, her kidneys were mined with balloon looking cysts.

Back home in Bartlesville, I read all I could about the disease. I joined Facebook groups. I met other TSC families in Oklahoma. I researched, stalked the best nephrologist of the country, the one who specializes in renal involvement in TSC, until I got an appointment for my daughter. We followed him to Cincinnati and then to Memphis. The years passed, and Atenea, eight years old, knocked most of the labels down. She proved them all wrong. She does not have seizures anymore and has excellent grades at school. She even plays soccer. She is kind, sweet, sensitive. However, she still exhibits symptoms of both TSC and PKD. Her blood pressure is still high, and her kidneys are the size of a football. We only see the nephrologist once a year now, but this does not mean she won't get worse. In a couple of days, she is going to have surgery. They are going to drain the cysts full of liquid she has all over her kidneys because they are at risk of rupturing. After that, they are going to give her a new medicine that controls the growth of her tumors.

Since I moved to Oklahoma, life has been a rollercoaster of emotions and strange situations. My former self broke into a million pieces, and I became an agglomerate, a patchwork of personalities and beliefs. I have turned a hundred years old since I left my friends, my place. I have seen my oldest daughter stand on the border between life and death. I have also seen my husband go through hell and come back. I have seen him change, into a shadow: drugs eating him alive slowly and carrying us, his family, with him. These extreme experiences, when I believe I had finally touched bottom, made me feel so estranged I started wondering about my identity. Many times I wonder who I am. Did I dream about the artist who only wanted to sell necklaces at the fair? Or am I dreaming about the mother, the worker, the student who struggles with time, money, and life? The only thing I am certain is about the distinct voice inside of me that is growing slowly, ready soon to be heard.

The Struggle

VERONICA WOLF

In my twenty-nine years of life I have experienced more than anybody could imagine. You don't think so? Well, let me tell you a story about my life. I was starting my senior year of high school when I had my first child. At the age of seventeen, I did not know what to expect about being a mom. The one thing I knew for sure was that I had to finish school. Right after I graduated in 2005, I worked full-time and went to school full-time at Tulsa Community College as a single parent. I was overwhelmed with everything, and I was trying to keep my head above water. Well, that didn't last too long because I ended up losing my job and failing half my classes. In a way it kind of worked out, because I became more focused on my studies and my child. I had been missing out on my child's first milestones of life.

After being single for three years, I decided to date again, and it didn't turn out to be so great. I ended up pregnant *again*! The relationship ended right before I gave birth to my second daughter. So, can you imagine being twenty years old with two kids? Because I sure couldn't. I quit going to school because I had morning sickness and was in and out of the hospital. Then, after I gave birth, I just focused on caring for my girls.

When my kids were old enough for me to leave them with someone, I decided to go back to school. Being so young at that time, I was still wanting to live life and hang out with friends. I didn't get too crazy or anything; I still knew I had responsibilities at home. I was content to be living my life as a single parent, going to school, and raising my kids. Two years went by, I was thinking I would be single forever. Well, I was wrong, and I met someone through a friend. At first I wasn't *that* interested in him, but he tried his best so I gave him a chance. We jumped out of the gate right into a relationship, and five months in the relationship I got pregnant again.

This pregnancy was planned because we both agreed that if it happened, it happened. I quit going to school *again* right in the middle of the semester due to the morning sickness. However, our relationship had started to go downhill when I found out I was pregnant. We were fighting all the time. He was drinking a lot and traveling to different powwows. Neither one of us had a job, and I was really getting tired of feeling lonesome. Nine months later I had my first son. My son was only a couple months old when his father and I split up. But we still saw each other for about a couple months, and me being the dumb one and not using protection, I ended up pregnant again two months later.

This pregnancy was different because neither of us wanted that to happen again. I was in a constant battle in my head, and the father and I decided to abort the pregnancy. Well, that didn't happen because I couldn't live with myself killing a baby. That's how I saw it. So we decided to adopt the baby out to a couple. The lady that was adopting the child went with me to the ultrasound appointment to be of moral support. That was the day that I found out I was going to have twins, the day that changed my life forever. I couldn't live with myself giving up on these kids without trying to be their parent. I finally made up my mind and decided to keep the twins. I know I broke some peoples' hearts, but in the end it was worth it to me.

Raising five children by yourself is rough. The children got older, though, and I was in my right mind. In 2011, now in a good place, I decided to try the school thing one more time. If it didn't work out then I was going to go find me a job. I managed to make good grades and pass my classes. There were times when I couldn't go because we had no babysitter or the kids were sick. But somehow I made it through. In 2013, I finally graduated from Tulsa Community College with an associate's degree in Liberal Arts (Native American Emphasis). My plan was to get my bachelor's degree in Native American Studies. I couldn't move somewhere where I didn't have any help with my kids. My mother was the only one who financially helped support me and the kids, so I had to limit my choices to schools that were close to home. One of my professors, Steven Woods, suggested that I go to Rogers State University (RSU) for their Communications program.

In August 2013, I started my new journey at Rogers State University. I had to drive forty-five minutes to school and back each day. At that time, all my kids were in school, so I didn't have the trouble of finding a daycare or babysitter for them. But let me tell you, it wasn't easy going to school full-time and raising five children. There were times when I didn't sleep for two days in a row or would fall asleep at night with the kids and fail to get my homework done on time. My oldest daughter played competitive basketball and my second-oldest daughter was (and is) dyslexic and attended occupational and speech therapy. Can you imagine what my life was like? I was running around with my damn head cut off.

During my second year at RSU, I was involved in a car wreck and hurt my shoulder. Due to my injury, I was limited to one arm. I still managed to make it to school and do my homework and turn it in. Only in that same semester, I ended up failing a class; yes, I was disappointed in myself, but I just told myself to do better next time.

Just when you think nothing else could go wrong, it did. My *very* last semester at RSU I was caught up in a violent domestic situation where my best friend would have lost her life if I had not intervened. I was pistol-whipped on the left side of my forehead. I had a black eye, a locked jaw, and a bruised arm. I was not trying to miss any days of school but for something like that I had to. I was missing out on one important class that I needed in order to graduate. I had to bear the pain because I couldn't be under the influence of prescription pills *and* drive forty-five minutes to school. Overcoming that domestic violence situation and finishing school were the highlights of my life. I graduated from RSU in May 2016 with my bachelor's degree in Communications (TV and Radio option). If it weren't for my professors being so understanding about my life situation, I would've never made it through school.

The path I chose in life wasn't easy, but I made that path for myself. Life was never easy for me. I grew up in a single-parent home. We were poor living on the north side of Tulsa. I went to a ghetto school with other kids that had a similar lifestyle. I was hanging out with the wrong crowd, and I was already drinking alcohol and smoking cigarettes and weed in the sixth grade. My mom was hardly ever home because she worked so much. I was heading down the wrong path. I could have easily given up and done nothing with my life. My life didn't turn out the way I wanted it to, and if I'd known then what I know now (like how hard juggling five kids and going to school is), I would've gone to school first before having kids. On the plus side of things, though, my children were my motivation for continuing and finishing school. I think I would've given up on school a long time ago if I never had any kids. I never thought I would have my bachelor's degree at the age of twenty-nine. I was not going to let a car wreck or a domestic violence situation keep me from graduating.

A boy name Joseph Looks Twice once said, "In life there's a clear road and there's a muddy road; the rich kid takes the easy road and the poor kid takes the muddy road and helps build up strength." I feel like the poor kid who took the muddy road because I had obstacles thrown in my path and I was poor (not like homeless poor, but the kind where I just had enough to get by with what I needed). In my mind, I didn't want to be another statistic as a Native American female who has a lot of kids but no education and is living off the government. I tried my best to make it to school every day (which didn't happen). I tried to turn in *all* my assignments and homework (which didn't happen either), and I tried to pass all my classes (which definitely didn't happen). Yes, it was disappointing when I failed, but I couldn't let it get to me. I sure in the hell didn't make straight A's in school. My determination is what got me through that muddy road.

I got myself into some of these challenging situations, and, no, they were not the smartest choices, but they were consequences of the choices I made. I am living with my consequences every day, and it takes a strong-willed person to get through it all. I'm going to tell you right now I'm not a person to cry when things get tough, but when I was at my breaking points I cried numerous times and wanted to give up—not only in school but in life in general. I wanted to run away from my kids and school just to have it easy, but I couldn't just sit there and cry and do nothing about it. I would sit there long enough to let my frustration out, then I would talk to myself. The things that I would tell myself were, "You're almost there, Veronica, you can't give up now, you can do this." Plus the encouragement I got from family and friends helped boost my confidence. Just like that, I got myself motivated and continued.

If I had known my life (love, trauma, birth, money, trust, sex, motherhood, acceptance, break-ups, hard times, tolerance) was going to be so hard, I would've done things differently or asked for instructions on how to deal with certain situations. I knew I couldn't control all my situations, but though it wasn't easy, I changed them to make the situation better. I'm not a perfect person, but I have learned and lived a lot. I think having a strong mentality is what has helped me in the long run, though in my case it took me a while to learn. I may not be able to get my dream job, but I'm able to get a good, decent job that pays well so that I can support my children. I'm grateful to have lived a hard life at a young age because I know now that I can handle anything and everything. If there's one thing that I've learned in my twenty-nine years, it is that no matter how great you may think life is, it will always throw you a curveball. It all depends on how you as a person handle that curveball. Life is what you make of it.

Diagnosis: Major Depressive Disorder

JENNA BUSCHMANN

You hear about psychiatric hospitals purely through the media instead of through the eyes of the patients. You see them presented in horror movies with old women gibbering in nightgowns, or you see them romanticized in young adult novels. Whichever way you view them, mental hospitals are places for people who are not "normal." The people who inhabit rehab centers and psych wards are people who make you nervous. They are people who some think deserve to be studied like lab rats. They are people like me.

I entered the psych ward the day after my boyfriend of two years left my life. I viewed this as a pathetic breaking point. I, the leader of a Tulsa feminist chapter and self-proclaimed badass, should not be sobbing as if my lungs were taken from me just because a boy doesn't want to date me anymore. I, the woman who has chided girls for reading *Twilight* because it teaches them to be dependent on men, should not be clawing at my face in agony just because a man deemed me not worth his time. Yet there I was, rocking back and forth in what I can only call hysterics. I felt as if the walls were folding in and the floor was crumbling beneath me. My head was playing a song that felt like a punch with each word. "He doesn't want you he doesn't want you he doesn't want you."

Then I started thinking about the woods behind my house. Only weeks earlier, my boyfriend, two friends of ours, and I had gone hiking and hunting for tree burls. My boyfriend had wandered away from us to walk on the solid ice that covered a small pond, and I had stretched out on a cold, blue-gray rock and stared into the bleak sky. I had felt still and peaceful just lying on the stone. Now, the ache to have that kind of peace washed over me, and my brain took that ache and transcribed it into something much darker. Suicide. Soon I was scanning my brain of all the methods and ways I could accomplish complete stillness. I had created a plan that I believed would be a good alternative to all the chaos raging inside my heart and head.

My mother was with me the morning I toyed around with death. She is one of the most wonderful women anyone could ever hope to meet. She laughs so hard that she hushes herself mid-sentence. Her cheeks are full and apple-red, and her eyes sparkle when she talks. She is sixty this year, but her heart and her spirit will always be a full-blown seventeen. My mom did not look seventeen on the day I planned to leave, though. She looked a thousand years old. I knew she could feel me trying to go, and I knew how hard she had taken the death of my father just six months prior. So, though my plan was still fresh in my mind, I told my mom to drive me to the hospital so I could be admitted. It was the hardest sentence I have ever spoken, but it was the strongest thing I have ever done.

The hospital waiting room was full of people with the flu or broken bones, and I felt overwhelmingly insignificant being there. I was telling myself that my pain was not valid in comparison to theirs and that I was weak for being so torn up over a boy. Yet they admitted me, though they looked at me as if I had two heads. When you check into a hospital for suicidal tendencies, the nurses don't know what to do with you because they can't see the parts of you that are sick. They want to take your pulse and make you pee in a cup. They don't know what to do when you tell them you want to stick your head in a bag. Three hours of sitting on a hospital bed went by. I fell asleep crying and shivering in my paper-thin gown. The lights snapped on, and a security guard informed me to come with him because he would escort me and my mother to the psych ward.

On the drive, the guard and the nurse, who were required to accompany us, flirted with each other. She was outrageously pregnant and he was remarkably older, yet they teased and smirked as if I didn't exist in the backseat. I was half grateful to be invisible for a moment. We arrived, and the two departed without a word. Inside of the lobby, the walls were painted as if someone used snot as the color sample. A woman with a goiter the size of a bread loaf wrote down my information and called me "baby girl" every other sentence. She had stiletto heels, and, as she led me to the elevator up to the patient ward, it was clear this was the first day she had worn them. She teetered back and forth every step.

They checked my body for drugs and counted all my tattoos. I bent over and coughed in a bathroom that smelled like soup. They miscounted my tattoos four times, despite my telling them how many I had five times over. They made my bed and put me in clothes I would never wear anywhere else. They took my shoelaces and took my blood and pee for the second time in four hours. It was past dinnertime, but I was handed a plate with stuffing on it that was more of a liquid than a solid, and Spam. When I tried to cut into my Spam with my spork, the tines bent all the way back and broke off into the meat. I took this as an omen.

An older woman in a bathrobe across the room laughed at me. I looked up, and I know that I must've looked like a wild animal digging through a dumpster. My eyes felt heavy in my sockets, and my mouth was completely dry and pale.

"The only thing worth eating is the snacks. Don't even try with that meat," the woman told me with a sleepy smile. Part of me was relieved to have someone else there who was also disgusted with the food. Another part of me was terrified that I would be in a hospital like this when I reached her age.

The TV only played two shows: *The Big Bang Theory* and *Home Improvement.* Both shows have never been high on my list, but still I sat staring at the screen. Another older woman whose dentures did not fit sat beside me to rest her back against the column I was hiding behind. She told a dirty joke to me, whistling through her fake teeth, and burst into laughter. I smiled for the first time, more because of how loud she was than because of the actual joke. We talked about books and her bipolar disorder. She didn't ask why I was there, and I was relieved. We then watched in silence as a schizophrenic woman taught us how to seal a chip bag without any clips. It was the first time I felt at ease that day.

When we slept, the lights had to be on full blast. I felt like a snake under a heat lamp and buried my face into my starched sheets. They gave me meds that made the walls expand and retract but also put me to sleep. I did not dream. In what seemed like minutes, I was being woken up by someone pronouncing my name wrong and telling me to pee in a cup. It was six in the morning, and I missed.

Breakfast was something else unappetizing, and I spent the entirety of it asleep on the plastic couch in the rec room. A handsome young nurse tech woke me up when it was time for me to attend my first psychiatrist appointment. The nurse tech was the only person who ever treated me as if there were no difference between normalcy and mental illness. He would tell me about great taco stands around town and ask about video games we played on the outside. He never asked me about why I was there or what was I going to do once I "healed." He just was there, and I was there, and it was the most relieving feeling.

My psychiatrist was a Chinese man with lazy eyes who sat uncomfortably close to me and reeked of fish fingers. When he wanted to make a point, he would emphatically slap my crossed leg with his hand. I still do not like this man at all. He reviewed my case in soundbites.

"You feel hopeless?"

"Helpless?"

"No reason to live?"

"Your father died?"

"Why does your boyfriend not love you?"

Within fifteen minutes, my day was doomed. I wandered back to the rec room like a boxer leaving a fight. Everything about me ached. I sat so sullenly that the older women asked the nurses if I could go to a different room because I was scaring them. Finally, my therapist appointment came.

My therapist had slate-gray hair that hung like a tapestry, shielding her face from mine. On the other side of the tapestry, I silently wept. We barely spoke to each other that first day. She just let me cry and stare out the window as snow fell all over the city I had fallen in love in. I looked at the skyscrapers peeking behind the clouds and knew the boy I was in love with was in one of them making coffee. I felt so incredibly worthless that I was locked away in a mental institution while my ex was fully capable of handling a job and laughing with friends or even just listening to music. I was jealous of his sanity and happiness. My hour was up quickly.

The rest of the day melted away. They handed out our night meds, and I took them silently in my corner. Again the older women complained that I was stressing them out with my sadness. This time, though, I was instructed to sit next to them. Without a word, the loudest of the women brought out two packs of Uno and dealt me in. The other women went to sleep. Soon the men who were in rehab for narcotics came to play. Then the new girl, who was much younger than I and still in her hospital gown, sat next to me to watch. The drugs kicked in full swing for everyone, and we found ourselves playing by new rules invented by us. If I were asked to play a game like that again, I would not be able to recreate the rules. At one point in the game, someone shouted, "You're crazy!" and the whole table burst into laughter. This was what healing began to look like.

The second day, I started to feel better. The Uno game was brought up during breakfast, and I cracked a smile. People noticed.

"Look, the girl knows how to smile; she's just been fooling us the whole damn time!" cried out one of the narcotic boys. I smiled wider in embarrassment, and the other patients laughed at my bashfulness. No one on the outside would consider me shy. But when everything is stripped away and I am forced to just be acquainted with myself, there is timidity.

My friends visited me that night, and they cracked jokes about the nurse techs who wouldn't let me use pens. They talked about throwing me a party when I got home. And they told me I was brave. I finally started to believe them. After they left, something changed in me. I wanted to be healthier. I wanted to be as likable as I felt when I was with them. I wanted to love myself more than anyone ever had. That's when the treatments started to work and the therapy started to click for me. I started to talk to others in group therapy and connect with their hurts. I finally could see that what I considered failures in my life did not reflect on who I was as a human being. I could accept myself.

In my last days at the hospital, I ended up mentoring two new girls that were younger than I. Their problems were vastly different from my own, but instead of feeling as if my own issues were invalid, I could see them from a new perspective. In our sickness, we found company. Knowing that girls younger than I could hurt so bad made me reevaluate my own grief. Perhaps seeing me, a girl their own age, helped them know it was okay to feel the way they felt. By taking care of them and making sure they ate when I ate and slept when I slept, I could see myself as someone worth having around.

Mental institutions are not terrifying. They are uncomfortable and strange, but they are incredibly precious to have available. It is important to admit we need help. You can't walk on a broken foot, and you can't live with a broken brain. I was sick for a very long time, and I will always have my struggles. I have anxiety and depression on my good days, just like on my bad days. The difference is, now I know I am someone worth living through the bad days. I am valuable enough to take care of myself. I was not pathetic for being upset about a boy. I was not pathetic for going to a hospital. I will never be pathetic. I simply was hurt, and sometimes that hurt needs to be healed the hard way. I would pee in a million cups and cry a thousand tears if that meant that I would be able to love myself. Admitting myself to a hospital was the absolute scariest thing I have done, but it was easily the most rewarding. I am not abnormal for it. It was not horrifying to be in the presence of druggies and psychos. It was not romantic to be around young people with unpredictable moods and backstories and hang-ups. It was familiar. It was important. Accepting that I was crazy was the sanest thing I have ever done for myself, and I continue to do it every single day.

Cultivation

Silt

YASMINDA CHOATE

Some people walk calmly and deliberately into the pond of life. Their ripples are predictable and measured, and the silt stays firmly packed at the bottom as they step carefully and see through to the bottom. Others, like me, cannonball in, whooping and hollering, kicking up the silt, muddying the path, and making far-flung ripples the results of which we may never fully know. We may miss the safety of seeing our path, but we're never bored.

I don't remember living in Gila Bend, Arizona. I do remember sitting on my dad's lap as we drove a rig in a sea of sand. My sister, who is two years younger, has memories that go back to her earliest years on the planet. I remember dirt. I remember my fourth birthday party. Soon after we moved to Sasakwa, Oklahoma, from Arizona, both my mom's and dad's sides of the family converged to sing at me and eat a cake made by my maternal grandmother and dyed with purple Kool-Aid. My paternal grandfather and I walked out to the garden patch together to bring in a couple of the watermelons that we'd carefully tended in the red clay dirt of Oklahoma during that first summer.

I remember sobbing at the window the next week when my cousin Gene, who was one year and three days older than I, walked up the long driveway from our paternal grandparents' home to catch the school bus for his first day of kindergarten, leaving me behind. I remember five months later, in January, when my mom brought home my youngest sibling, a brother, from the hospital.

I don't recall caring much, but I did enjoy that my grandma from Tulsa had stayed with us for a few days.

I remember hunting with my dad. Squirrel, rabbit, deer—they were all fair game. I remember the first deer I "helped" take down. It was evening, and Dad left me sitting next to the carcass as he went to get help to carry it out of the woods. It seemed like forever until he came back, but I wasn't afraid. I experienced ridiculous pride from that hunt. I don't know if I knew how tight money was at that point or if family lore implanted this memory; regardless, our family needed that meat to survive by that point.

The family business, Choate Landleveling, run by my paternal grandfather, my dad, and dad's two brothers, failed during that first year in Oklahoma. Grandpa, for all his good qualities, was a shit businessman. Our family ended up bankrupt even after selling all the heavy equipment at auction. My grandpa and uncles both went on the road for work. My dad stuck with us.

The next ten years are a blur. My mom had a series of jobs—computer technician, insurance salesperson, substitute teacher—so she could contribute to the family fortune, but mostly she took care of my sister, brother, and me. My dad found a job in Oklahoma City, roughly a hundred miles from our home. Each morning, he left before we got up. Most nights, he returned just before our bedtimes.

I always knew when my dad was preparing to leave for work. Sometimes I could manage to pull myself far enough out of sleep to go and kiss him goodbye before he left at 5:30 A.M. Most mornings, though, I just inhaled the scent of brewing coffee, listened for the clinking noises as he scooped some change from the large pile at the end of the bar counter in the kitchen, and snuggled more deeply into my little twin bed. His long days generally ended with a homecoming around 7:30 P.M.

My mom handled the day-to-day work of living. She got us off to school, checked homework, signed forms, and chauffeured. I never wondered if Mom would show up because she rarely left. Dad, though, worked hard to show up. I remember him, still in grease-soaked work clothes, standing in the back of the school auditorium as I performed in Christmas plays and talent shows. I remember him, still grimy from turning wrenches, leaning over the fence at my softball games. Mom coached softball and led my Girl Scouts troop. She read stories every night—and I couldn't help but overhear her soothing voice reading to my siblings long after I outgrew bedtime stories.

We had family gardens. My grandpa spent an entire summer teaching me to grow corn. We cooled off hiding from the summer sun in the corn patch once the corn grew tall, and the soil was dark beneath the stalks. Mom handled the beans and potatoes that we later canned in glass jars. Squash grew wild, and, just after we unloaded a bag on the neighbors, a bag would always appear on our own doorstep. Fat zucchinis and plump tomatoes and watermelons ready to burst their juices all over my face grew in the dark tilled dirt of our pastures.

When our house burned, I was two weeks shy of being fourteen. It was near the end of July, and I had just begun taekwondo lessons. My mom, brother, and I were all at the studio. Those lessons, I suppose, were our saving grace. Or maybe not. Regardless, we weren't home when the fire began. The three of us saw the smoke from the highway well before we turned down our dirt road. Mom stopped the truck midway down the hill to our house when we saw the flames shooting out the window. It was all my brother and I could do to hold her back from running into the inferno, and it wasn't until we reminded her that our sister was at an aunt's house that she stopped struggling. My cousin Gene ran over from next door to tell her that he'd called the volunteer fire department. By the time the fire fighters arrived, though, nothing much could be done.

We had a moment of good cheer when my dad's gun cabinet in the back bedroom, my parents' room, went off. The resulting gunfire, as the ammunition met the fire, led to several careless volunteer fire people and townsfolk ducking and covering. We had a moment of bad cheer when my father came upon the spectacle of his house ablaze and half the town in the road watching. He, too, stopped mid-hill and barreled through the crowd until he laid eyes on my mother. His aunt Alice, who was my grandma's sister, died that day. For the most part, it was a shit day.

The sun rose the next day, and my family, for all of our faults, started turning manure into fertilizer. My parents began the tedious process of paperwork. Insurance and home-buying and should-we-move-away questions fell to them. My siblings and I, staying with our grandparents during that time, began the almost gleeful process of sifting through donation bags for clothes to start school, shoes that fit, and personal necessities. I'll never forget my Aunt Susie, my dad's youngest sister, showing up with toothbrushes and Bibles and fresh underwear the morning after we lost everything. I'll never forget my Uncle Gene and Aunt Janice inviting us to stay with them and their own three children in their small two-bedroom trailer when it became clear that we couldn't stay with my grandparents and another aunt who lived there. I'll never forget my mom, taking a semester out of nursing school, managing to make staying in my dad's large metal shop building seem like an adventure.

We moved into a new house in October, three full months after the house burned. Mom went back to school a semester later. A year after that, she graduated and fulfilled a lifelong dream of becoming a registered nurse, just as her mother before her had been and as her second daughter was destined to become. Her college graduation, more than any other event, set me on a course that I am only now able to clarify.

I spent my last two years of high school, the two years immediately following my mom's graduation, as a student at the Oklahoma School of Science and Mathematics. I then attended East Central University, where I earned my bachelor's degree; pursued graduate coursework at Oklahoma State University; and experienced the birth of my only child. My infant daughter and I moved home to Sasakwa for her first year of life before I accepted a position as a grant writer at a community college in North Texas. I completed my master's degree at Texas A&M University–Commerce one month before I returned home to the red dirt and family ties of Oklahoma.

After all of my education and wandering, I still haven't conceived of what I want to be when I grow up. When I consider *who* I want to be when I grow up, the path seems easier. I want a good reputation in my career. I want to be a person of integrity. I want to laugh every single day. I want to cultivate—the earth, relationships, minds.

I lucked into a faculty position at a local community college a year after I returned to Oklahoma with my five-year-old daughter in tow. I teach developmental and first-year writing, English as a Second Language, and technical writing—no, I teach *people*. Human beings with their own dreams and goals and desires. Human beings who often arrive at college without a firm grasp of those dreams, goals, and desires. I adore them. My mother tells me that I was destined to teach. She says that I spent my earliest years learning to do things and then teaching those things to my cousins. If job satisfaction is any measure, Mom knew.

Of course, problems exist in any system. At the end of spring 2014, I received a letter stating that my teaching contract would not be renewed. I took stock even in the midst of my panic. The one thing that stuck the most firmly is that I don't want to move again. My return to Oklahoma has been refreshing. I spend my springs planting—flowers, vegetables, berry patches. Spring also brings the babies—chicks and ducks. I spend summers harvesting and canning and eating my produce (and a tad of dirt and maybe a bug or two) fresh off the vines. I release the poultry out to fertilize the yards and pastures naturally. I spend autumn hunting deer.

Winter always brings the expected sadness. I sit and gaze at my grow light, prescribed to fight the depression that comes on when the sun doesn't shine and it's too wet to play. Fortunately, the winters are short here in Oklahoma. The bad weather days intersperse with bright, shiny days. I work. I spoil my daughter shamelessly through all seasons. I accept and embrace the responsibilities that I created for myself.

I returned to school for one more round. I shudder to think of how difficult the pursuit of a Ph.D. might be without my family so close. My parents and siblings care for my daughter differently than I do. It's probably good for her to get other perspectives on how homes work. I'm certain it's good for me to escape into my mind's life through coursework again. The college found money in the budget to renew my contract after all, so I've had a few more years indulging in my teaching and life of the mind. However, I know I'm on borrowed time as a professor in Oklahoma during these lean years. Fortunately, I've lived the lean years before. I know how to keep things growing.

This story isn't a fairy tale, and I'm no princess in a tower. I'm a queen tending to my rather dirty and chaotic kingdom. I wouldn't undo a thing.

Strong Roots

A Reflection

GRACE E. FRANKLIN

Much of my creative voice is grounded in the pleasure of disrupting and challenging norms. Changing views of the world, to include my own, requires an assumption that my view is worth the uncomfortableness. It also requires resolving that I may be a bit different. Not alone. Different. When I describe physical beauty, I always include images of skin with melanin and larger frames. I find these unrepresented images most attractive. Clear porcelain skin and thin limbs never have the depth or attractiveness that various shades of brown skin and robust hips do.

    Beauty comes in many forms. I believe that in every way. Yet if the standard is the opposite of yourself, then you covet what you cannot have. What does that mean for a brown child to covet the total opposite of herself as a standard? How do you stand tall on roots not made to nourish your vision of yourself? After having a conversation with a close friend, I thought about life's lessons and divine instructors that have guided my vision of who I am in this world. How did I come to believe that our experiences, voices, and views as African American people are beautifully unique and deserve platforms of expression? Upon reflection, I came to see that events happened as interventions when I was a child. I was planted, then repotted in environments that nourished my soul. It was purposeful. This place that allows me to speak loudly, proudly, and without intimidation is not just about the color of my skin. It's the journey to love the skin I'm in.

My parents did a great job explaining and demonstrating that beauty doesn't have to be one thing. How could they not teach me that, considering I was a black girl in a predominantly white city, state, and country? That would be irresponsible. I understand now; they were also preparing me to hear my voice in a world they knew wouldn't always want to listen. It was important that I understood I had choices. Exterior voices do not define who I am or cause doubt once my decision is made. I was purposely raised to love every aspect of myself, including my skin, height, big body, growing intellect, creativity, sensitivity, and culture.

My parents both love to read. In the summer the list of books they assigned for me to read included such classics as *Their Eyes Were Watching God* by Zora Neal Hurston, *The Invisible Man* by Ralph Ellison, *and The Souls of Black Folk* by W. E. B. Du Bois. My mother gave me a poetry book called *Ego Tripping* by Nikki Giovanni, and I was hooked. My parents also made sure I understood the history of black people in this country. We were captured, enslaved, rebelled violently, escaped to freedom. One day we were emancipated, not because it was the right thing to do or because President Lincoln despised the institution, but as a strategic move to destabilize the south. We were free and we flourished. Oklahoma had more black settlements and cities than any state in the nation after the Civil War and up through the first two decades of the twentieth century. History, literature, politics, science, and art were taught to me by my parents from a broader perspective that emphasized the contributions of African Americans. Performances featuring African American artists were seen at least 3–4 times a year. The Alvin Ailey Dance Company or productions of *Porgy and Bess* and *The Wiz* fed my imagination. I was fully engrossed in my culture.

I was one of four black children in my class at a private school in Oklahoma City. It was close to my neighborhood but not in it. I attended that school from kindergarten to third grade. During those primary years, I learned a few things about how the world saw me. I was smart, fairly cute, fat, likeable, and black. My parents were professionals and wanted to make sure I valued my neighborhood and community at the same time they wanted the best foundation for my education. Most people outside of school in my life were black. The dentist, my parents' doctors, mechanics, cleaners, and drugstore owners were black men and women. My pediatrician was a Jewish woman. She was tough and sweet. She didn't prescribe much Western medication; instead she recommended more old-world and home remedies over antibiotics. She would always call me a smart, strong girl.

At school it was different. I wasn't the majority but the minority. All my teachers where white. It was a great learning environment. I enjoyed classroom time, recess, slumber parties, birthday parties, and many great memories. I had friends and teachers who liked me. It was fun. Until the third grade.

The first time I was called "nigger" was shocking, infuriating, embarrassing, and hurtful. My classmates and I had known each other since kindergarten. In the third grade, a boy I liked had a crush on me. Two things: I was taller than him, and I was a chunky girl. But he liked me. We always played together and he would give me candy. He was my friend. During recess a teacher jokingly told him to get out of my face and "give her a break." As if it was cute the way he was always around me. Under a bright Oklahoma sun a few boys were teasing him about me. He stood his ground. Again it was cute. The same group of boys said, "Kiss her! Kiss her!" He and I held hands—that was it. That was all. I didn't want to. He came over and said, "I'm gonna kiss you." I told him, "No, you're not." He tried, and I pushed him down. One of the other boys said, "You got hit by a girl. Are you gonna let a nigger push you?" Thomas didn't say anything. He got up and walked off. The other boys stood around still laughing. The boy who said that word so nonchalantly was quickly on the ground being slapped by that same girl he laughed about seconds ago.

My teacher explained that the boy was being mean but that I should have chosen a nonviolent method. I should have told the teacher on duty instead of slapping the taste out his mouth. I remember her saying, "You really could have hurt him." It was so confusing. In the midst of the most egregious and violent word thrown at me, *I* needed to consider how *I* could have injured *him*. I felt attacked again. I cried loudly and asked for my mother. My mother and father both came. On that day the boy apologized and I did not. Neither my parents nor teacher could make me. I held out until the end of that week. I didn't want to apologize. I wasn't sorry. I'm still not sorry. That boy had called me the N-word and changed everything. Now I didn't trust any of my classmates. Now I knew how I was seen. I knew what they said about me in the privacy of their homes. Slumber parties and birthday parties continued as usual but never were the same.

After the third grade, I transferred to a predominantly black school. When I was older, maybe twenty-one years old or so, I asked my mother why they sent me to a different school. She told me that, after that incident, she could see me searching for myself and doubting who I was. I didn't want my hair braided with beads anymore; I wanted it pressed straight. Minor changes in how I spoke about black people, art, and hair gave her pause. There was a negative tone in my descriptions of what I had once loved. While driving me and my friend Jennifer home, she had overheard us talking. Jennifer wanted me to braid her hair like mine and add beads. I told her that her hair was much prettier than mine and that beads would make her hair ugly. My mother's heart broke for her daughter. She knew that a few months earlier, before the incident, I would not have responded with self-deprecation. In fact she had seen me braid my white girlfriend's hair before. Or at least try to, as little girls do. Next thing you knew I was at a school with many little girls that looked like me. I was back to braiding hair and loving my beads. She and my father made a choice to secure my roots. To ensure I knew I could be and love my natural self. Maybe they could have done that while I continued my private education. Maybe I would have found my balance, lowered my guard, and been able to push all the exterior voices away while developing my own. Or maybe my voice would have been lost in conformity. I think they made the right decision for their child.

    I don't remember that car ride at all. In fact, I don't remember much of my time at that school after the incident that removed a bit of trust from my childhood. It wasn't just a word. It was a storm that loosened the soil around my roots. I wasn't as secure, so I was attempting to balance myself. I hope I would have found my center on my own. Luckily the vessels tending to me knew a better way. I am thankful each day for purposeful parenting.

Teaching Topsoil at Risk of Blowing Away

LENZY KREHBIEL-BURTON

Someday, I hope my children will be able to forgive me.

My seven-year-old daughter and infant son are loved, clothed, fed, and have a stable roof over their heads. They regularly get to see their grandparents, great-grandparents, and other older members of our extended family. They have access to cultural events and opportunities available through our tribe.

Although they will undoubtedly cherish those memories when they are older, the trade-off is a bit steep, as it requires us to live in a state that seems hell-bent on mortgaging their future. When my brother and I attended our neighborhood elementary school in midtown Tulsa twenty-something years ago, every student was exposed to instruction in at least one foreign language—two if you were in the gifted program. When we went on to middle school and high school, there was no question in our minds—or our parents'—that we would have access to all sorts of classes that our family's previous generations could have only dreamed of when they were growing up in rural Oklahoma, such as Advanced Placement Calculus and college-level Russian.

It's 2018, and my daughter is now an elementary school student in the same public school district that her mother and uncle attended as children. That same district is also bracing for another round of cuts in state aid—this time to the tune of up to $12 million. While the same passion and drive that I saw among my teachers growing up is still there among the faculty at my daughter's school, this spring marks the second straight school year where I can't honestly tell her whether her favorite teachers will be back in the fall. The low teacher turnover rate that marked my elementary years is a foreign concept to her, as are the notions of having foreign language or drama classes available during the school day.

My husband and I are trying to fill in the gaps as best we can, but as much as we want public education to thrive in our home state, we both know that the opportunities available to our daughter right now through the public school system fall short of what she deserves. Letters, calls, and emails to the state legislature seem to have been largely ineffective, although I am hopeful that the spring 2018 teacher walk-out is a first step of many toward rectifying the situation. My state representative is a former public school teacher and seems to get why parents and teachers are frustrated. He's also a member of the minority party, so his potential impact is limited.

A teacher friend of mine has made references to Oklahoma being at risk of becoming a "Dust Bowl of the mind," since twenty- and thirty-somethings are deciding to pursue opportunities elsewhere for any one of a host of reasons. I already see it in my own family. My younger brother and two of my three first cousins bolted for the state line as soon as they were old enough to support themselves. All three have made it clear they're not moving back if they can help it, in part because of the slow starvation of public education.

"I will only come back to Oklahoma if I can't get a single offer anywhere else, and I do mean anywhere else," said my brother while wading through the job opportunities available to an aspiring academic. He's now an assistant professor at a state institution more than one thousand miles away.

The other first cousin and I have stayed behind due to family obligations and a shared hesitation at the possibility of casting aside more than a century's worth of roots in this state.

Unless things start improving soon, however, I will more than likely encourage my own children to strongly consider doing just that and following in their uncle's footsteps when they are older.

Period, Exclamation Point

AMANDA RUYLE

The physical experience of being born biologically female and making it to menopause is one drenched in the blood of creation. This may seem melodramatic, and it is, but it's also true. Every month we magical, modern, liberated creatures make a little nest out of blood and tissue inside our fucking bodies, just in case our birth control fails and a baby gets put inside us by an irresponsible and (often) drunk man. If that little nest is left egg-free, it has to dribble out from between our legs into and onto various products designed to allow us to leave our bathrooms long enough to smash the patriarchy. Some people have light and airy periods that are really no bother, and those people are the worst. (Just kidding. Sisterhood.) Others have pain and such a dizzying loss of blood that they may eventually choose to surgically remove their uterus to stop the onslaught. Periods can bring heartbreak for those who are trying to conceive, or relief for those who are happy to keep their uteruses empty of fetuses. Every month it is a warning sign from your body that there better be some good-ass food in the house to eat.

While the period experience is personal, it is also deeply communal among women and other uterus-havers who bleed. The monthly blood ritual is often maligned and placed at the center of anti-woman jokes and sincerely held beliefs that view women as the weaker sex (looking at you, incels), but in reality this liquid life force is a primal and visceral part of the continuance of our species that connects women to one another and to creation. Periods are also a part of the apparently mystifying process that keeps the "Best Dad Ever" mug industry in business, so please, think of the economy the next time you get the heebie jeebies when the subject arises. It is true that you don't have to bleed to be a woman, but every one of us came from a person who bled, probably on her favorite pants and her best bed sheets, so we as a culture should buy menstruaters chocolate and an abundance of pillows as a simple "thank you." Looking back, I like to think all my years as a young girl spent praying for my period were because I understood how holy and profound the whole rigmarole was, but really I think I was just impatient and ready for the great sin signal from Eve, the original nasty woman.

On the day my neighbor, who was a grade below me, still in elementary school, and already bouncing around with bra-filling boobs, told me she got her period, I played it cool for about three minutes before coming up with an excuse to get the hell out of there. I ran across the street, in the front door of our cracker box house, and flung myself onto the bunk bed I shared with my two younger siblings. I sobbed into my pillow, not chanting as much as dramatically warbling, "I will never become a woman, I will never become a woman," my mantra of prepubescent injustice.

All of my born-female friends were already bleeding, like every month! They had tampons and pads and got to skip gym class because of Aunt Flo. Being given permission to skip gym class at Eli Whitney Middle School, one of the most pro-gym schools in Tulsa, Oklahoma, thanks to an overenthusiastic Mr. Seawright, was a major win, and one that required actual bleeding from orifices. Even if you did have to "suit up" in the gold T-shirts and black polyester gym shorts that lived forever in between one's butt cheeks, you were allowed to sit on the sidelines and skip the cherry pickers and sit ups, or, if you were supremely lucky, get out of swim safety week.

Swim safety week was a special kind of hell. It happened in the basement of the school, in a pool reminiscent of the one in *Jennifer's Body*, back when Oklahoma could still fund stuff like water for pools. The water was greenish gray and opaque, like if you dumped a wheatgrass shot into a glass of skim milk. If there was a body at the bottom, there would be no real way to tell, outside of accidentally touching it with your feet while treading water until the whistle blew. The air hung heavy with chlorine fumes; our eyes stung and our throats burned as we stood along the edge of the pool, shivering in our mandatory one-piece bathing suits, praying for a lightning storm or sudden cardiac arrest. If you didn't own a one-piece, you got to swim in your gym uniform, which, in retrospect, was not at all in line with swim safety week considering how heavy the shorts became once they came into contact with water. Unless of course you were shedding uterine lining that week, then you got to skip the entire undignified and presumably toxic experience.

Now, don't go getting it into your head that period privilege only extended to gym class. The women who moved among us in the halls of Whitney also got to ruin pants in public and skip trips to the water park and have their own heating pads and carry little bottles of Midol in their purses, which sounded like little maracas keeping time to the movement of their mature and womanly hips. Meanwhile, to my dismay, the crotch of my plain briefs stayed a pristine white, and I participated in gym class three times a week for three years.

Late bloomers will tell you that the girls who get boobs and blood early are the lucky ones. They are the standouts in the middle school hallways, the objects of nearly all the pre-pubescent male attention. They get asked to go steady and get invited to the school dances. They look amazing in swim suits, even one pieces. They get to hand their training bras down to friends like me who were still waiting for their boobies to sprout. Now that I am a jaded and experienced woman of almost forty, I realize that girls who develop early face their own set of challenges. I've heard it said that the attention that comes from getting boobs early, when girls still feel like girls and years away from womanhood, is uncomfortable, and, having been around plenty of chest-staring men in my life, I believe it. Also, having had my period for upwards of twenty-seven years now, I know that periods are actually not that fantastic. But middle school me was in a hurry.

The day I got my period was a disaster, and nothing like the Playtex Portables advertisements had primed me to expect. My mom was at work, waitressing at a hotel restaurant, basically abandoning me in my most desperate hour. It's fine, now. We've talked it through, she had to work, tampons are pricey, bitches gotta eat, and so forth. It was a Saturday and I was bored, home with my dad and younger brother and sister. I'd gone to the bathroom, and was most likely reading an Herbal Essence shampoo bottle, trying to discern if it was the sodium lauryl sulfate or the dimethicone that made those ladies in the commercials feel so good. There I sat in the pullman bathroom, perched on the toilet seat, which at one time had been a luxurious padded number, but now had a crack so big in the vinyl that if you moved, you'd pinch your ass so hard you'd get a blood blister. Finishing my business, I gingerly shifted my weight, hoping to avoid the scorpion sting of my toilet seat, wiped, and noticed a tinge of red. That seat had drawn blood before, but this was different. Could it be my period? Impossible, since I already knew I would *literally never* get my period. Shocked to have my internal reality challenged, I jumped on my bike and rode around the block a few times, shaking a little and checking in with myself to see if I felt any different. Did I? Did I suddenly have boobs? A checking account? A carefree lifestyle and white pants I liked to exercise in? I didn't. Hypothesis proven, no period. Or so I thought.

I rode home and casually strolled back to the bathroom to check again, this time avoiding the pinching toilet seat all together, and, sure enough, Mother Nature had come through for me! I apologized to her for calling her a snobby, cliquey bitch so many times and checked under the sink for Mom's supplies. I was pretty sure she wasn't so old that her period had stopped, but she was at least thirty-five, so who really knew? All that was available to me was a gigantic box of hulking paper-towel-roll-sized tampons. Tampax to be precise. The kind with the cardboard applicator. No pads, no dainty little tampons in pretty pink applicators, just massive, post-birthing-babies-sized cotton realness. I was terrified. I knew this was not the product for me. All sorts of horrible images of my mother's privates flashed before my eyes, and I started to black out, but then the real horror set in.

I was going to have to tell my dad.

Dad, the man who made us say "windy" instead of fart. As in, "Who windied?" The man who banned *The Simpsons* and rap music and cute underwear. My family wasn't exactly sex positive, nor did we discuss fluids, unless they went into or leaked out of a car. I did not want the first person I told about this cataclysmic event to be my dad. A man! A man that happened to be my dad! He was not going to like this little literal development one bit. However, I knew if I could play this off, I could ride my bike to my friend's house; she lived a few blocks over and she'd have a cornucopia of brand-name period accoutrements. She was the grizzled old woman of periods in our group. I think she started hers before I was off of training wheels; I knew she'd have something less potentially medically unsafe for me to use, and it'd probably even be lightly scented.

Quick note about my dad: at this point he had already earned a reputation for being strict and frightening. He insisted on walking me into every middle school dance to "take a look," which meant grilling the chaperones and listening to make sure the DJ wasn't playing any of that "rap crap." For nearly two decades he owned two pairs of jersey two-tone gym shorts that looked like shorts on shorts but were really just a fancy fabric illusion, which he wore every minute he was not at work. He loved to pair those shorts with a hyper-color T-shirt that had been through the dryer, contrary to the washing instructions, so it was forever a baby-shit green, and his work boots, which were black, lace-up, steel-toed combat boots. His facial hair was the stuff of legend within the community of frightened children he walked among, my peers included. My freshman year he would earn the nickname Fu Manchu, after he broke up a party I hadn't told him about. The mustache that hung several inches off his face did nothing to soften his menacing appearance. He liked to look scary. He wanted every boy in the tri-state area to understand that he knew how to dissolve a body in acid and would happily do so if the occasion arose. He was not the gentle and cooing father of the tampon commercials, and, as I've already touched upon, my mother had abandoned us (for like six hours, but still), so I had to woman up and just give him the facts.

I left the bathroom and hung a right, taking my first walk as a woman down the long dark and doorless hallway that connected the living room to the rest of the house. The voices of my matriarchal ancestors echoed in my ears, "Eve was trash; we bleed to atone." I walked a little faster. But not too fast because would speed make the bleeding worse?

I casually approached my dad who, apparently having not heard the voices of the Ghosts of Uterine past, was sitting unfazed in his green chair, one of several dozen he would acquire at garage sales over the years. There he sat in his two-tone gym shorts, boots laced up should some defensive action need to need taken, watching Bill Dance reel in the big ones on TBS, oblivious to the world-altering information that I, his first-born and most treasured child, was about to impart. I stood there looking as cool and casual as The Fresh Prince of Bel-Air, and tried to get one over on him.

"Hey Dad, can I ride over to Veronica's?"

"Why?"

"Uhhhhhhhhhhhhhhhhh ... for fun."

Now I had blown it. Any pause or hesitation in a sentence delivered by an eighth-grader was cause for serious alarm for Mr. Manchu. In his mind we were all going to hump each other and do drugs, and no way would any period-free daughter of his be doing that crap, even if it was biologically impossible for her to get pregnant. I realized I just had to just give it to him straight. I gathered my resolve, and with as much high drama as I could muster, dropped the hammer.

"Dad! I'm a woman now!"

"What the hell does that mean?"

Jesus H. Christ, he was going to make me say "period" right to his face! Couldn't he tell just by how mature I suddenly looked?

"I got my period!" I blurted out, fully aware that it was natural but also feeling my first little sting of womanly embarrassment.

Dad grabbed the handle of his gently used and fairly priced recliner and shot up, sputtering a bit, gave me one hundred dollars, and told me to go, no questions asked. (The part about the money is a lie, but I think every person should get one hundred dollars from a national fund on the occasion of their first menses. Period supplies are ridiculously expensive, and not optional.)

I mounted my bike and rode to Veronica's house, who quickly hooked me up with supplies and organized a last minute "Amanda is a woman now" sleepover with our group of girls. Once they all gathered, they took turns calling the cute boys in our class to tell them I was finally a woman, embarrassing both the boys and me. The last thing a pubescent boy wants to think about is the shedding of uterine linings, and the last thing a newly minted woman wants to admit is that this period stuff is not all it's cracked up to be.

Since the beginning of my monthlies, I've spent time around thousands of menstruaters, tried on many personalities and lifestyles, and given birth to two children. I've found that some believe in the holy power of "Moon Time," and that if you just surrender to the glory of it all and steam your yoni, all will be well. I've known those who have to use personal time and sick days every month to deal with the side effects of their periods, and others who use hormonal birth control to stop it all together. Despite these differences, one thing remains: the managing of our biological functions can be tiresome and expensive. And although women comprise fifty percent of the U.S. population, lawmakers (who are still predominantly male) see it fit to disregard our autonomy and humanity while crafting and passing laws limiting our ability to manage our reproductive and physical health. From taxing tampons and pads, thereby adding to the already high cost of owning and maintaining a body that gets periods, to making contraceptives and abortions difficult to obtain, to defunding Planned Parenthood and, most recently, proudly making being designated female at birth a pre-existing condition, they force us to live and bleed in a culture that shames us. So the next time some jackhole makes a joke implying that you are being crabby or sensitive because you are on your period, steal his money and make it rain pads and 'pons on members of the Blood Club. We bloody well deserve it.

Navigation

Going Home

JARI ASKINS

Like most everyone else who went to college, my focus after graduation did not include returning to my hometown. I was selected for the job I wanted, one which required my traveling to numerous college and university campuses throughout the county, but it was only a one-year contract. The second year after graduation, I returned to Oklahoma and, while working for a bank in downtown Oklahoma City, began making decisions and taking risks that would change my life.

First, I decided to go to graduate school. Nothing interested me, but I was intrigued with the idea of going to law school. No one in my immediate family was a lawyer, but I knew the attorneys who were leaders in my church and my community. My application was accepted, and I began a three-year journey toward a law degree that had never before been part of my plans. After the bar exam, I intended to practice oil and gas law, probably in Tulsa, but a chance encounter with a Duncan lawyer at a motion docket in Cleveland County offered an opportunity to return to my hometown and to practice in my area of interest. The dilemma—do I stick to my goal of moving to Tulsa or do I accept a job offer in Oklahoma City or do I take a risk and move back home to Duncan to practice the kind of law that motivated me.

After convincing myself that "home" would be a good place to learn how to be a lawyer, I decided to give myself two years in Duncan, bought a house there, and went to work. Life was good. I became more confident in my legal abilities and started to think about moving. And then the phone rang. The district judge asked me to accept the position of special judge!

How could this be happening to me? I never even planned on going to law school and now, less than two years after receiving my license to practice law, I was asked to be a judge! Was I smart enough? Could I be successful? Self-doubt invaded every part of my being. The district judge convinced me that I could learn whatever law was needed, but he persuaded me to accept by emphasizing the importance of judicial temperament and demeanor, two traits he believed I had.

So, I took the oath, donned the black robe, and began my life of public service in a courtroom at the Stephens County Courthouse in Duncan. I learned much in the eight years I served in that judicial capacity. Most important, I learned a lot about listening to people and solving problems. And, always, I tried to maintain an even temperament and calm demeanor. You see, I knew that although sometimes I might make an error in judgment, the people who came into my courtroom should feel like they had been treated fairly. I tried to treat everyone—litigants, defendants, attorneys, witnesses—the way I would want my family and friends to be treated if roles were reversed.

Because I genuinely like people, I truly enjoyed my time as a judge. However, a former teacher planted a seed by suggesting that I run for office in the state legislature. I dismissed the notion at first, but the seed took root and the idea grew. That teacher saw something in me that I had not seen in myself. I decided to try a new path of public service in the Oklahoma Legislature. After being elected state representative in 1994, I began learning how to be a legislator, amend laws, and help constituents. As I progressed in my legislative career, I was frequently asked to be a panelist or speaker, especially for groups of women or girls. When invited to share my rules to success, I harkened back to my time as a judge.

MORAL COMPASS

Consistently throughout my career, I have shared three guideposts that keep me focused, that help my moral compass stay true. The first: treat other people the way you want to be treated. When I was on the bench, adhering to the Golden Rule, or my version of it, was foremost on my mind. It was the same when I served in the Oklahoma Legislature. Whether answering questions from legislators, talking with staff, or helping constituents, I tried to remember that each person deserves to be treated with respect. Many times this was harder than you think! When you have a good idea and try to convince your colleagues to vote with you, the debate can become heated. My goal was to keep an even temperament, display a calm demeanor, and not take comments personally. In the legislature, today's foe may be tomorrow's supporter.

My second guidepost: if you believe it, you can achieve it. Coaches know this philosophy and often use it to motivate their teams. The reverse is also true: if you don't think you can, you won't. Reaching your goals will not occur if you do not believe in yourself and in your own abilities. This mantra became more important after I made the decision to run for statewide office. Few believed that a state representative from a small city in southwestern Oklahoma could become lieutenant governor. I believed. My family and friends believed. Through their efforts and the hard work of my campaign staff, we finished first in the primary, the runoff, and the general election. But "believe and achieve" applies to more than sports and politics.

Each of us faces decisions in our personal life. The approach to those decisions and the ability to handle the result of our choices are guided, in large part, by our belief in ourselves. Losing does not mean failing. Sometimes the effort of trying uncovers sources of talent not previously known. Even if a door closes in front of you, new windows will open if you are resilient and willing to take a risk, and if you believe in yourself.

As a child, my parents bought two panels to hang in our bedrooms. My sister and I had one that read "Rules for Little Girls to Live By," and my brother's contained similar "Rules for Little Boys." The rules were mostly different; however, the last one was the same for boys and girls. "Stand for something or you will fall for anything." That's my third guidepost. Even as a ten-year-old, I knew those words were important. However, I had no premonition of the significance those words would play later in my life.

I love public service but have never liked bitter partisanship. The former judge in me still tries to understand all sides of a position or argument before making a decision, trying to support the best idea regardless of where the idea originated. Politics can make that difficult. I chose a public service arena that relied on partisan politics, but that did not mean I had to give up my own voice or my own integrity.

During every contested election when I was a candidate, there were specific points in time when I was asked, often encouraged, to go a different direction with my campaign—to go negative. Some of the prepared ads were really good, impactful; but I was not always comfortable with the type of impact. One time I acquiesced and a negative ad appeared on television. As soon as I saw it, I knew I had made the wrong decision. We replaced it as soon as possible, but the ad still ran for a few days. I did not stand for my own beliefs but had fallen for the oft-used counterattack of negativity. Never again! I had learned my lesson. After that, any response or rebuttal my campaign staff crafted emphasized my positives, not my opponent's negatives. This allowed me to stay true to my personal beliefs and not succumb to traditional strategies.

ROLE MODEL

Not until I was elected lieutenant governor was I comfortable with the title of role model. Yet if I wanted to have an impact on young girls and women, I needed to use every opportunity to encourage their dreams. I wondered if hearing about my personal journey could possibly motivate someone else to pursue a plan, be open to change, choose a new goal.

I was fortunate to be raised in a two-parent household. My dad was self-employed, and we all pitched in to help the family business. My mother was a woman of strong character and a leader in many civic activities. Dad could be found behind the scenes, quietly doing his part in his own way to make our community a better place in which to live and raise a family. Both my parents were my role models. They gave me encouragement and confidence to discover my passion and potential. In learning as a child and young adult to believe in myself, I learned that I could try and fail and live to try again.

I really do not like the word "fail." Some of my most interesting jobs have come after falling short of my original goal. Whether it is "finding the silver lining" or "making lemonade out of the lemon" in a bad situation, I always look for that open window when a door has been closed. Family and friends in my life modeled that behavior and attitude for me. Every one of us needs to understand that someone is watching us and learning from us. Only I have the ability to determine what they will see from me.

A few years ago I came across a quote from Melinda Gates that has stayed with me. "A woman with a voice is by definition a strong woman. But the search to find that voice may be remarkably difficult."

Hopefully, I can make the journey a little less difficult for someone on the road behind me.

Just Be Nice

EMILY DIAL-DRIVER

Parents and other relatives give all kinds of advice, some of it consistent, some of it not.

Some of their words can resonate throughout our lifetimes, sometimes coming out of our mouths later, unexpectedly, causing us to think, "Whoa. That's what Mother used to say. That's what Mother used to say that I thought was so stupid, and I just said it. She's there in my head and talking through my mouth. Noooo."

Sometimes advice from relatives is valuable. The constant mantras can yield important information. My grandfather was a veterinarian and a rancher. He and my grandmother had some rules. One of them was "If you take it out, put it back—like it was." Of course, we didn't play with any of Granddaddy's belongings, which included medicines in tempting glass apothecary jars with ground-glass stoppers. Very appealing, but no touching. The "take it out, put it back" was about kitchen items, horse tack, grain buckets, books—all the items that we were allowed to touch but had to replace.

Then there was "If you open it, close it." This applied to house doors and windows, cabinets, drawers, and, especially, gates. Gates! If a child opened a gate and the cows/fowl/animals in pens, some of which were ailing, got out, that child was in *such* trouble. No one wants to chase cows or corral geese or hunt down a sick dog.

Related to veterinary work was the admonition "Wash your hands." We heard that one, of course, before every meal. That's not surprising, but, due to his an encyclopedic knowledge of the diseases transmittable from one denizen to another, my grandfather would say, "Wash your hands" on many occasions: after we came in from the pasture, after we went to get a jar of okra from the cellar, and, even after we pushed open the screen door and stood on the porch, touching nothing but the hot Oklahoma afternoon air. We had very clean hands.

The one all-purpose saying, the saying we heard most consistently, almost as much as "Wash your hands," was "Be nice." It had various iterations: "Now, you be nice," "That's not nice," "Is that nice?" "Play nice," "What's nice about that?" "When are you going to learn to be nice?"—and more.

"Be nice" is kind of a wimpy-sounding caution, but it was bigger than it sounded. "Be nice" meant, among other things, "Don't say something mean about someone," and "Don't do something mean to someone."

All that's very "nice," but the saying also meant "Don't just stand there when someone else practices meanness and not do something about it; it's up to you to help the victim of the meanness." That's a much more proactive stance than just "Don't be mean." That puts responsibility on the witness or hearer to make a positive move, even in the face of peer pressure and in more uncomfortable situations. That means standing up for the downtrodden, for the weak and meek, for the right. No matter what.

That's a tough thing to learn and a tougher thing to do. For one or more of us four sisters (all of us members of the Methodist Church), it might mean uncomfortable action. On one occasion, when my sister was riding the school bus, nasty things were said about Jewish people; my sister felt compelled to stand up and announce, with heart pounding so hard she shook, to her bus mates, "You can't say those things; they're not right. Besides, *I'm* Jewish." She doesn't know how they took that statement because, she says, her vision disappeared and then she got off at her bus stop. But, she said, it was *hard*.

That simple (right, simple) statement "Be nice" also meant "Be honest." Always. We saw that played out when my father realized he'd received too much change in a transaction and turned the car around and drove back several miles to return the extra dollar he'd been given in change. One child whined "Daddy, I want to go home." His answer was, "We don't cheat people." My mother added, "It's not nice." We learned to count our change very carefully and *never* to accept too much. It wasn't right. It wasn't honest. It was cheating. It wasn't "nice."

Even a faceless bureaucracy was to be treated nicely. One didn't cheat on taxes because it wasn't nice. Eavesdropping led one of the sisters to that conclusion, which she passed on to the entire sisterhood. An overheard conversation between parents and another couple turned to the subject of the IRS and upcoming tax filings. The other couple was discussing (bragging?) about the shady accountant (of sorts) they had found to make sure they had all the breaks he could make—or make up—on their tax forms. Later, my mother commented that she had at first liked the couple but had mostly changed her mind after hearing their conversation: "They aren't very nice, trying to cheat on taxes like that."

"Nice" today seems just to mean pleasant, even faked pleasant. Both a college professor I know and a friend of mine have accused those of us in the southern and south-central United States of being fake people, fake "nice" people. Both have said something to the effect that it's hard to know what people from these areas actually feel because they're "all so *nice.*" My friend said people smile and nod and ask, "How are you today?" and then walk away, not actually wanting a response. She wails, "Why do they ask if they don't want to know? Why can't they act like they feel? They're just always nice." The college professor said, "This unrelieved pleasantness, this niceness, it all makes me very uncomfortable. I always think one of them is going to smile at me in passing and then turn around and stick a knife in my back."

Both of those people—and many more—think of "nice" as being pleasant (but not necessarily meaning any pleasantness). In the Broadway musical *Into the Woods*, the witch sings about ineffectual people caught in a situation they cannot seem to resolve: "You're so nice. / You're not good, / You're not bad / You're just nice. / I'm not good, / I'm not nice, / I'm just right." In those cases, "nice" becomes a code word for looking "sweet" and feeling and/or acting "tart"—or being mean or double-dealing. "Nice" is code for fakery.

But "nice" has other meanings, more akin to how my grandparents and my parents, especially my mother, "coded" it. Under "nice," *Merriam-Webster's Dictionary* adds, to "pleasing," "agreeable," and "socially acceptable," the words "particular" and "appropriate." The *Oxford English Dictionary* uses "pleasing" and "agreeable" but not "socially acceptable," and adds "fastidious," "refined," "precise," "careful," "strict," "carefully accurate," "attentive," and "demanding close consideration or thought."

"Appropriate" ("nice") actions, according to my parents and grandparents, were honest, were kind, were based on "right." "Nice" meant "close consideration *and* thought," and was to be based on "Love your neighbor as yourself," with the realization "your neighbor" is sometimes not warm or pleasant or welcoming or resembling you or acting like you or anyone you know. But, whoever they are, they are your neighbors.

All the coding of "nice" was reinforced by our watching television as a family. When, on *M*A*S*H*, Frank Burns says about Radar O'Reilly, "I knew I should have ripped the stuffing out of the little bugger when I had the chance," one of us commented, "Frank Burns is always so mean. He doesn't know how to act nice." When Cordelia quips to Willow in the first season of *Buffy the Vampire Slayer*, "Good to know you've seen the softer side of Sears," one of us said, "That's kind of nasty. She could be nicer." When Sheldon on *The Big Bang Theory* says to Raj, "You're afraid of insects and women. Ladybugs must render you catatonic," one of us snickered, "Even if it's funny, that's kind of mean. Mean humor. That's not nice."

So acting nice meant not acting—not acting mean, not acting exclusive, not acting hurtful, not being offensive. Acting nice meant action—acting to protect, acting to prevent harm or discomfort, acting "right." These events occurred sporadically, but consistently. And sometimes they were not entirely successful. Sometimes they resulted in negative consequences for the purported rescuer, but, with trepidation, rescues were still attempted. After all, those tormentors were not *nice*.

I think we all should always remember: Be nice.

The Button

AURA THOMAS

August 19, 1998: Such an ordinary Wednesday. I was eight months pregnant with my second son. I was big as a house and struggling to keep up with my two-year-old son, Jacob, who I swear could climb straight up a glass wall. After a full morning of keeping Jacob entertained with the garden hose, our entire yard was flooded, the flowers were waterlogged, and the water bill was headed higher than the mortgage payment. I decided to load Jacob into the car and head for the local Burger King to let him burn off some energy in the big hamster tubes of the Burger King Play Place. After arriving at the restaurant, I quickly realized I'd made a mistake. The place was packed with screaming kids and exhausted mothers. I was trying hard to keep track of my son in a sea of toddlers who were all the exact same height with medium-brown hair.

The combination of swollen pregnancy ankles and soaking wet shoes from Jacob's flower watering left me feeling less than social, but a woman with a kind face approached me and pulled me into a conversation. She told me she was visiting from near Springfield, Illinois. In fact, she and I were from neighboring hometowns. We had been to all the same places but couldn't seem to make a connection of knowing any of the same people even in such a tiny world. We talked about our shared but separate memories of life in the small community we grew up in. She even helped me corral Jacob when he broke free from the herd of children and tried to escape to the parking lot. She told me she was visiting her brother-in-law who had been diagnosed with adrenal cancer just a few months earlier. She said the cancer was extremely rare, but when it did appear, it was typically in children and less commonly in adults. I appreciated her warm personality and help with my son, but I had reached the end of my energy and decided to wrestle Jacob's shoes back on him as I prayed there would be a nap in my near future. The woman never gave me her name, or if she did, I have no memory of it. But even as I was leaving, she continued to tell me more about her brother-in-law's adrenal cancer, including details about his diagnosis. "The adrenals sit right on top of the kidneys and the cancer is often treatable if found early," she said. I thanked her for her help, told her goodbye, and went on my way.

August 20, 1998: I got the news. The baby was measuring large at thirty-five weeks along, and the doctor wanted to have one final look on ultrasound to make sure all was well. I arrived at the ultrasound clinic, dressed in the only thing that still fit, a worn-out denim jumper that buttoned down the front, from the top of the Puritan-looking collar, to the bottom of the dowdy, ankle-length skirt. Underneath, I wore a white T-shirt, which made me look much the same way Winnie the Pooh does, squeezed into his equally unflattering red top. I was wearing the only shoes that would go on my feet, which had swollen to the size of bread loaves. I pulled into the parking spot at the clinic, and, as I stepped out of the car, I stepped on the hem of my skirt. Buttons flew everywhere as they popped off my jumper and hit nearby cars like shrapnel. I could hear the pinging and cringed as I saw each button take flight. I scrambled around the parking lot pulling my dress together like a bathrobe. I could only find a single button on the ground. I picked it up and held it tightly in my hand as I walked through the doors of the clinic, embarrassed and tired. I asked the attendant for a safety pin, needle and thread, or anything that would help me hold together the yards of ugly denim fabric that now hung wide open, showing my much too short T-shirt and giant pregnancy grannie panties. Finding no help, I held the button tighter in my hand, dug in my fingernails, and felt tears well up as I sat there waiting, feeling exposed.

My name was called and I waddled back to the ultrasound area. The technician began the scan and cheerfully told me my baby boy was perfect in every way. With one month remaining in my pregnancy, he was already weighing in at more than eight pounds. Yet the words of the woman I had met the day before, in the chaotic restaurant, had replayed in my head the night before the scan. Replaying conversations was nothing new to me. I frequently obsessed about saying the wrong thing or hoping I didn't offend someone, but this was different. I wasn't focusing on my words. I was focusing on hers. As the technician finished the scan, I asked her to check on more thing, his kidneys and adrenal glands. The technician switched her focus and began to scan the baby's kidneys, and her demeanor suddenly changed. Her face went pale as she scanned the baby's right adrenal gland, revealing a golf-ball-sized mass. She asked me to lie still while she found a doctor to review the finding. She left the room, and I was left with my thoughts of the conversation with the woman in the restaurant. I knew exactly what was happening as I continued to clutch the single button in the palm of my hand. I knew my child had cancer, and I wished I could go back twenty minutes earlier when my biggest concern was my exposed stomach, tattered dress, and the tiny button in my hand.

The door of the exam room flew open, and doctors poured in to see the mass on the screen. I was told my baby appeared to have a textbook case of neuroblastoma, a childhood cancer of the central nervous system, affecting fewer than seven hundred children each year, worldwide. Although neuroblastoma was suspected, a biopsy was need to confirm the suspicion. I was told to go home, tell my husband about the mass, and come directly back to the hospital so labor could be induced, the baby could be delivered, and testing could begin.

August 21, 1998: I met Adam. He came into the world at 7:15 A.M. He was a big, pink, fat baby and was perfect in every way, but before he drew his first breath, his battle with cancer had begun. He would be one of the lucky ones. The years ahead would be filled for him with surgery, scans, scares, and huge fears, but he would survive and thrive. He has grown to be nearly six feet, eight inches, a popular, handsome young man headed to college and living a beautiful life that almost didn't happen. Each day, when he steps out the front door of our house, he passes a small shadow box containing the single silver button that I kept from the day he was diagnosed—a constant reminder of how quickly life can change. Adam's life was saved by the grace of God and a total stranger who felt compelled to tell me the details of a relative's battle.

Don't Tempt Me!

SHERRY MORGAN

Tall, slender, blond, blue-eyed with a ready smile and carefree attitude, Darryl was a high school senior in my first-hour English literature and composition class. A little bit mouthy making comments like "that's cool" and "who knows" while smiling and looking at others during the discussion, he still seemed to mean well. It was a hot, sweaty day in August, 1970, prior to air-conditioned classrooms, and I was dressed in my best Sunday clothes, wearing high-heeled shoes and panty hose. It was my first year of teaching. Through what began as a near catastrophe, Darryl and I became good friends.

I noticed—or rather heard—him during the first two days (Thursday and Friday) of school and thought he might represent a potential problem. (Beginning teachers are paranoid about potential problems.) On the following Monday he kept his head down on his desk most of the hour and when asked to participate in the oral grammar exercises, he grumbled some comment like "I don't feel like it." I, flippantly and in my best new teacher style, replied, "Either keep your head up and participate or get out!" He retorted with a sneering "Don't tempt me!" To which I again flippantly, but feeling nervous inside, quipped, "I'm not tempting you; I'm just stating a fact!"

Class resumed with Darryl upright and tension in the air until the lessons finally ended. After class, a boy I knew from the community stopped by my desk and said politely, "Mrs. Morgan, I'm sure you don't know, but I'm sure you want to know: Darryl's brother died over the weekend."

Suddenly I remembered reading in the newspaper about a Reese boy who had died as a result of injuries sustained in Vietnam. The circumstances were horrible; he had been in a tank that had been hit and had exploded. The young man was taken to Japan and lived several days before mercifully dying. I was stunned and saddened and explained that I certainly didn't know. Blah! Blah! Blah! I rambled the error of my innocence. I was so sorry!

At lunchtime I learned from another teacher that word had spread through the high school quickly—probably within a few minutes. The next day Darryl was back in class, head high and participating. After class, I stopped him and put my hand on his shoulder. I couldn't put my arm around him because he towered above me. As I looked up to his clear blue eyes and the straight, even teeth showing in his smile, I told him that I was sorry and that I really had been completely unaware of the sorrow in his life. I told him I appreciated his coming to class and trying. He touched my elbow with his hand and gently said, "I know you didn't know; I probably shouldn't have been here; thanks."

From then on, this high school athlete and his friends were my friends the entire year and still are to this day. The apology opened doors for me, literally and symbolically. I never opened a door to the building; Darryl or one of his friends always met me at the door each morning. Of course they had to be silly and bow or act frightened like they *had* to open the door. Darryl's friend Pat said, "How else could we do this and the other guys not make fun?" When I walked into the building each day, I smiled and waved as "the group" booed, hissed, whistled, laughed, talked loudly about me or something, but I knew that I was welcome—they were glad I was there.

I know the apology influenced all my students because that first year went more smoothly than I could ever have dreamed with 36 students in each of my 5 classes. (That's 180 students total!) When I encounter these former students from the class of 1971 at reunions (they always invite me) or any other place, they hug me and tell me how much they loved me as a teacher, how much they learned in my class, and how successful they were in college, especially in English classes. I always thank them and emphatically state, "I got better."

Agak-agak

CORDELIA SANTA MARIA

I would watch as her hands gently worked the flour and butter together. She would pinch a tiny piece of the resultant dough and rub it between her thumb and forefinger. Sometimes she added a little more water into the mixing bowl, other times a dollop more butter. When her fingertips told her the texture was perfect, she would roll the dough out and use our old-fashioned copper cookie cutters to make the circles we needed. Not far away, a bowl of homemade pineapple jam would sit, waiting to be spooned onto the dough. The jam smelled wonderful, all golden and sweet and rich. It would take hours to boil the grated fruit, sugar, and water down to the consistency perfect for these pineapple tarts, with lots of stirring and watching involved.

"Ma, how do you know how much water to add?" I'd venture, as my sisters and I helped to roll out more pastry and cut out more circles.

"To what?" she'd answer distractedly, eyes on everything at the same time.

"The dough."

Silence for a few seconds while her hands kept busy. "Just *agak-agak*. When the dough is right, you'll know."

Agak-agak. A compound word in the Malay language. The root word—a single *agak*—is a verb, meaning "to estimate." A double *agak* turns it into an adverb, meaning "more or less." My mother used this precise measurement of *agak-agak* in her cooking a great deal. For those of us trying to learn her recipes, this meant we were stuck with that same delightful measurement. It was frustrating because vague measurements didn't help budding cooks. Well, it was frustrating for me, at least. I liked exactness and certainty, and fly-by-night measurements were disconcerting.

The *agak-agak* method of cooking is not as uncommon as you might think. In fact it's the only way humans cooked for a very long time and is still the only way some of us cook today. To those who learned to prepare meals this way, it is silly to assume that the amount of each ingredient used should be exactly the same every time. Sometimes the honey is sweeter than usual, so you use less of it. Sometimes the fresh ginger is too mild, so you use more.

My father, however, would tell you about his Auntie Gertie, who would use *exactly* two chili peppers if that was what the recipe called for. No more, no less. If the peppers she happened to buy at the market that morning were smaller than usual, or less hot than usual, well, too bad. *Exactly two* were going into the dish she was making.

The *agak-agak* method is much less about being vague or lazy, and much more about seeking the right balance with the circumstances or ingredients you're given. You employ all the five senses when cooking this way, with a good pinch of experience and practicality to guide you. Recipes, if you follow them at all, are a rough guide rather than a strict formula. You can even find yourself cooking in someone else's kitchen, disadvantaged by the unfamiliar, and still wing your way to a successful meal. Which is quite the life lesson in many ways. It teaches you to trust yourself, and that trust grows with time and practice.

My mother was an amazing cook. She made complex Eurasian curries drawn from my father's side of the family with the same aplomb as she did her native Cantonese dishes. My father would sing high praises of her ability to get the taste of a dish "exactly right." She would stand in front of the two-burner gas stove in our little kitchen, deftly using her long-handled turner and big, black wok to transform mere ingredients into nourishing meals for her family. It was alchemy, really, and seemingly born of instinct. She didn't worry about precision when she was in the kitchen. She trusted in her abilities, and we trusted her.

Nevertheless I didn't always trust her in every aspect when I was growing up. Perhaps because the roles of our parents back in the day seemed so set—Mom stayed at home, Dad went to work—I couldn't see my mother as possessing any other talents or skills that, you know, *mattered*. I would shed tears at a mistake I'd made in an art assignment for school, and she would calmly tell me it didn't matter, showing me how to turn the mistake into a neat little feature. I would cry even more because what did my mother know about art anyway. I would learn later that my mother was an incredible artist, who had traded in her career at a well-known advertising firm to become a stay-at-home mom for us. She knew exactly what she was doing when she rubbed an old toothbrush—dipped in paint—back and forth against an old hair comb, creating a beautiful, even spray of color across the blank canvas. Just as she knew what she was doing when she created life-like roses out of crepe paper, or gorgeous bead necklaces with a crochet needle and jewelry wire.

When I first arrived in Oklahoma, I struggled with a sense of displacement. I was so far from the life I had become accustomed to in Malaysia, and then Australia. I had uprooted and re-settled countless times in between. The move to Oklahoma was for marriage, for love, but as happy as I was to be making a home with my husband, I felt a sadness I hadn't felt before. Perhaps it was the anguish at having to start life all over again in a new country, perhaps it was the sheer geographical distance that dispirited me. I knew traveling to visit my father and siblings was going to be more difficult from now on. With each move taking me farther and farther away from my roots and my support network, this recent upheaval was especially emotional for me. Oklahoma seemed brown and flat, rural and dull. I found myself missing the stunning landscapes and bustling energy of the places I'd lived in previously. I was disappointed in myself. Where was my usual sense of awe and joy at a new adventure? And worse, how long was I going to feel this way? I couldn't hear my own dependable instincts over the loudness of my fear of uncertainty.

It took me a while to remember that, like the *agak-agak* method, there was no formula or recipe for this new life I was leading. I would have to roll with my circumstances and get to know the ingredients I was working with. I had survived huge changes before, and I could find the strength and flexibility to do it again. Sure, I didn't have the same wide-eyed zest I did when I was nineteen and leaving home for my first big adventure overseas, but I had wisdom and experience on my side now. And a deeper faith that all things happen for a reason.

These days I find so much peace in Oklahoma's subtle beauty. My husband and I love taking long, scenic drives on country roads, often with no destination in mind. I see the redbud's gorgeous shades of pink, red, and maroon in spring, and it delights me. I thrill when a scissor-tailed flycatcher swoops across our windshield and settles on a fence. . Lake Claremore sparkles spectacularly on sunny days, and I find myself not missing the ocean quite as much. Oh, and the hawks do make lazy circles in the sky, just like the song says. It is a common sight in Oklahoma, but I never want to take it for granted—after all, I could end up moving again!

Although there are things I will always miss about the places where I've lived, I have learned not to yearn so desperately for them. If we are constantly fighting the present because we miss the past, where would we find the time or energy to build for the future? There is a lot of beauty in the small things in life that we often don't see because we're over-occupied with wishing things were different. I don't want that for me. I want to feel firmly in the now, wherever I am, and notice all the good stuff.

As I stand in front of my own stove thousands and thousands of miles away from the land of my birth, I have carried on my mother's tradition of winging it in the kitchen. The *agak-agak* is strong in me. I make meals that are a mix of this cuisine and that. I am a culinary rebel and can't ever seem to follow a recipe to the detail. I rarely measure out ingredients, and no two meals ever taste quite the same. But life is more colorful this way, and I am okay with that.

Adjusting the Bible Belt

VICKI MAY THORNE

Like many other states in the South and Southwest, Oklahoma likes to declare itself the "buckle on the Bible Belt." The belt in question is undoubtedly a chastity belt, given how strict moral values tend to be in the South. In Oklahoma, this belt is most likely a large "championship bull-riding"–style belt, embroidered in leather and with a large, gleaming silver platter of a buckle. Wearing such a belt and buckle affirms that sexual purity is essential, central, and a shining centerpiece of Christian morality.

Christian moral influence is very strong in Oklahoma, and tends to skew to the conservative side, largely because of the evangelical roots of many churches. Before statehood in 1907, Christian missionaries began moving to what was then Indian Territory to evangelize, convert, and subdue American Indian populations. Christian "values" of education, civility, and modesty were ultimately used to support the Land Run of 1889, as a literal opportunity to subdue and tame a wild land, full of "wild Indians."

My family moved to Oklahoma when I was five. I refused to get out of the car at the first restroom break after we crossed the state line. I was certain that "wild Indians" would ride out from the windswept plains to attack our car. Fortunately for me, the Wild West had been sufficiently tamed by the 1980s, and most Native Americans I would meet would practice conservative, Christian religion, just like me. But as it turned out, the legacy of those early

Christian missionaries would lead to many more culture clashes in Oklahoma, no tomahawks required.

My family moved from suburban Dallas, Texas, to Claremore, Oklahoma, the hometown of Will Rogers, a humorist who loved to skewer politicians and self-important religious people in equal measure. We immediately became active members of First Baptist Church in Claremore. My father received his ordination as a Southern Baptist minister when I was eight and began working as a "bi-vocational" minister shortly after; he had a day job in sales recruitment for a men's tailoring company and pastored or preached on the weekends.

My father is a rabid evangelical, delighting in door-to-door evangelism, short-term medical mission trips to Central America, and "church planting" in the unreached regions of rural Oklahoma. On Sundays for about three years, my family drove our blue Oldsmobile to the far northeastern corner of the state, almost to Kansas, to try to save a dying country church.

The church, Wimer Mission, had one main room, a drafty foyer, and beautiful hardwood floors. It was whitewashed, with a matching outhouse and a modest steeple. Its grounds were literally cut out of a grazing pasture, and were bordered by barbed wire, waving grasses, and curious cows. My father preached and proselytized, my mother played the piano, and my little sister and I sat in the front pew, singing from the Baptist Hymnal with gusto. I swung on the whitewashed wooden church gate, my Sunday dress flaring in the hot summer wind.

The little church was dying, like most do, because there were no young people attending. There were plenty of people in the area, but they were just very spread out. The cows outnumbered the residents 100 to 1. We visited them all—the residents, that is, not the cows.

The little country church grew under my father's energetic efforts. Families brought their kids, and we had children's church on the floor by the gas heater. Senior citizens dusted off their Sunday clothes and the ranchers put on their newest Wranglers. Babies were dedicated and common-law couples asked to be married, as part of their "getting right with God."

Shortly after our time at Wimer, my parents decided that the local public school wasn't doing a great job teaching my little sister and was a corrupting moral influence on my sixth-grade self. We left behind the secular institution of public school to be home-educated (or homeschooled). We participated in the Christian Home Educators Fellowship (C.H.E.F.), where all educational components (especially sex education) were filtered through an extremely conservative, Christian lens. My sex education was cold and scientific, at the hands of my brilliant but slightly prudish mother, who had a master's degree in Radiation Biology. College degrees were somewhat of a rarity in the Oklahoma homeschooling community. When I began to menstruate, my mother sat me down for a thorough discussion of body functions and sexual activities (to my horror). This new information was tinted by a strong emphasis on sexual abstinence and the horror and possibilities of (heterosexual) rape. Both my sister and I recall the emphasis on rape in our sexual education, particularly as something that you could bring on yourself if you didn't follow the rules for modesty and conservative sexual behavior. My budding sexuality was exclusively framed in a heterosexual and hysterical context.

To that end, the family rules dictated that I was not allowed to date until I was sixteen, but, as a homeschooled teen, there were not a lot of (male) options. In addition, my church youth group, where I lusted over cute boys from the public schools, sponsored a True Love Waits initiative, and I signed the abstinence pledge as a matter of course. In the even more conservative homeschool community, the notions of "courtship" and only "dating for a mate" emphasized sexual constraint and relational restriction. With the emphasis on marriage and keeping oneself sexually pure (i.e., virginal), same-sex relationships were essentially erased. I did not know any "out" gays or lesbians, and didn't really know anything about them; they didn't exist in my world.

At seventeen, I finished my homeschool studies and graduated from "May Academy." I earned an academic scholarship from Oklahoma Baptist University (OBU), where I would major in English. It was at OBU that I started to notice a loosening of the Bible Belt on myself.

I chose OBU for my undergraduate education for largely academic reasons—good rankings, solid core courses, an Honors program—but the underlying "Christian" roots definitely appealed to me too. In fact OBU was one of four Christian universities that I toured and applied to; influenced by my conservative religious upbringing, I did not apply to any public universities. Also, there was scholarship money available at OBU for active members of Southern Baptist congregations.

The school had antiquated and detailed rules on moral behaviors, and all students signed a code of conduct. The code of conduct addressed all manner of conservative mores from co-ed dormitories, alcohol consumption, and dancing on campus—all absolutely prohibited—in line with the Southern Baptist tradition. In addition, there was an anti-gay policy prohibiting homosexual expression and relationships. I never really noticed that policy in particular; it didn't seem to apply to anyone I knew on campus.

While at OBU, I was educated about topics adjacent to homosexuality, never about it. In our core biological science class, I learned about intersex individuals as a biological reality, but there was no discussion about homosexuality in the natural world. In the social sciences, the Human Sexualities class was forbidden fruit to me; it was an advanced sociology and psychology course and generally considered off-limits to anyone outside those degrees. However, my chosen major of English literature taught me more about sexuality and desire, and various expressions of that desire, than anything else at OBU did. The arts were indeed a "hotbed of liberalism," as I had been warned by my church elders; literature, drama, music, and chorale opened up the possibilities of other ways of being and doing, even if most sexual themes were greatly suppressed.

During this time, I began to notice the lack of diversity on campus. OBU's student population was almost completely homogeneous—85 percent of the students were white, and 100 percent were either practicing Christians or didn't mind being at a Christian university. But when everyone is the same, the ones who are different really stick out. For example, I noticed there was a theater guy who never dated anyone, although he was very social and universally well liked. There was a girl a class above me who wrote her Honor's thesis about Foucault and "enforced heteronormativity." That was a new one for me. Heteronormativity was a concept I wasn't familiar with, or so I thought. When I was twenty, I worked one summer with an incredibly handsome and charming guy who attended Baylor University, another Christian school with a strict code of conduct, who was strangely uninterested in any of the girls on our team. All the girls loved to hang out with him and giggle about how silly the other guys we worked with were. None of these people were "out" in any way, yet in retrospect it seems glaringly obvious: due to social pressure and university policy, they weren't *allowed* to be out.

College is a hormone-soaked time, especially at OBU. While flirting and "going for coffee" were rampant, casual dating or "hooking up" were distinctly absent. Furthermore, the expectation was that couples who were dating were doing so with an eye toward the long term, and any sexual exploration was off-limits until marriage. Because "recreational" sex was not condoned, many *many* couples got engaged by the spring of their senior year, resulting in many stale jokes about "Ring by Spring" and getting one's "M.R.S." degree. Because the university reinforced the lessons and expectations that our conservative parents and church families had instilled in us, marriage was the only approved route for sexual expression on campus. Homosexual experiences, on the other hand, could be punished, up to and including expulsion.

My own experience with sexual expression was highly informative. As a twenty-two-year-old virgin, I marveled that anyone could be sexually active and get anything accomplished in their real lives. After I became sexually active, I was consumed with the physicality of sex: the desire, the drives, and the need. Ironically, my first sexual partner was a former classmate from the OBU English Department and rather more knowledgeable than I expected him to be.

And then came the lightbulb moment: sex wasn't that big of a deal. It was intimate, yes. But having premarital sex didn't change who I was or make me less of a moral person; it made me more aware, more understanding. I understood what it meant when people said that you don't have to learn your sexuality—it just is.

A few years later, I would meet and fall hard for my future spouse. We met in a singles group at church (of course), and were casual acquaintances for almost a year before we finally noticed each other. We started dating, and soon entered a long-distance relationship, when he moved away to attend graduate school. We only survived through regular visits, which quickly turned into sleepovers. Even though we were adults in a committed relationship, I felt I had to lie to my parents when they questioned me about the sleeping arrangements. We got engaged fourteen tortuous months later and married only four months after that, largely in part because we knew that moving in together unmarried would not be allowed by our families.

The first year of marriage was a major challenge. We were poor in only the way that graduate students with unpaid internships can be. But we hung together and made it through the stormy journey to full-time employment. Newlywed sex was certainly an important part of our ability to hang together. We were madly in love: all the love songs on the radio were about us, distance was a trifling obstacle to be overcome, and poverty only meant we spent more time together. Our love was True, and it wasn't waiting for anyone.

Marriage, in my experience, is significant for its inferred meaning. What marriage *means* for someone can vary, depending on religious upbringing, rejection or acceptance of said religious upbringing, economic situation, sexual compatibility, and other factions. For me, getting married was about being able to *be* together (both physically and mentally) and deciding to be with that person both legally and matrimonially. Choosing to involve the federal government in your relationship signals a certain level of seriousness. Finally we were declaring the trueness of our love, in front of friends and family and God.

As it stands, marriage is both a legal status and a cultural one. Because it is both, there is significant tension around who can legally get married, even in Oklahoma. Culturally, America still values romantic love, highlighting it, adoring it, and promoting it exclusively. Our culture is obsessed with love: the mental, emotional, physical, and sexual nature of it. This has not always been the case; marriage as a legal status has historically benefitted families involved in a domestic partnership arrangement. Throughout most of European and American history, fathers would arrange a marriage between two of their offspring, literally for the propagation of the species. The "bride price" varied, based on several negotiation points; beauty, health, and desire were all part of the negotiation. The greater the desire, the higher the price.

But in 2015, all that changed. After years of lobbying and countless legal battles that went all the way to the U.S. Supreme Court, the definition of marriage was expanded nationwide to include same-sex couples. A mere nine months before, in October 2014, same-sex marriage had become legal in Oklahoma, thanks to the legal suit of Mary Bishop and Sharon Baldwin, a lesbian couple from Oklahoma.

Yet the cultural view of marriage had already shifted by that time; gay and lesbian couples abounded on television. "Same Love," an anthem to the inclusiveness of love, was nominated for a Grammy in 2014. The repeal of "Don't Ask, Don't Tell" in 2010 ungagged members of the military from hiding their sexuality. "Legalizing gay marriage" was a political bone for state and national lawmakers to wrestle over.

Proponents of denying legality of marriage equality appealed to ancient mores about the purpose of marriage. In the Bishop-Baldwin lawsuit, the opposition defended marriage as a right available only to "heterosexual couples to encourage procreation and provide a mother and father for children." Ironically, Oklahoma has one of the highest divorce rates in the nation, confirms a News 9 report, "Divorce Rate Increases despite Oklahoma Marriage Initiative."(December 2, 2013). In fact the Center for Disease Control's informational webpage on "Reproductive Health: Teen Pregnancy" points to risk factors in many southern Bible Belt states, such as elevated divorce rates and lower levels of parental education and income, all by a significant and consistent margin. The dominant Christian culture in the South still insists that marriage follow historic models—man and wife—for procreation. But southern mores no longer mirror the majority of Americans' understanding of the purpose of marriage.

During these tumultuous years, a dear friend of mine, an OBU graduate and divinity student, not only personally encouraged me to explore the issue but happily officiated at a same-sex wedding for another friend of mine from OBU (who, I realize in retrospect, had probably identified as a lesbian while a student, but was not "out" at the time). I trusted this friend as an academic and as a Christian. That friend showed me that it was safe to consider and accept that a person could be both a Christian and gay.

In fact, maybe gay people were just normal people.

Maybe, as the marriage equality movement insisted, Love is Love.

Maybe marriage isn't just a strict, boxlike biblical notion, like I had been taught in both my church and my cultural experience.

Why then shouldn't marriage be available as a legal status to everyone who wants to legally ratify his or her partnership? Although I personally chose to get married as a willing participant in the dominant religious culture, everyone should get a chance to validate their Great and True Love in a way that is meaningful to them! My love and my relationship were not somehow more important just because they happened to be heterosexual. And if non-heterosexuals have been disenfranchised legally for literally thousands of years, legal marriage is likely an important part of this validation. The truth is, over thousands of years, since Biblical times, marriage, both legal and cultural, has always been a mutable concept. As humans we have married for many reasons: safety, alliances, childbearing, wealth, love, obligation, and more.

I began to see that marriage as an institution is evolving, expanding, including.

It's moving toward "tolerance" and "acceptance" and "support."

My nephew, one of the younger members of my extended family, who joined the army to escape small-town Oklahoma, recently announced via Facebook that he was gay. No one was really surprised, and the vast majority of his Facebook friends (including most immediate family members) expressed acceptance. Most responses to his announcement focused on loving him as a person, without necessarily voicing support for his sexuality. A notable exception was his biological father and stepmother, who expressed rejection, claiming their response was due to their "Christian" beliefs—although they were not regular church attenders. They did not speak to him for well over a year; eventually, though, they too came to an acceptance of their son as a gay man.

My nephew and I attended Tulsa Pride last summer, a first for both of us. A wide variety of organizations, civic groups, dance clubs, and churches participated in the celebration. It was the church groups that made the greatest impact on me. They smiled and waved, joyous yet brave.

After that Pride day, my nephew and I talked about his future plans, which included his casual declaration that he probably would not get married until after he retired from the army. On another occasion, he told me about reporting a superior officer during basic training for using a gay slur; the officer was quickly disciplined. He was adamant that his rights as an LGBTQ person be recognized; I could not have been more proud.

The growing crowds at Tulsa Pride, the progress of many mainstream Christian denominations (with the notable exception of the Southern Baptists) toward accepting and welcoming LGBTQ persons, the growing numbers of LGBTQ persons in elected leadership and religious leadership, and the acceptance of some of my religious family members around concepts like "gay marriage" are proof that culture and religion continue to be intertwined and that both can adapt and adjust. The Bible Belt doesn't need to be restrictive; it can be encompassing, encircling, embracing.

Contributors

RILLA ASKEW is the author of four novels, a book of stories, and a collection of creative nonfiction, *Most American: Notes from a Wounded Place*. She is a PEN/Faulkner finalist, recipient of the Western Heritage Award, Oklahoma Book Award, and a 2009 Arts and Letters Award from the American Academy of Arts and Letters. Her novel about the Tulsa Race Massacre, *Fire in Beulah*, received the American Book Award in 2002. Rilla's essays and short fiction have appeared in *Tin House*, *World Literature Today*, *Nimrod*, *Prize Stories: The O. Henry Awards*, and elsewhere. She teaches creative writing at the University of Oklahoma.

JARI ASKINS has served the people of Oklahoma for more than thirty years in a variety of roles ranging from judge to legislator to lieutenant governor. She currently serves as Administrative Director of the Courts where, under the supervision of the Chief Justice and the Oklahoma Supreme Court, she coordinates judicial operations and personnel throughout the state. When Jari was sworn in as Oklahoma's fifteenth lieutenant governor in 2007, she achieved the rare distinction of having served in all three branches of state government. Born and reared in Duncan, Jari is a proud Oklahoman, whose signature accessory is her Oklahoma pin.

SARA N. BEAM's formative years were split among several small towns, first in southeastern Oklahoma and then in Fort Smith, Arkansas. She graduated from Hendrix College in 2002 with a B.A. degree in English. After moving to Tulsa, she completed the University of Tulsa (TU) English Master's and Doctoral Degree programs in 2010. She is Applied Assistant Professor of English and Director of the Writing Program at TU. Her academic interests include teaching, written composition, women's and gender studies, visual rhetoric, and childhood studies. Her scholarly work includes co-editing and writing sections of the 2015 book *Children's and Young Adult Books in the College Classroom: Essays on Instructional Methods*. In the Tulsa community, Sara is involved with the St. John's Center for Spiritual Reformation and is a supporter of The Little Blue House at TU.

RHONDA BEAR, formerly incarcerated, is now Program Manager for Stand in the Gap's Women in Transition program. She is founder of His House Outreach Ministries and She Brews Coffee House. She began her education at Tulsa Community College and completed it at Northeastern State University with a B.A. in Social Work. Advocacy against excessive sentencing for women at the legislative level is her passion. She has a wonderful husband, three children, a son-in-law, daughter-in-law, and five amazing grandchildren, and is happy to live in Oklahoma.

MERLEYN BELL is a fifth-generation Oklahoman and an art director with more than fifteen years of experience in publication design. She has worked for clients across Oklahoma, receiving numerous awards for her work in *Oklahoma Humanities* and *World Literature Today*, among other publications. In 2018, Merleyn was elected to the Oklahoma House of Representatives, becoming the first African American to represent her hometown of Norman in the state legislature.

SHARON BISHOP-BALDWIN is a freelance writer and editor who lives in Broken Arrow, Oklahoma, with her wife, Mary, and their five cats. After a twenty-one-year editing career at the *Tulsa World*, Sharon resigned from the newspaper in 2014 to write a book about the decade-long Oklahoma marriage equality lawsuit, which brought same-sex marriage to the state in October 2014 after the U.S. Supreme Court declined to hear an appeal of the case. Sharon and Mary were the lead plaintiffs in the case, and *Becoming Brave: Winning*

Marriage Equality in Oklahoma and Finding Our Voice is Sharon's recounting of the couple's story. A licensed wildlife rehabilitator, Sharon is working on her second book, which will focus on wildlife rehabilitation.

RUTH ASKEW BRELSFORD taught theater and speech for twenty-nine years in both public and private schools, at all grade levels, and in inner-city, suburban, and rural settings. Those experiences shape her advocacy now as a Court Appointed Special Advocate (CASA) volunteer, mediator, and prison reform advocate. Ruth lives with her husband, Les, in a log cabin in the woods with dogs, cats, chickens, and grass-fed, gentle cows. She teaches Creative Writing and Conflict Resolution at Jackie Brannon Correctional Center. Through her affiliation with the Latimer County Arts Council, she is an advocate for the arts and loves to tell stories to kids.

JENNA BUSCHMANN lives in Tulsa with her partner, who loves dogs, and her cat, who is not a dog. She is currently working on her B.A. in English as well as her people skills. Jenna has received awards for her writing from the Tulsa City–County Library as well as from *The Tulsa Review* for works published in that journal.

YASMINDA CHOATE plants herself in Sasakwa, Oklahoma—the only place that's ever felt like home. She spends her time there growing tomatoes and caring for poultry, cats, dogs, and a daughter on her family farm, Poor Boy's Dream. Yasminda teaches English at Seminole State College in Seminole, Oklahoma, and is one exam and a dissertation away from completing a doctorate in Higher Education Administration at the University of Oklahoma.

TAMYA COX-TOURÉ grew up in both Des Moines, Iowa, and Tulsa, Oklahoma. After graduating from Oklahoma City University School of Law, then receiving Admission to the Bar, she worked for the ACLU of Oklahoma as its first legislative counsel. She has served on numerous panels and presented on a variety of topics focusing mainly on race equity. Her honors include the AC Hamlin Award from the Oklahoma Legislative Black Caucus, the John Green Community Service Award from the Association of Black Lawyers, the Faith and Freedom Award for the Oklahoma Religious Coalition for Reproductive Choice, the Torch Award from Freedom Oklahoma, and the Ada Louis Sipuel Fisher Award from the Oklahoma Bar Association Diversity Committee. Late in her contributed essay, Tamya mentions a new relationship; happily, she and Jabari Touré were married in the fall of 2018.

JENNY YANG CROPP is the author of the poetry collection *String Theory* (Mongrel Empire Press), a 2016 Oklahoma Book Award finalist. She grew up mainly in Lawton, Oklahoma, and holds a B.A. in English from the University of Oklahoma, MFA in creative writing from Minnesota State University–Mankato, and Ph.D. in English from the University of South Dakota. She began her full-time teaching career at Cameron University in Lawton and recently moved to Cape Girardeau, Missouri, where she started her dream job, teaching creative writing as Assistant Professor of English at Southeast Missouri State University.

ARIELLE DAVIS is the co-founder and owner of Reflections Media Tulsa, a service that creates visual and audience space for people to make their dreams a reality, and co-creator of The DL Travel Channel, which documents travel inspired by literature. An alumna of Booker T. Washington High School in Tulsa, she earned a B.A. in Communications from Rogers State University. She describes herself as a motivational speaker, aspirational author, article addict, information provider, inspiration seeker, and practical being.

PRIYA DESAI lives and works in Oklahoma City, where she grew up. She volunteers as co-executive director of the Oklahoma Call for Reproductive Justice and also serves on the Board of Directors for the United Nations Association of Oklahoma City. In addition, she is a cofounder of Oklahomans for Paid Family Leave and is a proud member of the National Network of Abortion Funds and SisterSong. Priya holds a B.A. and M.A. in Social Work with an emphasis in Administration and Community Practice from the University of Oklahoma.

EMILY DIAL-DRIVER is Professor of English and Humanities at Rogers State University. She has authored textbooks, articles, plays, poems, and telecourses, and is co-editor of *Voices from the Heartland* (vol. 1), *The Truth of Buffy*, *Fantasy Media in the Classroom*, and *Children's and Young Adult Books in the College Classroom*. She is the author of *Conjunction: A Novel of Murder and Manners*, *Excursions: 15 Short Stories*; *SideWalks: Collected Poems*; and *A Play Collection: One Adult and Four All-Ages*. Having won local awards for service, publication, and teaching, she also received, in 2014, the Oklahoma Medal for Excellence for teaching in regional institutions and community colleges.

JULIET EVUSA is Professor and Greg Kunz Endowed Chair of Communications, as well as Assistant Director for Academic Enrichment, at Rogers State University. In 1993, she received her B.A. from the University of Maharaja Sayajirao, Baroda, India, eventually becoming a Social Services Officer with the Ministry of Cultural and Social Services in Nairobi, Kenya. In 1995, Juliet accepted a position with the Cooperative Bank of Kenya, where she served as a Foreign Exchange staff member for three years. In 1997, she was awarded a full scholarship at the University of Ohio, Athens, where she received dual M.A. degrees in the Schools of International Affairs and Telecommunications. She later received her doctoral degree in the university's School of Communications in 2005. Fall 2017 marked the thirteen-year anniversary of Juliet's tenure at Rogers State University. Thanks to her recent appointment as the Greg Kunz Endowed Chair of Communication, Juliet will spend future summers in Kenya to work on a video-ethnography that will explore the ways in which gender, underserved locations (rural and slums), and education interrelate to create an environment of multiple vulnerability for underprivileged Kenyan students attending secondary schools. She currently resides in Claremore, Oklahoma, with her supportive partner Patrick and their two sons, Ambula and Devin.

GRACE E. FRANKLIN is a published poet, playwright, actress, and director. Born in Oklahoma City, she attended Lincoln University in Jefferson City, Missouri. She has been a featured spoken-word artist in Atlanta, Dallas, Baltimore, and Washington, D.C. She recently released her third book of poetry and CD, *Up from Red Clay*. In October 2014, Grace co-founded OKC Artists for Justice, whose mission is to ensure that women of color have an opportunity to receive justice and national attention as they struggle with disproportionate rates of violence and sexual assault. Recently she was seen on TV One's Roland Martin Now, Democracy Now, Al Jazeera, and BBC America. She was a panelist at the Take Root Conference 2016: Red States Perspective on Reproductive Justice, where she and others discussed the regional complexities of women of color in the South in relation to race, religion, and economics. She has discussed community organizing as a panelist for the Women of Color Network, Inc. (WOCN) Economic Policy & Leadership Southern Regional Forum. In recent years, at Columbia Law School panels focusing on the Daniel Holtzclaw trial in Oklahoma, Grace discussed community organizing around issues of violence against African American women. She received the Woman of Action Award from the National Organization of Women (NOW). Grace is committed to the spiritual, political, and physical liberation of women of color through advocacy, community work, and policy changes.

KALYN FREE is a Choctaw woman, a self-proclaimed "Sovereignista," an unapologetic Democrat; an attorney specializing in environmental and American Indian law; a former elected district attorney; a campaign professional; a social activist; a fierce advocate for tribal sovereignty, the environment, equality, women's rights, human rights and organized labor; a proud associate member of the United Steelworkers; and a lifetime member of the NAACP. She has been a public servant in Washington, D.C., and Oklahoma, and has been active in tribal, state, and national political campaigns for more than thirty years. Her raison d'etre are the three men in her life—her beloved eleven-year-old German Shepherds, Wegas and Ofi, and her husband, Steve Bruner—and her family.

In the back seat of an Oklahoma City police car and at her wit's end, having already spent twelve years in prison with more to go, defeated after a life of generational abuse, crime, and addiction, **SHAUNTE GORDON** did not even know God could change her life. But He changed her forever ten years ago. Now she experiences restoration, great joy, hope, and success through She Does Odd Jobs With Integrity as a productive member in society in the most wonderful community in Oklahoma.

EDEN HEMMING started writing poetry at the age of ten and was awarded the Most Likely to Write the Great American Novel Award by her sixth-grade teacher. She co-owned an internationally known record company, Digitalis Industries, for thirteen years, writing and editing for *Foxy Digitalis* for ten of those years. In the meantime, she earned two degrees in anthropology from the University of Tulsa. Her greatest accomplishment is learning how to be herself in a world that always seems to be telling her what she shouldn't be.

KATIE RAIN HILL is a transgender advocate living in Oklahoma. She transitioned during her sophomore year of high school and was the first open transgender student to graduate from a school in Oklahoma. She has spoken at several high schools and colleges in the country about supporting transgender students. Hill has been interviewed by England's *Daily Mail*, has appeared on ABC Television's *20-20*, modeled in the 2014 Barney Spring Campaign, and has been profiled regularly in both national and international newspapers. She has recently published her first book, *Rethinking Normal*. Katie graduated with two B.A.s, in Anthropology and Sociology respectively, from the University of Tulsa.

SPRING HOUGHTON hails from Holdenville, Oklahoma, and currently resides in Tulsa. After earning a B.A. from the University of Oklahoma, she moved from Norman to Tulsa to pursue an M.A. in English, with concentrations in women's and gender studies and film studies. These days, her interests in reproductive justice have led her into the health sciences, and she is studying to become a Registered Nurse-Midwife.

LEANNE HOWE (citizen, Choctaw Nation of Oklahoma) is an author, playwright, and poet. She connects literature, Indigenous knowledge, Native histories, and expressive cultures in her fiction, creative nonfiction, and poetry. LeAnne is the Eidson Distinguished Professor of American Literature at the University of Georgia, Athens. She makes her home in both Athens and in Ada, Oklahoma.

DEBORAH J. HUNTER is a Tulsa poet and spoken word artist. Her grandparents and their families made their way to Oklahoma from various places in the South. Settling in Tulsa, they survived the 1921 Greenwood Massacre, escaped the area, and returned to rebuild. She credits her poetic voice to having grown up surrounded by the rhythmic speech patterns of her grandmother, aunts, and uncles. None of them ever talked to her about the hardships they endured. In her job as a certified behavioral health case manager, Deborah is an advocate for the homeless and those with mental illnesses, and she often expresses her advocacy through her poetry and performances.

PAMELA KINGFISHER is an enrolled member of the Cherokee Nation, born to the Bird Clan. She farms organically on her grandmother's allotment land in northeastern Oklahoma, where she works with bees and medicinal plants. Pam has been a consultant to the nonprofit field for the past nineteen years, providing services in organizational capacity, policy, and programming. As a direct descendent of the Cherokee Beloved Woman, Nanyehi (One Who Goes About), Pam has visited 78 American Indian reservations, 52 states, and 8 foreign countries, sharing and collecting stories with a camera in hand.

A lifelong Oklahoman, **LENZY KREHBIEL-BURTON** is a Tulsa-based freelance journalist. Her regular client list includes the *Journal Record, Fairfax Chief,* the Citizen Potawatomi Nation's *Hownikan, Osage News, Reuters,* and the *Tulsa World.* When she and her husband, Jacob Burton, aren't chasing their two children or their assorted pets, they can often be found hiding in the woods or curled up with some primo literature.

MARY M. MACKIE is originally from Boston. She is Professor of Creative Writing and Literature at Rogers State University and poetry editor of the *Cooweescoowee.* Four of her plays, *Unrequited to the Nth Degree, Closing Time, Sweet Dreams Are Made of This,* and *Reading Izzy* have been produced by the RSU Theater Program. Her poems have appeared in *California Quarterly, Vermont Literary Review,* and *Windmill,* and her poem "fantom mother" was published recently in *Red Earth Review.* . Mary is working on a poetry collection entitled "Conversations with My Mother," and continues to search for a publisher for her novella "Below the Salt."

NANCY MICHNO is a student at Rogers State University pursuing her B.A. in Liberal Arts as an English major. She was born and raised in Argentina listening to *tango* and *chacareras,* drinking *mate,* and eating Abuela's orange cake. She loves to paint and make enamel copper jewelry. When Nancy was twenty-three years old, she moved to Bartlesville, Oklahoma, where she exchanged the sea for the lake, and the overcrowding of the city for the silence of the buffalo, the ethereal dance of the bald eagle, and the wisdom of the weather forecaster announcing a tornado warning. In Oklahoma she learned what love was, crafted into two little goddesses she called Atenea and Helena. Above all, in Oklahoma she discovered her writing voice.

JEANETTA CALHOUN MISH is a scholar, poet, prose writer, and the 2017–18 Oklahoma State Poet Laureate. Her most recent books are *What I Learned at the War,* a poetry collection; and *Oklahomeland: Essays.* Jeanettta is director of The Red Earth Creative Writing MFA Program at Oklahoma City University, where she also serves as advisor to *Red Earth Review* and as a faculty mentor in writing pedagogy, professional writing, and the craft of poetry.

SHERRY MORGAN received her B.A. and M.A. in English Education from Oklahoma State University and taught twelfth-grade English and Creative Writing at Charles Page High School in the town of Sand Springs, winning Oklahoma Teacher of the Year in 1980 and the Valley Forge Freedoms Foundation Teacher's Medal. One or more of her students won local, state, and national writing contests each year she taught. She left teaching after fifteen years to accept a position as consultant and editor for Holt McDougal. The Oklahoma State University College of Education inducted Sherry into its Hall of Fame in 2009.

APOLLONIA PIÑA is an interdisciplinary researcher of Mvskoke, Xicana, Scots-Irish, and French lineage. She holds a B.S. in Cross-Cultural Epistemologies in Science and Math from the University of Oklahoma. Apollonia is the Tulsa chapter organizer in the Native-women-led nonprofit initiative Matriarch and developer of a Native-American-focused STEM camp for Native youth. Her research interests include indigenous perspectives in science and math, indigenous sexuality, and indigenous womanism. When time allows she enjoys scouting rare books, rock and roll, origin stories, and connecting the dots. She resides on Mvskoke lands in Tvlse, Okla Humma, with her son José.

AMANDA RUYLE is descended from Dust Bowl survivors, truck drivers, Yellow Dog Democrats, forcibly relocated people, and mouthy, outspoken women. A mother of two and a late bloomer who procrastinates as if it's a competition, she longs for the disciplined, focused life of a "real writer." She dropped out of college to travel and never looked back, so on paper she is rather unimpressive, but in person she will knock your socks off. If you can get her to leave the house.

CORDELIA SANTA MARIA was born and raised in Kuala Lumpur, Malaysia. After completing her Bachelor's of Science in Psychology in the beautiful north woods of Minnesota, she lived and worked in both Malaysia and Australia before making her way back to the United States.. There are few things that make her happier than sitting around a table with family and friends, and sharing great conversation and home-cooked food. She is a self-professed foodie who loves sampling cuisines from all over the world. She currently resides in Claremore, Oklahoma, with her husband and son, and their goofy dog, Winston.

ELLEN STACKABLE is the founder of Poetic Justice, an organization that facilitates restorative writing classes for incarcerated women. She has taught English and writing for more than seventeen years at Tulsa School of Arts and Sciences. In March 2014, she helped start Poetic Justice, working with incarcerated women at the Tulsa County Jail. Poetic Justice classes give a voice to the voiceless and empower women to change as they engage in self-reflective, therapeutic writing. Poetic Justice now has twenty volunteers who teach classes to incarcerated women every week at the Tulsa County Jail, Mabel Bassett Correctional Center, Eddie Warrior Correctional Center, and Kate Bernard Correctional Center. Every Tuesday, you can find Ellen at Mabel Bassett surrounded by incarcerated women, who are becoming poet warriors.

Originally from St. Louis, Missouri, **AURA THOMAS** has called Oklahoma home for more than ten years. She works full-time helping new students at the University of Tulsa adjust to college life. She is also a small business owner and social media consultant, and is passionate about raising awareness and funding pediatric cancer research.

VICKI MAY THORNE is a former southern-fried Baptist and proud homeschool graduate. A native of Claremore, she earned degrees in English from Oklahoma Baptist University and the University of Tulsa. She taught composition and Writing for the Professions at the University of Tulsa, Rogers State University, and Tulsa Community College before transitioning to the more lucrative field of grant writing. Now a full-time freelance writer, Vicki teaches grant writing, mentors young professionals in the nonprofit arena, and explores interfaith issues as a board member for Tulsa Interfaith Alliance. When not perched on the edge of a chair at her kitchen table, Vicki is exploring Tulsa's parks, museums, and flea markets with her spouse and two kiddos.

UREKA WILLIAMS is a native Tennessean who has lived in Oklahoma for the past eighteen years. She has a B.A. degree in English and Spanish (emphasis in Culture) from Fisk University, Nashville, and an M.A. in English Language and Literature from the University of Tulsa. While at Fisk, Ureka was editor of the *Fisk Forum*, president of the W.E.B. DuBois Honor Society, and a United Negro College Fund Undergraduate Andrew W. Mellon Fellow. Ureka was member of the inaugural faculty of the Tulsa School of Arts and Sciences and is currently Associate Professor of English at Tulsa Community College. Captivated by images and narratives, Ureka enjoys portraiture, biographies, documentaries, and investigative reporting. Ureka lives in Tulsa with her husband, Thomas, son, Gentry, and daughter, Claire.

JANICE WILLSON lived in Colorado and New England before moving to Oklahoma as a child. After completing a degree at Northeastern State University, Tahlequah, she pursued a teaching career in northern China. During her time abroad, she survived long Manchurian winters, witnessed riots at the U.S. Embassy, and experienced the excitement of living in an Olympics host city. After two decades overseas, she returned to Oklahoma to pursue new adventures. She now serves as a Language Testing and Assessment Specialist at Yale University.

VERONICA WOLF is a descendent of the Creek and Seminole tribes. Born in Claremore, she grew up in North Tulsa and is now residing in Oklahoma City. She graduated from Rogers State University with a B.A. in Communications. Veronica is the mother of five children.

www.ingramcontent.com/pod-product-compliance
Ingram Content Group UK Ltd.
Pitfield, Milton Keynes, MK11 3LW, UK
UKHW041305180426